The Forgotten Men

CRITICAL ISSUES IN CRIME AND SOCIETY

Raymond J. Michalowski, Series Editor

Critical Issues in Crime and Society is oriented toward critical analysis of contemporary problems in crime and justice. The series is open to a broad range of topics including specific types of crime, wrongful behavior by economically or politically powerful actors, controversies over justice system practices, and issues related to the intersection of identity, crime, and justice. It is committed to offering thoughtful works that will be accessible to scholars and professional criminologists, general readers, and students.

For a list of titles in the series, see the last page of the book.

The Forgotten Men

SERVING A LIFE WITHOUT PAROLE SENTENCE

MARGARET E. LEIGEY

RUTGERS UNIVERSITY PRESS
New Brunswick, New Jersey, and London

Library of Congress Cataloging-in-Publication Data

Leigey, Margaret E.
The forgotten men : serving a life without parole sentence / Margaret E. Leigey.
    pages cm.—(Critical issues in crime and society)
Includes bibliographical references and index.
ISBN 978-0-8135-6948-2 (hardcover : alk. paper)—ISBN 978-0-8135-6947-5
(pbk. : alk. paper)—ISBN 978-0-8135-6949-9 (e-book (web pdf))—ISBN
978-0-8135-7365-6 (e-book (epub))
1. Parole—United States. 2. Life imprisonment—United States. 3. Capital
punishment—United States. I. Title.
HV9304.L395 2015
365.'60973—dc23
                                                    2014030635

A British Cataloging-in-Publication record for this book is available from the British
Library.

Visit our website: http://rutgerspress.rutgers.edu

Manufactured in the United States of America

For my mother

Contents

Preface: Death by Incarceration

A NATURAL LIFE SENTENCE. The other death penalty. Death by incarceration. These are the apt descriptions of life without the possibility of parole (LWOP), the most severe prison sentence possible in the United States. As the name suggests, inmates serving this sentence are ineligible for parole. Other than the vacating of a LWOP sentence by an appellate court, commutation is the only other theoretical means by which a LWOP inmate would be released from prison. However, the likelihood of release either through court order or executive clemency is virtually nonexistent. The most likely outcome for virtually all LWOP inmates is that they will die in prison.

There are approximately forty-nine thousand federal and state inmates serving life without parole in the United States (Nellis 2013, 1). Of the one and a half million sentenced inmates in this country (Carson and Sabol 2012, 1), about 3.3 percent are serving a LWOP sentence (Nellis 2013, 6). While still a small portion of the overall prison population, the number of LWOP inmates has increased precipitously over the last several decades to the point where there are now roughly the same number of individuals serving life without parole in the United States as the total prison populations of forty-three states (Carson and Sabol 2012, 22). Yet despite the severity of the sentence and the growth of the LWOP population, these inmates receive little attention. They are a group that has been forgotten.

Similar to inmates who receive the formal death penalty, LWOP inmates are executed by the State, though the process is much different. Their cases do not receive additional scrutiny from appellate courts to ensure the punishment is fair. Their deaths do not occur on a scheduled day and time after they have had the opportunity to say goodbye to loved ones and consume a specially requested meal. When LWOP inmates die, there are no abolitionists outside the prison protesting the unjustness of the punishment. Their deaths do not attract intense media coverage. Rather, for LWOP inmates, death is much more banal. The "execution," the eventual succumbing to disease, illness, or advanced age, is the culmination of a decades-long process fraught with the uncertainty of not knowing whether they will ever be released from prison and if not, when and how they will die in prison. Older inmates can expect to incur casualties, in particular to their social networks and to their physical health, over the course of three decades of confinement, the average length of a life sentence (Mauer et al. 2004, 12). Because of the length of time that LWOP inmates can expect to be incarcerated, it is difficult to maintain connections with the outside world. As their relatives grow old and die, their ties to the outside become increasingly splintered. Older LWOP inmates, themselves, are not immune to the aging process. They can expect to encounter many of the same medical conditions that older people face, yet they are in an environment in which they have little control over the quality of the medical care they receive. After struggling to carve out a life that is personally meaningful, and surviving a predatory prison environment, almost all can expect their deaths to occur in prison and without loved ones nearby. Death by incarceration.

The contention that "death is different" has led to greater oversight of death penalty cases (for an extensive discussion see Henry 2012). While the processes differ considerably, the ultimate outcome of the death penalty or death by incarceration is the same. This position is reflected in the following statement from Noah, who was sixty-three years of age and had spent almost half of his life serving life without parole (see Appendix A for more information about pseudonyms): "It dawns on you that, man, you know what? Man, you've got the death penalty. Really, you got the death penalty. [It's] not that you have a set date . . . but there's a slow death penalty because, see, you are sentenced to natural life that means until the rest of your life. And when it starts seeping in . . . chances are I'm going to die here."

Both sentences constitute a rejection by the public, as they send the message that the offenders are unworthy of ever reentering society, either because of the severity of the offense or because of their perceived dangerousness. Yet, given the comparative size of the populations and the number of offenses punishable by each, death by incarceration has a far wider reach than the formal death penalty. The LWOP population dwarfs the death-sentenced population, forty-nine thousand versus thirty-one hundred (Snell 2013, 1). Moreover, there are more offenses (e.g., rape) and types of offenders (e.g., habitual property offenders) eligible to receive life without parole than the death penalty.

Despite the size of the population, the heterogeneity of LWOP-eligible offenses and offenders, and the low likelihood of release, researchers have devoted little time to examining the offenders' correctional experiences, and correctional administrators have been remiss in developing prison programming to address their needs. Therefore, the purpose of this book is to give voice to twenty-five older men who are serving LWOP sentences. Based on in-depth interviews conducted in the fall of 2006 and in the fall of 2011, *The Forgotten Men* provides unprecedented access into the lives of men who are serving the most severe prison sentence imaginable. In 2011 all of the men were at least fifty-five years of age and had been incarcerated for at least twenty years, though half of them had been incarcerated in excess of thirty years.

While this book centers on the experiences of a small group of older long-term inmates, their collective story can be seen in a broader context. First, these inmates are survivors of a life spent confined. For this reason alone, their lives arouse curiosity. What kind of lives have they created for themselves? How have they coped with permanent confinement? Listening to their accounts of life in a sparse and often violent world provides insight into the resiliency of the mind and spirit. These men serve as proof that the psyche can withstand a variety of stresses and losses. Second, these men are aging under special circumstances in controlled facilities that were not designed for them. As will be discussed more fully, their biological ages and how old they feel vary widely from their actual chronological ages. Most men reported that they felt younger, and in some cases decades younger, than their actual ages. Due to the monotony of prison life, they claim that prison has preserved them. At the same time, they experience medical problems similar to those of older people residing in free society. Almost all have at least one physical health condition, though comorbidity is common. In contrast to the decline in physical health, most believe that their mental health has improved over the course of confinement. They claim that maturation has made them self-aware, patient, and less impulsive. Because of their self-growth, combined with the length of time they have been incarcerated and their low likelihood of recidivating, the men feel as though they should be permitted to reenter society. However, release is highly improbable and dying in prison is the reality for most of the permanently incarcerated. In the five-year interim period between interviews, three men died (Thomas, Anthony, and Samuel), and Walter has died since the second interview.

While the population and the conditions of confinement are unusual, there are themes present in the men's accounts that are universal—including adaptation, survival, finding meaning in life, redemption, and hope. Finding purpose in life is a commonly held desire by most people, including the men featured in this book. Over the two decades they have been incarcerated, they have struggled to find meaning in their lives. Most have made efforts to better themselves (through education, for example) and have positively contributed to the prison through their advocacy, mentorship, and service to other inmates

This book also raises important questions regarding the meaning of life. What is the value of a life spent incarcerated? Hope of release is fundamental in many of the men's belief systems. They have never relinquished the hope that they will one day be freed. This hope of release, however remote, profoundly shapes their behavior. They work to make themselves as attractive for release as possible by avoiding trouble and seeking out opportunities for self-improvement. They protect their physical health by exercising and monitoring their diets so they could have active lives in society should they be released. For some, their lives revolve around their pursuit of release. This glimpse behind the walls forces us to contemplate not only the meaning of life but the human costs of punishment.

Chapter 1 traces the history of life without parole and frames the major arguments in the LWOP debate. The men featured in this book are introduced in Chapter 2, and a typology of their different offenses and other biographical information are presented. Chapter 3 examines the pains of permanent imprisonment, most notably the separation from loved ones, institutional thoughtlessness, and the indeterminacy of the sentence. The coping strategies employed by the men to manage a LWOP sentence are presented in Chapter 4. In Chapter 5, the physical and mental health of the men and the two possible forms of release from a LWOP sentence—sentence modification and death, with the latter being the most likely outcome—are examined. The final chapter presents policy recommendations and calls for a reexamination of the current use of life without parole in the United States.

ACKNOWLEDGMENTS

I AM INDEBTED TO the many individuals who have made this book possible. I thank the Department of Corrections of the mid-Atlantic state which allowed me to enter its prisons and the prison staff who assisted me in 2006 and 2011. This book would simply not exist without the participation of the twenty-five men interviewed. I appreciate their willingness to discuss deeply personal subject matter and their patience in answering my many questions. I believe that their stories are important and need to be heard. I hope I have accurately captured and communicated the experience of permanent incarceration.

I am grateful to the staff at Rutgers University Press for their support of this project and especially Peter Mickulas for his help and guidance through all phases of the publishing process. I also would like to acknowledge the thoughtful feedback provided by the two reviewers, Ron Aday and Susan Miller. This book is undoubtedly better because of their suggestions.

I thank my former colleagues at California State University, Chico and my current ones at The College of New Jersey for their support and encouragement of this project. I feel fortunate to have been in collegial environments during the conception and completion of this book.

I have been privileged to have had gifted teachers at all levels of my education, and it is probably not a coincidence that I became a teacher myself. I credit my English teachers at Red Land High School in Lewisberry, Pennsylvania, for helping me become a better writer. I thank my professors at Indiana University of Pennsylvania for fostering my interest in criminology. I am grateful to my professors at the University of Delaware for helping me develop my own identity as a teacher and a researcher. My mentors Ronet Bachman and Eric Rise have always provided me with good counsel. I thank them for their advice and also their insistence that I write this book.

I am blessed to have a strong personal support system. I thank my parents for giving me the confidence to pursue my own path and for their encouragement and love. My mother is a constant source of support, and I lean on her often. Usually the longest relationships in people's lives are the ones they have with their siblings. I am happy that I get to go through life as the middle child sandwiched between my older sister, Katie, and younger brother, Dan.

My siblings are two of my biggest cheerleaders, and they never allow me to take myself too seriously. I thank my two closest friends, Jess Hodge and Jill Russell, for the support and laughter their friendships bring. I would also like to thank my other friends from graduate school. I feel fortunate to have crossed paths with them, especially Rita Poteyeva, Lauren Barsky, Bonnie Wu, and Whitney DeCamp.

Lastly, my husband, Eric, brings a level of meaning, not to mention logic, calm, and organization, to my life that would otherwise be missing. I thank him for his inexhaustible patience and understanding. If not for him, the highs of life would not be as high and the lows would be even lower. I thank my lucky stars that I have him as a partner.

The Forgotten Men

CHAPTER 1

The Rise in the
Permanently Incarcerated

THE MEN FEATURED IN this book were part of the first wave of inmates across the country to receive formal sentences of life without parole (LWOP). While the United States has always allowed for life terms, and even the denial of parole eligibility with some, the formal sentence of life without parole is a creation of the twentieth century (Mauer et al. 2004, 4; van Zyl Smit 2002, 54). Several states—including the mid-Atlantic state where the men in this book were incarcerated—had already implemented the sentence when LWOP statutes were increasingly adopted and more frequently imposed in the 1970s. In 1982, twenty-one states authorized life without parole (Stewart and Lieberman 1982, 15); by 1996, the number had risen to thirty-four states (van Zyl Smit 2002, 55). As of 2013, the federal system and every state (other than Alaska) authorize the sentence (Nellis 2013, 3).[1]

As state after state began adopting LWOP legislation, the number of permanently incarcerated inmates skyrocketed. In 1992, there were approximately ten thousand LWOP inmates in the United States (Maguire et al. 1993, 633). By 2003, the size had tripled to thirty-four thousand (Mauer et al. 2004, 10). In 2008, the population was estimated to be approximately forty-one thousand inmates (Nellis and King 2009, 3), and in the last five years, there has been a 22 percent increase in the LWOP population up to forty-nine thousand inmates (Nellis 2013, 1). LWOP inmates now account for a larger portion of the total prison population and a larger portion of the life-sentenced population than ever before (Nellis 2013, 5). The number of LWOP inmates—both in raw numbers and as a portion of the total prison population—has sharply risen. Less than one-quarter of one percent of the US prison population was serving life without parole in 1965 (Appleton and Grøver 2007, 600). The rate remained stable until 1974 when the ratio of LWOP inmates to total inmates began to increase steadily to its present figure of about 3.3 percent (Nellis 2013, 6).

Researchers at The Sentencing Project have amassed the most comprehensive information to date on LWOP inmates in the United States. Table 1.1 displays the total number of LWOP inmates in each jurisdiction and the percentage of LWOP inmates in the total prison population. While every jurisdiction besides Alaska authorizes life without parole, the actual imposition of the sentence varies widely both in terms of the total number of LWOP inmates in the jurisdiction and as a percentage of the jurisdiction's total prison population. In raw counts, twelve states have less than one hundred LWOP inmates as compared to the five jurisdictions with the highest number: Florida (7,992), Pennsylvania (5,102), Louisiana (4,637), California (4,603), and the federal system (4,058) (Nellis 2013, 6). In terms of portion of the total prison population, the percentage of LWOP inmates is less than 1 percent in ten states, much lower than the five states with the highest percentages: Louisiana (11.5 percent), Massachusetts (10.3 percent), Pennsylvania (10.0 percent), Delaware (9.6 percent), and Michigan (8.4 percent). It is important to note that in six states (Illinois, Iowa, Louisiana, Maine, Pennsylvania, and South Dakota) and in the federal system, all life sentences are parole ineligible (Nellis 2013, 4). Unless serious changes were to take place in sentencing and correctional practices, it is expected that the growth of the national LWOP population will only continue.

LIFE WITHOUT PAROLE: SUPPORT AND OPPOSITION

In the 1970s, rehabilitation, the dominant reason for punishment in American corrections since the country's inception, was eclipsed by retribution, incapacitation, and deterrence. As the crime rates in the United States, in particular the violent crime rate, began to climb in the 1960s (Uniform Crime Reports 2010), a shift in correctional ideology occurred. Instead of reforming offenders, prisons needed to punish them because of the harm their crimes caused (retribution), to protect the public (incapacitation), to make an example of them to would-be offenders (general deterrence), or to make the punishment experience as unpleasant as possible in order to prevent future offending (specific deterrence). As it is not concerned with the ability of an offender to become law-abiding, life without parole exemplifies the departure from rehabilitation and the embrace of a law and order or tough on crime ideology.

IN SUPPORT OF THE SENTENCE

The proliferation of life without parole was born from two sources of dissatisfaction: the continued existence of capital punishment and the perceived leniency of judges and parole boards. Because of its punitive nature, yet also an alleged respect for human life, LWOP is supported by an unlikely caucus of tough-on-crime proponents and death-penalty abolitionists. The primary rationales for the punishment are examined more fully below.

Rationale One: Better than the Death Penalty

In the eighteenth century, the prominent scholars Cesare Beccaria and Jeremy Bentham offered early support for life imprisonment as an alternative to capital punishment. Both believed that permanent incarceration was a more severe sentence, and as a result a better deterrent, than the death penalty. In *On Crimes and Punishments* ([1764] 1995, 68), Beccaria asserted: "Permanent penal servitude in place of the death penalty would be enough to deter even the most resolute soul: indeed, I would say that it is more likely to. Very many people look on death with a calm and steadfast gaze, some from fanaticism, some from vanity. . . . However, neither fanaticism nor vanity survives in manacles and chains, under the rod and the yoke or in an iron cage; and the ills of the desperate man are not over, but are just beginning." Similar to the notion of permanent penal servitude advanced by Beccaria, in *The Rationale of Punishment* ([1811] 1830, 194–195), Bentham argued: "The contemplation of perpetual imprisonment, accompanied with hard labour and occasional solitary confinement, would produce a deeper impression on the minds of persons in whom it is more eminently desirable that that impression should be produced, than even death itself."

One hundred and fifty years later, after the death penalty was reinstated in the wake of *Gregg v. Georgia* (1976), the anti–death penalty movement reconsidered its strategies in its fight against capital punishment. In addition to humanizing the death-sentenced and calling for direct action and civil disobedience by movement supporters, abolitionists wrestled with endorsing life without parole as an alternative to the death penalty. According to Herbert H. Haines in *Against Capital Punishment: The Anti–Death Penalty Movement in America, 1972–1994* (1996, 135), "the credibility of the anti–death penalty movement hinges on its ability to provide a convincing answer [to the question:] '*If not the death penalty, then what?*'" Even within the anti–death penalty movement, pressure exists to appear tough on crime, as a faction within the movement maintained that in order for the abolition of the death penalty to be seriously considered, a tough alternative needed to be promoted. If a formal death sentence was abolished, then death by incarceration is the next best penalty in a first-degree murder case in order to meet the retributive demand that punishment should be proportional to the severity of the offense. Considering it to be the lesser of two evils, some within the movement supported the strategy to endorse life without parole. However, this proposed action did not gain widespread support as others criticized the sentence for being as

LWOP Inmates by Jurisdiction in Total Number and
as a Percentage of the Prison Population

	Total Number of LWOP Inmates	% of Prison Population[*]
Alabama	1,507	4.7
Alaska	0	0.0
Arizona	441	1.1
Arkansas	528	3.6
California	4,603	3.4
Colorado	606	2.9
Connecticut	70	0.6
Delaware	386	9.6
Florida	7,992	8.0
Georgia	813	1.4
Hawaii	47	1.3
Idaho	122	1.7
Illinois	1,600	3.3
Indiana	113	0.4
Iowa	635	7.7
Kansas	21	0.2
Kentucky	99	0.4
Louisiana	4,637	11.5
Maine	55	2.6
Maryland	380	1.8
Massachusetts	1,045	10.3
Michigan	3,635	8.4
Minnesota	102	1.1
Mississippi	1,518	6.8
Missouri	1,063	3.4
Montana	53	2.2
Nebraska	236	4.9
Nevada	491	3.9
New Hampshire	79	3.0
New Jersey	70	0.3
New Mexico	0	0.0
New York	246	0.5

	Total Number of LWOP Inmates	% of Prison Population
North Carolina	1,228	3.3
North Dakota	27	1.8
Ohio	408	0.8
Oklahoma	780	3.0
Oregon	180	1.3
Pennsylvania	5,102	10.0
Rhode Island	32	1.3
South Carolina	988	4.4
South Dakota	181	5.0
Tennessee	317	1.6
Texas	538	0.4
Utah	105	1.5
Vermont	14	0.7
Virginia	774	2.1
Washington	623	3.7
West Virginia	276	3.9
Wisconsin	229	1.0
Wyoming	28	1.4
Federal	4,058	1.9
Total	49,081	3.3

Source: Reprinted from Nellis (2013).

Note: Hawaii and Virginia did not respond to several requests for data in 2012; therefore, 2008 figures are provided for these states. The federal system eliminated parole in 1987; the parole-eligible lifers listed here were convicted before 1987.

[*] The author calculated the percentage of LWOP inmates in the prison population using the total prison population estimates provided in Nellis (2013).

inhumane as the death penalty. Instead of promoting an alternate penalty, abolitionists against life without parole argued that the appropriate answer to the question, "*If not the death penalty, then what?*" is "The alternative to the death penalty is *no* death penalty!" (Haines 1996, 135, 138).

Whether explicitly promoted by the anti–death penalty movement or not, life without parole has been perceived as the only viable alternative to the death penalty. In some non–death penalty states, such as West Virginia, the mandatory sentence for first-degree murder is life without parole (W.Va. Code R. §61-2-2 2013), and in many death penalty states (for example, Texas and Alabama), if the jury opts not to impose the death penalty, then life without parole is the mandatory sentence (Death Penalty Information Center [DPIC] 2013d). In recent years New Jersey, New Mexico, New York, Connecticut, and most recently Maryland abolished the death penalty, establishing life without parole as the most severe penalty available (DPIC 2013c). Overall, the attractiveness of life without parole is claimed as one of the primary reasons for the decline in capital punishment, as reflected in the following statement by law professor James Liebman: "Life without parole has been absolutely crucial to whatever progress has been made against the death penalty. . . . The drop in death sentences—from three hundred and twenty in 1996 to one hundred and twenty-five last year [in 2004] would not have happened without LWOP" (quoted in Liptak 2005, para. 37). By 2012, the number of death sentences imposed in the country had further declined to seventy-eight (McLaughlin 2012, para. 8). Regional differences in execution rates suggest that the use of the death penalty is becoming increasingly isolated to the South and West. Only about one-fourth of death penalty states (nine of the thirty-three) carried out an execution in 2012. Of them, four states (Texas, Mississippi, Arizona, and Oklahoma) were responsible for 75 percent of the executions (McLaughlin 2012, para. 6).

Public opinion polls have consistently noted waning support for the death penalty, especially when life without parole is included as a sentencing alternative. According to Gallup, in 1994, global support for capital punishment crested at 80 percent, the highest since the organization began polling on the issue.[2] More recently, global support for the death penalty has held steady at around 65 percent, representing the lowest level of support since the mid-1970s (Newport 2010). However, when those polled were asked to select between the death penalty and life without parole, support for capital punishment fell 15 percent from 64 to 49 percent, a level of support similar to the 46 percent who preferred life without parole. As there has been a documented decline in support for capital punishment, there has been a corresponding rise in support for permanent incarceration. In 1986, 35 percent of respondents preferred life without parole over the death penalty; in 2001, support had climbed to 42 percent; and ten years later, support had reached its apex of

46 percent (Newport 2010). A recent poll in North Carolina indicated that support for life without parole is buoyed when the provision of restitution is added. Of those polled, 68 percent (n=600) supported the replacement of capital punishment with life without parole plus restitution (H. White 2013, paras. 2, 4).

Haines was insightful in his forecast that "more than any other single issue, the matter of what that answer [to the question of an alternative to the death penalty] should be has the potential to split the movement into pieces" (1996, 135). In the twenty years since Haines's prediction, life without parole has served as a fault line in dividing the abolition movement. Some within the movement continue to assert that the only way in which the death penalty will be abolished is through the promotion of permanent imprisonment. This faction also maintains that when capital punishment is repealed, a critical gaze can then be cast on life without parole, as reflected in the following statement from Richard Dieter, director of the DPIC (Burns 2013, para. 9): "Right now, life without parole is the alternative if you want to get rid of capital punishment. As long as you have the death penalty, life without parole appears to be a gift. If we got rid of the death penalty, then life without parole would be left as the most extreme punishment, and I think attention could then be focused on its negative aspects."

Nowhere is the internal division within the anti–death penalty community over life without parole better demonstrated than in California's failed Proposition Thirty-Four. In November 2012, with Proposition Thirty-Four (i.e., the Death Penalty Initiative Statute), California voters had the opportunity to abolish the death penalty, leaving life without parole as the maximum penalty for first-degree murder. The ballot measure would apply retroactively to the approximate seven hundred persons who at the time were sentenced to death, including the high profile inmates Scott Peterson, Richard Ramirez, and Richard Allen Davis. The proposed legislation mandated that persons convicted of murder must work while incarcerated, and their wages could be allocated to victim restitution funds. Proposition Thirty-Four also required that $100 million, a portion of the state's savings if the death penalty was banned, be allocated to aid law enforcement in investigations of murder and rape cases (California Secretary of State 2012a, para. 1). The proposition was narrowly defeated, 52 percent against and 48 percent in support (California Secretary of State 2012b, 69).

The ballot measure was championed by influential individuals and organizations.[3] In articulating its support, the Northern California Chapter of the American Civil Liberties Union (ACLU) and Amnesty International USA emphasized the reversibility and the lower cost of life without parole, two common reasons that permanent incarceration is argued to be a preferable punishment over the death penalty (ACLU of Northern California 2013b, para. 2; ibid., 2013e, para. 2; Butkus 2012, para, 6).[4] Life without parole allows the potential for redress in wrongful conviction cases. Citing the statistic that 140 death-sentenced inmates, including three in California, had been wrongfully convicted, the Northern California Chapter of the ACLU posited that abolishing the death penalty is the only way to protect against the execution of the innocent (ACLU of Northern California 2013e, paras. 1–2).

In addition, supporters of Proposition Thirty-Four attempted to appeal to fiscal conservatives by highlighting the exorbitant expense of capital punishment. According to a study conducted by Judge Arthur L. Alarcón and Paula M. Mitchell (2011), California has spent $4 billion on the death penalty since its reinstatement in 1978. The estimate includes (1) pre-trial and trial costs [$1.94 billion], (2) costs related to direct appeals and state habeas corpus petitions [$925 million], (3) costs related to federal habeas corpus petitions [$775 million], and (4) costs of incarceration [$1 billion]. At the time of the study, the State had executed thirteen individuals since the reinstatement of the death penalty in 1978. Studies from other states ranging from Tennessee, Nevada, Washington, Kansas, Indiana, North Carolina, Florida, and the federal government confirm the expense of capital punishment (DPIC 2013a). While quite expensive in its own right, life without parole is less expensive than the death penalty, primarily because it eliminates the costs of appeals required in death penalty cases. The SAFE California website emphasized that, "In contrast [to capital punishment], murder cases in which the prosecution seeks life without possibility of parole have none of these special requirements. Instead, such trials are conducted like any other criminal trial and usually are completed in a matter of weeks. A prisoner sentenced to life imprisonment without the possibility of parole is also entitled to only one tax-payer funded appeal, a process that is usually completed within eighteen months after conviction" (ACLU of Northern California 2013a, para. 3). In describing its organization as "a proud supporter of the campaign," Amnesty International USA estimated that California's repeal of the death penalty could save the State $130 million annually (Butkus 2012, paras. 5–6). As maintained by the ACLU of Northern California, this funding would be better spent on law enforcement, violence prevention, and education (ACLU of Northern California 2013b, para. 4).

In an effort to galvanize support from law enforcement associations and victims' rights groups, Proposition Thirty-Four supporters emphasized that the statute would reduce trauma for victims' families, lead to compensation to victims' families through restitution, and improve the functioning of the criminal justice system in that more seriously violent offenders would be punished. As stated above, the ballot measure would require those convicted of murder to work while incarcerated and their wages could be earmarked for victim restitution. According to the SAFE California website (ACLU of Northern

California 2013g), which has the tagline "Justice That Works. For Everyone," each year 46 percent of reported homicide cases and 56 percent of reported rape cases remain unsolved. Proposition Thirty-Four supporters argued that the $100 million presently spent on capital punishment would be better used in assisting law enforcement in the apprehension of serious violent offenders (ACLU of Northern California 2013g, para. 2). Furthermore, the SAFE California Fund website posited that the death penalty is "broken beyond repair" and "a false promise" to murder victims' families because "death penalty trials in California take an average of twenty-five years from conviction to execution, and more inmates end up dying of old age or illness." Instead, with life without parole, "family members get peace of mind and can move on with their healing—rather than experiencing decades of traumatic court dates and delays" (ACLU of Northern California 2013a; 2013d, para. 2).

There are various reasons life without parole is considered a superior option over the death penalty. These include the reversibility and the lower cost of life without parole, as well as its certainty. The reversal rate of 10–20 percent in noncapital cases is substantially lower than the reversal rate of about 70 percent in capital cases (Henry 2012, 77). While capital punishment is touted as the ultimate penalty and the only guaranteed means to ensure that an offender never returns to society, in actuality it has a greater likelihood of sentence modification than other forms of punishment, including life without parole.

Rationale Two: Ensuring "Life Means Life."

The men who appear in this book were caught in the midst of changing societal views toward punishment. Some recalled initially thinking that, even though they had been sentenced to life without parole, they did not expect to spend the remainder of their lives incarcerated. Adam, who had been incarcerated for thirty-two years, alleged that he was told the following by his attorney: "You'll probably do about twenty, twenty-five years. They never let anyone die in prison." Anthony, a sixty-two-year-old habitual offender, recalled: "Yeah, at the time [of sentencing], . . . I felt that I would do maybe ten, maybe fifteen years, you know. I didn't think it would be as long as it was, you know, but since then a lot of the societal views have changed and things. . . . But, at the time, back in 1982, guys were getting life sentences, I mean for murder, and they were like doing seven, eight, nine years and getting out." Anthony's estimate was accurate to an extent. In 1982, the average length of time a life-sentenced inmate served prior to release was less than eight years (Minor-Harper and Greenfeld 1985, 10). In that same year, the mean length of time served for murder was less than seven years (Minor-Harper and Greenfeld 1985, 8).

However, as Leon S. Sheleff notes (1987, 73), these estimates are deceiving and present a distorted picture of release practices. First, under an indeterminate sentencing scheme, the maximum sentence for many offenses was life imprisonment; it was probably not the intent of the sentencing judge to confine most of these offenders for the remainder of their lives. Second, these estimates only take into consideration the length of time served for inmates who were released. They do not include the length of time served for those life-sentenced inmates who remained incarcerated or died in prison. Even prior to the widespread adoption of life without parole, Sheleff estimated that about half of life-sentenced inmates were never released from prison, especially those who received life imprisonment in lieu of the death penalty (1987, 73–75). As such, there was most likely a discernible gap between the crimes of murderers who were released and those who remained incarcerated (e.g., a third-degree murder conviction as compared to a first-degree murder conviction).

Nonetheless, the LWOP sentence was in part implemented to eliminate the discretion of judges and parole officials who have been criticized for being overly lenient in their sentencing and release decisions (Blair 1994, 198–199; Mauer et al. 2004, 4). The mandatory imposition of life without parole curbs judicial discretion in imposing a sentence that is perceived as being insufficient given the offense. Over the last three decades, the mean length of a life sentence has continued to climb; by 2004, the average had risen to approximately twenty-nine years (Mauer et al. 2004, 12).

The elimination of judicial and parole board discretion brought about by life without parole would be consistent with the punishment philosophy of retribution. This philosophy prizes uniformity in sentencing and the curtailment of discretion could reduce sentencing disparities. From this perspective, punishment should be based on the severity of the crime committed and the culpability of the offender (Cullen and Jonson 2012, 39–40). About two-thirds of inmates in the United States who are serving life sentences (including LWOP) were convicted of murder (Nellis 2013, 7); as such, from a retributive framework, a LWOP sentence is an appropriate sentence (especially in non–death penalty states).

As a non-utilitarian philosophy, retribution concerns itself solely with punishing offenders for the crimes they have committed. One of the most difficult arguments to refute for those who oppose permanent incarceration is retribution's directive that continued incarceration is warranted for serious offenders even if they no longer pose a risk to society. The men featured in this book argue that their decades-long incarceration should have satisfied the need for retribution. According to Francis, a sixty-eight-year-old habitual offender, "There's some point in time where people should have received their pound of flesh." In addition to the severity of the crimes they committed (most commonly murder), they maintain that their minimal threat to society should also be taken into consideration when determining the appropriateness of continued incarceration.

In addition to being compatible with some of the key principles of retribution, incapacitation can also be used to provide support for life without parole for the sentence virtually guarantees that an offender will be permanently removed from society and deprives him or her of the opportunity to recidivate. While commutation and pardon are theoretically plausible means by which LWOP inmates could obtain release, these are rare at either the federal or state level (Gill 2010, 21). At the federal level, only one life-sentenced inmate has received a sentence commutation in the last twenty years (Gill 2010, 22). A similar situation exists at the state level. For example, in California there have been over twenty-five hundred inmates who have received life without parole in the past thirty years; none has had the sentence commuted (Sundby 2005, 38). Other states, for example, Wyoming, expressly prohibit a reduction to LWOP sentences through executive clemency (Wyoming Board of Parole 2012, sect 2).

Rationale Three: The Exemplar of the Tough on Crime Movement

The use of life without parole extends beyond an alternative to the death penalty. While the number of death-eligible offenses has decreased in the last thirty years, the number of offenses punishable by a LWOP sentence has expanded. Either based on a single conviction or a series of convictions, a variety of violent offenses (e.g., murder, rape/sexual assault, kidnapping, robbery, and aggravated assault), property offenses (e.g., burglary and carjacking), and drug offenses are punishable with life sentences, including life without parole (Nellis 2013, 7). Three strikes legislation in thirteen states and the federal government mandate the imposition of life without parole on the final strike (Ogletree and Sarat 2012, 4–5). The mid-Atlantic state which incarcerated the subjects of this book has its own version of habitual offender legislation, which prescribes life without parole for repeat offenders. Four men (Francis, Anthony, Troy, and Samuel) were serving LWOP sentences following their designations as habitual offenders.

Policymakers use their support for life without parole and other harsh sentencing practices as evidence that they are tough on crime. Perceived lenient treatment of serious offenders is high risk, low reward. As Jessica S. Henry notes in *Life without Parole: America's New Death Penalty?* (2012, 69), "No politician ever lost an election because he or she denied a parole application." Yet, history contains several examples of political careers damaged when leniency—or perceived leniency—toward offenders backfires. Perhaps, the best known is the Willie Horton case. This incident served as an important lesson to elected officials of the high political costs associated with perceived lenient treatment of offenders. While on a weekend furlough, Willie Horton, a LWOP inmate incarcerated in Massachusetts, sexually assaulted a woman and physically assaulted her boyfriend (Baranauckas 2010, para. 3). In 1988, while trailing his rival in the polls (Irwin 2009, 13), Republican presidential nominee George H.W. Bush used the Horton case to attack Democratic challenger Michael Dukakis, then the governor of Massachusetts, for being "soft" on crime. Two important facts are often missing from the common narrative of this incident. First, the furlough program had a success rate of 99.5 percent (Barkow 2012, 201); thus, while not minimizing the seriousness of the crimes Horton committed, he is a serious outlier. Virtually all inmates who participated in the furlough program did not pose a risk to the public. Second, Dukakis was not directly involved in the decision to grant Horton's furlough (Irwin 2009, 13). Nevertheless, Dukakis paid for his perceived softness on crime, while Bush capitalized on his tough on crime image, ultimately winning the election.

More recent examples exist of how the perception of leniency—in these cases miscalculations in the use of executive clemency—can be manufactured into political currency. Mike Huckabee, former governor of Arkansas, was criticized for supporting commutation in Maurice Clemmons's case. In 2000, Clemmons had been sentenced to 108 years for theft and other offenses. Huckabee defended the commutation stating that the sentence was excessive given Clemmons's offenses and his status as a juvenile, and that it had been unfairly applied based on Clemmons's race. Also, Clemmons had already served more than ten years of the sentence (Montopoli 2009, para. 3). Following his release, Clemmons was killed by police in 2009 (Montopoli 2009, para. 4). At the time of his death, he was suspected of murdering four Washington policemen (Baranauckas 2010, para. 13). Huckabee was condemned for his involvement in Clemmons's release. In 2009, Tim Pawlenty, who was the governor of Minnesota and shared Huckabee's presidential ambitions, played up his law and order stance when he stated: "In Minnesota, I don't think I've ever voted for clemency. We've given out pardons for things after everybody has served out their term, but again, usually for more minor offenses. But clemency, certainly not. Commutation of sentence, certainly not" (Fabian 2009, para. 4). Two years later, Tim Pawlenty was on the other side of the controversy when he faced criticism for his involvement in the 2008 pardon of Jeremy Giefer. In 1993, nineteen-year-old Giefer was convicted of engaging in a sexual relationship with his fourteen-year-old girlfriend and received a jail sentence of forty-five days. Two years after his pardon, Giefer was charged with twelve felonies related to the repeated sexual victimization of a child (Karnowski 2010).

IN OPPOSITION TO LIFE WITHOUT PAROLE

As there are two groups that support life without parole, opposition to the sentence can be broadly divided into two camps. One maintains that life without parole is as inhumane as the death penalty and its use should be seriously curtailed, if not eliminated entirely. These opponents allege that due to the low likelihood of recidivism, permanent incarceration is unnecessary, especially given its cost. In contrast, another faction rejects life without parole as an acceptable replacement for the death penalty and argues that capital punishment is the only way to ensure an offender never commits another crime.

Rationale One: LWOP Is as Inhumane as the Death Penalty

As outlined above, some of the support for life without parole appears to stem not from the belief that it is a good punishment in and of itself, but because it is thought to be the lesser of two evils. Critics of life without parole allege that this is not a compelling reason to support its implementation and express concern that the implications of the sentence have not been fully considered (Sheleff 1987, 140). For example, research casts doubt on the contention that life without parole has replaced the use of the death penalty as the decline in capital punishment occurred regardless of when LWOP legislation was implemented ("Matter of Life and Death" 2006, 1847–1850). Instead, the proliferation of LWOP has now resulted in the majority of US jurisdictions having two severe punishments, instead of one, at their disposal. In fact, all thirty-two death penalty states also authorize LWOP (DPIC 2013b).

While LWOP supporters maintain that the punishment respects human life to a greater extent than capital punishment because it preserves life, life without parole has been criticized as inhumane because of its lack of parole eligibility (Appleton and Grøver 2007, 609–611). Sheleff (1987, 56) explained: "When a person is doomed to spend his final years imprisoned, with no (or few) prospects of release, then in terms of his human dignity, his individuality, his freedom, and his autonomy, one could well argue that the oppressive confines of a prison constitute as great an infringement of his basic human rights as a death sentence. In fact, when a prisoner is sustained emotionally by the hope of his eventual release, then the continued denial of such release serves only to add a touch of macabre psychological strain, a Tantalus-like situation of recurrent hope met by repeated rejection."

This position has been maintained by the Council of Europe since 1977, when its Committee on the Treatment of Long-Term Prisoners stated (22): "It is inhuman to imprison a person for life without any hope of release. A crime prevention policy which accepts keeping a prisoner for life even if he is no longer a danger to society would be compatible neither with modern principles on the treatment of prisoners during the execution of their sentence nor with the idea of the reintegration of offenders into society. Nobody should be deprived of the *chance* of possible release." In *Graham v. Florida* (2010), the US Supreme Court appeared to share this position but only for juvenile LWOP offenders convicted of non-homicide offenses.[5] Justice Anthony Kennedy, the author of the majority's opinion, reasoned, "A State is not required to guarantee eventual freedom to a juvenile offender convicted of a nonhomicide crime. What the State must do, however, is give defendants like Graham some meaningful opportunity to obtain release based on demonstrated maturity and rehabilitation" (845–846).

Both the ACLU and Amnesty International USA oppose the death penalty and oppose life without parole for juveniles (ACLU 2014a, 2014b; Amnesty International and Human Rights Watch 2005, 2014), but they support the penalty for adults. The Sentencing Project and Campaign to End the Death Penalty (CEDP) are two of only a handful of national organizations that oppose both punishments for all offenders. CEDP director Lily Hughes explained the organization's opposition to California's Proposition Thirty-Four, which would have abolished the death penalty and replaced it with life without parole (Burns 2013, para. 6): "[CEDP] has been troubled by the development of a more and more conservative approach to the question of death penalty abolition. We're one of the only anti–death penalty organizations that has a stance on life without parole: We don't view it as a just alternative. Anti–death penalty campaigners need to do more to address the way that the whole criminal justice system operates." Hughes rejected the strategy of endorsing life without parole in order to abolish the death penalty and then attacking it as proposed by Dieter. She countered: "Life without parole shouldn't be promoted by activists as a short-term strategy for [death penalty] abolition, only to try to return to the issue later and attack life without parole. [This won't work] once life without parole has been cast by campaigners as a just sentence" (Burns 2013, para. 10).

The men whose experiences are described in this book agreed that permanent incarceration is an inhumane punishment because of the low likelihood of release. After serving two decades in prison, some wished that they had received the death penalty instead of receiving life without parole, for they thought that life without parole was a worse fate than death. Joshua, who had been incarcerated for thirty-three years for the murder of a homeowner in a burglary that went awry, explained: "I think it's harder. I mean, you know, you probably wouldn't think that, you know, when you first got a sentence to be executed, but I've been around them guys too and I know [one guy] didn't want appeals and wanted to get it over with because they know the bottom line. At the very worst, they're going to die sooner than later. And for some of them, it was the later part that was the problem not the sooner part."

Some specifically identified the low likelihood of release as the reason why permanent incarceration was a worse punishment than the death penalty:

> Let's say a guy murdered a guy and he got the death sentence. Okay, his intent is to try and get his sentenced overturned so he can get life without parole, then once he get life without parole . . . he [would] just try to continue his pursuit [of] his appeal and then get maybe the LWOP taken off and get parole put onto it and so on and so forth. . . . I've never seen [it] happen . . . but I think a guy that's on death row, I think he would be a lot better off if they just went on and executed him as opposed to the life without parole because that's torture. That is cold-blooded torture to stay here, and like I said, I've been here twenty-nine years. (Karl)

> They decided to give me life without parole. The hard death penalty. We call it the hard death penalty. (Joshua)

> We have a guy in here right now he says, you know, it would be better if they just take us out back and shot us. (Victor)

Even inmates formally sentenced to death agree that life without parole is a worse punishment. For example, Julian Wright, Jr. (1991, 348) found that half of his sample of death-sentenced inmates rated permanent incarceration as worse than the death penalty.

While the men acknowledged that they should receive a harsh punishment because of the severity of the crimes they committed (most commonly first-degree murder), they believed that the positive changes they had made over their lengthy incarcerations should be taken into consideration. Victor, who had been incarcerated for twenty-six years for the murder of an acquaintance, argued: "It's a shame that [there are] so many people sitting in here that would not reoffend, that has had enough, that has changed enough, that has fixed their selves up to where they can stand on their own two feet and make the right choices, they will never get that choice. They will never get that chance." Instead of a LWOP sentence, the men supported a sentence of life with the possibility of parole (LWP), which would require them to serve a certain number of years (e.g., twenty-five) before they would be eligible for parole (see Chapter 6, Policy Recommendations).[6]

Rationale Two: Only the Death Penalty Will Do

As with supporters of California's Proposition Thirty-Four, opponents of the legislation were also influential.[7] Californians for Justice and Public Safety was the most outspoken organization against the proposed abolition of the death penalty and sponsored the website "Vote NO on Prop 34." In explaining its opposition, Californians for Justice and Public Safety (2013d, para. 1) alleged that life without parole is not a sufficiently harsh punishment and maintained that capital punishment is the only fair punishment for especially heinous murders: "The death penalty is given to less than two percent of all murderers in California. These murders are so shocking that juries of law-abiding citizens unanimously delivered the sentence." On the "Vote NO on Prop 34" website, descriptions of the gruesome crimes of death-sentenced inmates were used as evidence of the deservingness of the death penalty (Californians for Justice and Public Safety 2013d, para. 2).

Retribution is the punishment philosophy most compatible with this position. It requires a punishment that is commensurate with the harm caused; subsequently, if an offender took a life, then his or her life should be forfeited. These LWOP opponents argue that, even if offenders were to be incarcerated until their deaths, they still have some semblance of a life (Blecker 2010, 13–15). If they took a life, why should their lives be spared? Why do murderers deserve to remain alive when they deprived their victims of the same opportunity? Furthermore, LWOP opponents doubt that "life means life" and are concerned that laws could be altered in the future, which could allow for the release of LWOP inmates. To this group, there is no acceptable alternative to the death penalty; even permanent incarceration leaves too much to chance, as reflected in the following statement: "Prisoner rights advocates funded by the ACLU promise Californians that if we abolish the death penalty, these death row inmates will never get out. This promise cannot be made. History has proven otherwise" (Californians for Justice and Public Safety 2013a, para. 3). In support of this claim, the organization cited the statistic that 23 death sentences were commuted between 1958 and 1966, though no examples of the commutation of LWOP sentences were included. Instead of abolishing capital punishment, the organization advocated for changes to the death penalty (e.g., curtailing the appeals process), as evident in its slogan "Mend It, Don't End It" (Californians for Justice and Public Safety 2013b).

Opponents of life without parole also express concern that LWOP inmates continue to pose a risk to others. They could attack other inmates or correctional staff, and if they were to escape, they could endanger the public (Waldo and Paternoster 2003, 339). In fact, it was feared that, because of their parole ineligibility, LWOP inmates would have little incentive to behave in prison. When LWOP statutes emerged, LWOP inmates were predicted to be "a new breed of superinmates, prone to violence and uncontrollable" (Stewart and Lieberman 1982, 16). These early concerns have not come to fruition as empirical evidence repeatedly demonstrates that parole-eligible inmates serving shorter sentences pose a greater disciplinary problem than LWOP inmates. For example, Mark D. Cunningham and Jon R. Sorensen (2006, 693) reviewed the disciplinary records of LWOP inmates compared to four groups of long-term inmates with sentence lengths of ten to fourteen years, fifteen to nineteen years, twenty to twenty-nine years, and thirty or more years. While controlling for security level, they found LWOP inmates were less involved in potentially violent or violent misconduct than the inmates serving sentences of less than nineteen years. However, although the variation was small, LWOP inmates were more likely to be involved in potentially violent or violent rule violations than inmates with sentences in excess of twenty years.

Taking their analysis one step further, Cunningham and Sorensen (2006, 697) used survival analysis to estimate the time to committing a potentially violent disciplinary infraction for each group. They found that the mean survival times to the commission of a potentially violent act for LWOP inmates were significantly longer than the group of long-term inmates serving ten to fourteen years; however, the mean survival times for LWOP inmates were significantly shorter than inmates in the group serving at least thirty years. Even after accounting for other factors that are related to prison misconduct, including age at prison admission, gang membership, previous incarceration, and sentence offense, LWOP inmates had a lower probability than long-term inmates in the ten to fourteen years, fifteen to nineteen years, and twenty to twenty-nine years groups (698). Based on these findings, they concluded that LWOP inmates as a group did not pose a major problem for prison staff to manage.

This study is consistent with the bulk of empirical evidence that suggests that LWOP inmates have low involvement in prison rule breaking, violent or otherwise, than other populations of inmates. LWOP inmates are less likely to engage in serious disciplinary infractions and they have lower rates of disciplinary infraction than most other inmates. In fact, as they age, their likelihood of engaging in misconduct is further reduced. One of the most consistent findings related to inmate misconduct is that because of "maturation, loss of nerve, the association of age with prosocial normative orientations and conventional commitments, or some combination of these factors" (Flanagan 1980b, 359), older inmates are less likely to violate prison rules than younger inmates., The men were deterred from rule breaking, as the punishment would jeopardize the privileges they had worked to obtain.

Rationale Three: The Price Is Not Right

As might be surmised, permanent incarceration is expensive, though cheaper than the death penalty. The average cost of incarcerating an inmate for forty years is estimated to be approximately $1 million (Mauer et al. 2004, 25). The men in this book were aware of the tremendous costs of keeping them incarcerated for the remainder of their lives. As LWOP inmates grow old in prison, they require more expensive health care, which further increases the cost of confinement. The annual cost of caring for an older inmate is estimated to be about $70,000 (Mauer et al. 2004, 25), approximately three times higher than the annual cost for a younger inmate. The expense of their continued confinement is the reason that some opponents support the eventual release of LWOP inmates. In addition to the monetary costs, Victor alleged that "all of the people in here, to me, is a terrible waste of life, money, [and] space."

Rationale Four: Permanent Incarceration Is Not Necessary for Public Safety

Critics of life without parole further assert that life-sentenced inmates do not pose a threat to public safety, as statistics consistently demonstrate that older inmates and murderers have lower likelihoods of recidivism than younger inmates or inmates who have committed less serious offenses (Langan and Levin 2002, 7–8). The men were familiar with studies highlighting the low likelihood of recidivism for aging inmates convicted of murder and used them as evidence to support their release. Daniel, a fifty-seven-year-old inmate who had been incarcerated for thirty-one years, argued: "They deserve a second chance because the recidivism rate of murderers is not that high. I think that needs to be considered from the legislators and all of that because people just don't go out and commit murders."

In their often-cited examination of the institutional and post-release behaviors of *Furman*-commuted inmates in Texas, James W. Marquart and Jonathan R. Sorensen (1988, 686–689) found a low level of recidivism for released death- and life-sentenced inmates. In Texas, in order for the death penalty to be imposed, the capital jury must unanimously agree that the defendant poses a threat of future dangerousness (687). When the death penalty was declared unconstitutional in *Furman v. Georgia* (1972), death-sentenced inmates automatically had their sentences commuted to life with the possibility of parole (678). The Court's ruling created the necessary experimental conditions in order to determine how inmates who were believed to be so dangerous that they needed to be executed would behave if they were ever to return to the community (678). The institutional behavior of the 44 *Furman*-commuted inmates and the post-release behavior of the 28 among them who were eventually paroled were compared to 156 inmates originally sentenced to life with the possibility of parole (687). Based on data, 21 of the 28 did not recidivate (687). Of the seven who did, three committed technical violations of parole and four committed new felony offenses (two committed burglary, one committed rape, and one committed murder) (687).[8] Among the life-sentenced inmates, 109 were released and 18 recidivated (678). Twelve committed technical violations and six committed new offenses (four committed burglary, one committed robbery, and one committed rape) (678). None committed another homicide (688). These results suggest that juries overestimate the future dangerousness of serious offenders. Additional studies conducted in Pennsylvania (Pennsylvania General Assembly 2005, 4), Massachusetts (Black 1990, 68; Haas and Fillion 2010, 17), and California (Weisberg et al. 2011, 17) confirm the low recidivism of life-sentenced inmates. As such, from a public safety standpoint, it appears that there is little compelling evidence to justify the permanent incarceration of LWP and LWOP inmates en masse.

Rationale Five: No Evidence that Punitiveness Leads to General Deterrence

Deterrence is another important aim of punishment and can be used to provide support for life without parole in theory. According to the philosophy, and as advanced by Beccaria and Bentham, severe punishment can act as a general deterrent by discouraging others from committing similar offenses. However, evidence is scant that harsher punishments have a strong and lasting general deterrent effect as compared to less serious alternatives (Cullen and Jonson 2012, 74–77). While there are no studies that examine the deterrent effect of life without parole as compared to a lesser sentence such as life with the possibility of parole, there is no reason to expect that life without parole would have a general deterrent effect greater than other forms of punishment including the death penalty (O'Hear 2010, 5). In fact, Paul H. Robinson (2012, 140–142) contends that life without parole fails three perquisites to achieve a general deterrence effect: (1) Would-be offenders are unaware of the scenarios in which they could receive a LWOP sentence; (2) Would-be offenders, because of drug or alcohol use or emotional strain, are unable to conduct a rational cost-benefit analysis of whether to commit an offense; and (3) Would-be offenders determine that the costs related to the commission of the crime outweigh the benefits, yet the low likelihood of apprehension and punishment alongside the immediate benefits of the offense (e.g., money or alleviation of emotions) may cause the offender to risk the crime. The men's descriptions of their thought processes and behaviors leading up to the commission of the crime challenge deterrence's major assumption of offender rationality. One-third of the men claimed to be under the influence of alcohol, drugs, or a combination of both at the time of the offense. Several of the men described "snapping" and being incapable of thinking clearly. In addition, most of the men did not believe that they would get caught, or if they did, a sentence of life without parole would not be imposed. These sentiments are reflected in the following statements from George, who had been incarcerated since the age of thirty-seven and was now seventy-two, and Francis, a sixty-eight-year-old habitual offender who had been incarcerated for eighteen years:

> I didn't feel that I would [receive a LWOP sentence]. I had previous encounters with the law and they all ended in not guilty verdicts. (George)

> I did know that there was the habitual offender statute, [but] to be honest with you, though I knew it, I never thought I'd get [life without parole]. (Francis)

Rationale Six: International Use of Life without Parole

A cross-national review of life without parole is insightful. Along with the United States, nations in Europe (e.g., Bulgaria, Estonia, Hungary, France, England and Wales, Iceland, Lithuania, Malta, the Netherlands, Slovakia, Sweden, and Switzerland, and Ukraine), the Middle East (e.g., Turkey,) and Asia (e.g., Vietnam) also allow for the sentence (Appleton and Grøver 2007, 602; Penal Reform International 2007, 4; *Vinter and Others v. The United Kingdom* 2013, 25). However, two major differences exist in the use of life without parole internationally as compared to in the United States. First, other LWOP nations do not use the sentence with the same frequency as the United States. For instance, there are only forty-two English and Welsh inmates serving sentences equivalent to life without parole (Ministry of Justice 2013, 9) as compared to the approximate fifty thousand inmates in the United States (Nellis 2013, 1). Second, international human rights laws mandate that the possibility of sentence review and the chance of release must exist for adult LWOP inmates. Otherwise, the European Court of Human Rights held that whole-life tariffs (the equivalent of life without parole) would violate Article 3 of the European Convention on Human Rights (*Vinter and Others v. The United Kingdom* 2013).[9] The European Court explained why the lack of review and lack of potential release for the permanently incarcerated constitute a human rights violation, reasoning: "If such a prisoner is incarcerated without any prospect of release and without the possibility of having his life sentence reviewed, there is the risk that he can never atone for his offence: whatever the prisoner does in prison, however exceptional his progress towards rehabilitation, his punishment remains fixed and unreviewable. If anything, the punishment becomes greater with time: the longer the prisoner lives, the longer his sentence" (40).

Universal support for life without parole does not exist as other countries around the world (e.g., Andorra, Bosnia and Herzegovina, Brazil, Croatia, Columbia, El Salvador, Mexico, Montenegro, Nicaragua, Norway, Portugal, San Marino, Spain, and Venezuela) expressly prohibit the use of life imprisonment (Appleton and Grøver 2007, 601, 608; *Vinter and Others v. The United Kingdom* 2013, 25).[10] In theory, these countries could block the extradition of offenders facing life without parole, as other countries have done with offenders who could receive a death sentence (O'Hear 2010, 4). In addition, the United States is the only country in the world to allow juvenile offenders to receive life without parole (The Sentencing Project 2011, 1). In 2005, Amnesty International and Human Rights Watch estimated that there were at least two thousand individuals across the country serving LWOP sentences for crimes they committed when they were below the age of eighteen (1). In *Graham v. Florida* (2010), and two years later in the companion cases of *Miller v. Alabama* (2012) and *Jackson v. Hobbs* (2012), the US Supreme Court limited the use of life without parole for juvenile defendants as the sentence cannot be imposed for non-homicide offenses and cannot be mandatorily applied, respectively. It is important to note that these restrictions apply to juvenile defendants only.[11]

Rationale Seven: The Public Claims to Want More from Punishment

One rationale to explain why politicians embraced the tough on crime movement is that they were mirroring the opinions of their constituents (Applegate et al. 1996, 518). However, the American public might not be as punitive as commonly believed and, instead, have attitudes that are more comparable to the international use of life without parole. Although dated, William J. Bowers and colleagues (1994, 90) examined public support for a variety of LWP and LWOP provisions. They found that in five of seven states, a modified sentence of life with the possibility of parole in which there is parole ineligibility for twenty-five years and victim restitution received higher public approval than the death penalty. Furthermore, they also noted that life with the possibility of parole with twenty-five years of parole ineligibility and restitution was the punishment most likely to be selected by New York residents as the punishment that "does the greatest good for all concerned" (112). A sentence of life without parole was rated lowest by both New York and Nebraska residents on this measure.

While the above study is indicative of the public's approval of less severe versions of life without parole, public attitudes toward punishment may be even more nuanced. Public opinion toward the release of serious offenders in the abstract, as measured in the study above, may be substantially different from attitudes when release actually occurs, as suggested in the reaction to former Republican Mississippi governor Haley Barbour's decision in January 2012 to grant executive clemency to approximately two hundred inmates, including the commutations of four men who were incarcerated for murder (Jonsson 2012, para. 1; "Outgoing Mississippi Governor" 2012, para. 1). Barbour, a popular governor with a reputation as being a law and order proponent, had served the limit of two terms. Although it appeared that Barbour was entertaining the notion of running for president, his decision to use executive clemency in an unprecedented number of cases could have been indicative of his belief that his political career was ending (Jonsson 2012, para. 2). Of the four men incarcerated for murder who received executive clemency, three of the four had served approximately twenty years and the other had served more than ten years ("Outgoing Mississippi Governor" 2012, para. 1; Le Coz 2013, paras. 5, 40). While three of the men had served close to the sentence of life with the possibility of parole with twenty-five years of parole ineligibility that was supported in the Bowers et al. study (1994), public reaction was decidedly against Barbour's use of executive clemency.

After a legal challenge brought by Jim Hood, the Democratic attorney general, Barbour's use of executive clemency was ultimately upheld by the Mississippi Supreme Court (Mohr 2012, paras. 1, 3). Legislation to reduce gubernatorial clemency powers was introduced (Jonsson 2012, para. 19), and immediately after taking office, current governor Phil Bryant ended the decades-long inmate trustee program, in which inmates, including the four convicted of murder whose sentences were later commuted, worked in the governor's residence ("Mississippi Ends" 2012, para. 1). In fact, in a national poll of one thousand randomly selected participants conducted in March 2012, near the time in which there was heightened media coverage of Barbour's use of executive clemency, a sizeable majority believed that executive clemency should not be permitted in cases involving serious violent offenses, namely, rape (85 percent), murder (84 percent), drunk driving resulting in death (77 percent), or armed robbery (75 percent) (Angus Reid Public Opinion 2012, 1). The sample was divided on whether executive clemency should exist at all; 49 percent supported it and 43 percent opposed it (2).

How can this difference in public opinion polls be reconciled? It could be the case that the public has greater opposition to executive discretion and has an adverse reaction when sentences are modified in this manner. Perhaps, the public would be more supportive of LWOP sentences of twenty-five years of parole ineligibility if they were imposed by the courts as opposed to the reduction of sentences after the fact. These conflicting findings could also indicate that the public is less supportive of the release of serious offenders when it actually occurs than as suggested by polls in which the release of serious offenders is being discussed in the abstract.

Rationale Eight: Minorities Are Disproportionately Affected

Another source of concern for LWOP opponents is the disproportionate number of minorities who are sentenced to permanent incarceration. According to The Sentencing Project (Nellis 2013, 10), Black inmates account for over half (58 percent) of the LWOP population. Minorities are also disproportionately represented among the men featured in this book as sixteen of the twenty-five are of color. While retribution could be used to justify life without parole, it would not support disparate sentencing based on race or ethnicity. Instead, the punishment philosophy requires that offenders who committed the same crime and have the same culpability receive the same punishment, regardless of the offender's race or any other extralegal factor (Frase 2010, 55).

Rationale Nine: Lack of Legal Protections for the Permanently Incarcerated

Critics of life without parole allege that the sentence suffers from issues that are either not present or have been remedied in capital cases, including the absence of special scrutiny by courts, its arbitrariness, and its mandatory imposition. While LWOP inmates are sentenced to spend the remainder of their lives incarcerated, they are not afforded the same legal protections as their capital counterparts. In the adjudication of capital cases, meticulous attention is paid to ensure that laws are closely adhered to; the same diligence is not afforded to LWOP cases. According to former prosecutor Bennett Capers (Burns 2013, para. 13): "As a prosecutor, when I was confronted with a death-eligible case, [my team] would put in immense resources because we knew that judges would make sure to dot every 'i' and cross every 't.' But when defendants were facing life without parole or an equivalent, we'd treat those cases like part of an assembly line. Those cases become invisible. . . . We don't worry and lose sleep over the defendants who will never see the light of day again." Another personal observation from Capers is equally telling. In *Life without Parole: America's New Death Penalty?* (2012, 169), Capers claimed that he can remember many of the capital defendants he prosecuted but few of the LWOP defendants.

At the appellate level, LWOP cases receive no special measures of review, potentially allowing for legal mistakes to go uncorrected. In the United States, defendants convicted of serious felonies such as murder receive a court-appointed attorney to assist with their direct appeals (Simon 2012b, para. 3). However, only death-sentenced inmates receive a court-appointed attorney in state and federal habeas corpus proceedings (Egelko 2012, para. 6). As mentioned above, the odds of overturning a death sentence are much higher than those of overturning non-death sentences, including LWOP (Henry 2012, 77).

Anecdotal evidence from Alabama suggests that because of the additional legal protections in death penalty cases some capital defendants put forth a request to receive a death sentence at the penalty phase (Liptak 2005, para. 26). Returning to California's Proposition Thirty-Four, the CEDP contacted the more than 220 death-sentenced inmates in the state asking them if they supported the measure. Of the 60 who responded, 56 opposed it (Hughes 2014, para. 14). The primary reason expressed for their opposition was the loss of the legal protections they were entitled to because of their capital sentence. One death-sentenced inmate claimed that, if their sentences were commuted to life without parole, it would not be seen as a victory but instead as "taking a step backward in our ability to challenge our convictions" (Egelko 2012, para. 18).

Related to the lack of additional legal scrutiny provided to LWOP inmates, a subsequent issue is the arbitrary imposition of the sentence (Henry 2012,

83–87). Permanent incarceration is used to punish a wide range of offenders; as a result, it has been criticized for being used too loosely and not reserved for the worst offenders (Henry 2012, 83). In *Ultimate Penalties*, Leon S. Sheleff (1987, 118) argued that the varying lengths of a life sentence further compounds its arbitrariness. As there is no precise length of a LWOP sentence, one LWOP inmate could serve many more years than another. This lack of uniformity violates one of retribution's principal tenets that offenders who committed the same crime and have the same levels of culpability receive the same sentence. Finally, the mandatory imposition of life without parole, which is banned in capital cases, is another source of opposition. In thirteen states and the federal government, life without parole is the mandatory final sentence prescribed by three strikes legislation (Ogletree and Sarat 2012, 4–5). As a result, the specific details of the case fail to be taken into consideration by the judge.

Rationale Ten: Ignores Evidence of Rehabilitation

Similar to capital punishment, permanent incarceration conveys the message that the inmate is never meant to return to society. Hence, the punishment fails to consider the potential for LWOP inmates to be rehabilitated and to positively contribute to society upon release. While incarcerated, many undergo an "awakening" in which they accept responsibility for their offenses and actively pursue efforts to improve themselves (through education, vocational training, counseling, etc.) (Irwin 2009, 88). Life-sentenced inmates have created a variety of programs in prison (e.g., self-help programs) and work to assist other inmates and better the prison environment through tutoring, mentoring, ministry, and legal advocacy (Hassine 2009; Irwin 2009, 78–79; Tierney 2012, para. 12). As a result, opponents of permanent incarceration argue that it is unfair to continue to incarcerate individuals who have demonstrated evidence of rehabilitation and would not endanger the public if released. In reflecting this position, Irwin (2009, 126) contended: "[It is inhumane to hold] persons who, though they committed a serious crime, sometimes a horrible crime, have, through the years, matured into completely different human beings than the 'offenders' they were many years, perhaps two to three decades, ago. Most of these individuals not only experience the normal process of maturation through which immature, irresponsible, conscienceless, often psychologically disturbed, and socially disconnected young people 'grow up.' But they also, through the imprisonment experience, gain insight and remorse, and vigorously participate in programs to improve themselves."

THE US SUPREME COURT AND
PERMANENT INCARCERATION

In the post-*Furman* era, the US Supreme Court has narrowed the categories of death-eligible offenders for it has ruled that it is unconstitutional for
the mentally insane (*Ford v. Wainwright* 1986), the mentally retarded (*Atkins v.
Virginia* 2002), and juveniles (*Roper v. Simmons* 2005) to receive the death penalty. The Court has also prohibited the use of the death penalty for the offense
of rape either of an adult (*Coker v. Georgia* 1977) or of a child (*Kennedy v. Louisiana* 2008). The mandatory imposition of the death penalty (*Woodson v. North
Carolina* 1976), including a mandatory death sentence for LWOP inmates who
commit homicide while incarcerated (*Sumner v. Shuman* 1987), has also been
banned. During the same time period, the only category of offender whom
the Court has expressly made LWOP-ineligible is juvenile offenders convicted
of non-lethal offenses (*Graham v. Florida* 2010). Additionally, only juveniles
cannot receive a mandatory LWOP sentence (*Jackson v. Hobbs* 2012; *Miller v.
Alabama* 2012).

The constitutionality of life without parole as a sentencing option in
capital cases appears to have been accepted by the Court in non-capital cases.
In *Schick v. Reed* (1974), the Court upheld the constitutionality of President
Eisenhower's commutation of a death sentence to life imprisonment that
included the stipulation of parole ineligibility. The US Supreme Court has
also (with few exceptions) upheld the constitutionality of LWP and LWOP
sentences for adult habitual and drug offenders. The Court affirmed a sentence
of life with the possibility of parole for habitual offenders in *Rummel v. Estelle*
(1980), in which the defendant had been previously convicted of two property
crimes and whose life-sentence-triggering offense was felony theft. In *Harmelin v. Michigan* (1991), the Court determined that a mandatory LWOP sentence
for Harmelin, who was convicted of possession of 672 grams of cocaine, was
constitutional.[12] More recently, the Court affirmed the twenty-five-year to life
sentence prescribed by California's Three Strikes legislation in *Ewing v. California* (2003) and *Lockyer v. Andrade* (2003), in which the triggering offenses were
shoplifting golf clubs and video tapes, respectively.

There has been only one notable exception to the Court's deference to
the legislative branch in defining sentencing parameters for adult defendants.
In *Solem v. Helm* (1983), the Court ruled that the punishment of life without
parole under a South Dakota habitual offender statute violated the Eighth
Amendment for Helm, who had been previously convicted of seven non-
violent offenses. The Court has imposed greater restrictions on the use of
juvenile life without parole. However, the three juvenile LWOP decisions
described above affect only a small portion of the total LWOP population;
less than 5 percent of LWOP inmates are serving sentences for crimes they

committed when they were juveniles (Nellis and King 2009, 3). Although restrictions have been made to limit juvenile life without parole, juveniles could nonetheless still spend most of their lives incarcerated. For example, in Iowa, the sentences of all thirty-eight juveniles serving life without parole were commuted by the governor to parole-ineligible sixty-year terms (Wiser 2012, paras. 1–2).

CONCLUSION

There are more LWOP inmates incarcerated today than at any other point in US history. Over the last four decades, the number of LWOP inmates and the ratio of LWOP inmates to the total prison population have steadily increased. Today, every jurisdiction in the nation (besides Alaska) permits the sentence. The rationales for the use of life without parole center on its toughness and its mercy, as the sentence is supported because of the limited likelihood of release of inmates yet also because it spares human life. In contrast, some LWOP opponents argue that it is an insufficient alternative to the death penalty, while others base their opposition on the grounds that life without parole is as unjust as the death penalty because of how it is utilized, including the crimes punishable with permanent incarceration, the characteristics of the defendants who receive it, the low likelihood of release, and the lack of additional legal safeguards provided to LWOP inmates.

What is less clear is how aging LWOP inmates perceive the punishment. As such, the purpose of this book is to examine their perceptions of permanent incarceration and how they have coped with their decades-long separation from the free world. In the next chapter, the twenty-five men are introduced.

CHAPTER 2

The Forgotten

PRIOR TO ENTERING PRISON to begin serving life without parole, the men had ordinary lives. Most were young men in their twenties and thirties. Seven had earned high school diplomas or the equivalent. Four (George, Gabriel, Francis, and Adam) had attended college, and Charles had graduated. Many had families. Nine were married, and twenty-one were fathers. The men worked, predominantly in trades including construction, carpentry, auto body repair, and welding. Five were small business owners. Two were police officers. Seven had served in the military. Two had immigrated to the United States.

While their lives were unremarkable, they were not without turmoil. As children, Anthony, Robert, and Thomas were placed in foster care. Thomas and Anthony also shared another commonality: both had spent more than three-quarters of their lives incarcerated. In surveying his life, Thomas, who was sixty-eight years of age and had been incarcerated for twenty-one years, surmised: "I'm a child of the State. . . . I've spent most of my time inside rather than outside." Most of his life had been spent in one total institution or another (Goffman 1961). As a child, Thomas was placed in an orphanage after the deaths of his parents; as a teenager he was confined to a mental hospital; and as an adult, he had served several jail and prison sentences prior to receiving life without parole. One other LWOP inmate spent time in a mental institution as a young man, and another as an adult.

Matthew, who at the age of seventy-three was one of the oldest men in the group, also experienced difficulty over the course of his life. He believed that his anger issues stemmed from childhood. His father was a sharecropper, and Matthew described growing up in poverty, living in a house without basic amenities such as electricity, running water, or an inside toilet. The oldest of ten, Matthew was forced at a young age to assume responsibility for his younger siblings; over fifty years later, Matthew was angry that he had missed out on a carefree childhood. As an adult Matthew also experienced traumatic life events. One of his children was born with a congenital heart defect and died at the age of three.

Other negative life events were also mentioned. During the Vietnam War, Charles routinely witnessed combat-related deaths. Though he survived, he was sprayed with the harmful herbicide Agent Orange. Upon returning to the United States, Charles was diagnosed with combat fatigue syndrome, later his diagnosis was elevated to post-traumatic stress disorder. Serving in the Navy during Vietnam, Alan witnessed the death of a serviceman when a steel cable broke free and dismembered him. Personal relationships were also strained. Almost one-third of the men were divorced, and three were separated from their spouses. Eight admitted to using drugs regularly, including heroin, PCP, crack cocaine, and marijuana, or having a substance abuse problem. Seventeen had been jailed or imprisoned previously, commonly for non-violent offenses (e.g., burglary), although drug possession and trafficking, driving while intoxicated, and motor vehicle theft were also reported. Eight men had been incarcerated previously for a violent offense, most commonly for robbery or assault. One individual had been incarcerated previously for attempted rape.

THE MEN

The pseudonyms and select demographics of the twenty-five men are displayed in Appendix A. Most were young men when they entered prison to begin serving permanent incarceration. Eight were in their twenties, ten were in their thirties, five were in their forties, and two were in their fifties. At the age of twenty-two, Troy was the youngest of all the men when he entered prison, and at the age of fifty-eight, James was the oldest. The mean age at incarceration for the group of twenty-five men was thirty-four. At the time of the first interview in 2006, the men ranged in age from fifty to seventy-five with a mean of fifty-nine. At the time of the follow-up interview in 2011, the mean age had increased to sixty-four and all the men were between the ages of fifty-five and eighty. Minorities were disproportionately represented in the group. Nine of the men were White, fourteen were Black, one was Hispanic, and one was Asian. With regard to social attachments, seven men were married when they entered prison. Twenty-one had children. Prior to the current sentence, the group's level of education ranged from the sixth grade to a college degree with an average of about ten years of schooling. In 2006, the average length of time served for the crimes described below was about twenty-four years, with a range of fifteen to thirty-one years. Five years later, for the nineteen who remained incarcerated and consented to a second interview, the mean length of time served had increased to thirty years with a range of nineteen to thirty-six years.

A TYPOLOGY OF THEIR OFFENSES

Twenty-one of the men received sentences of life without parole following a conviction of first-degree murder. The remaining four received LWOP sentences following their designations as habitual offenders. Fifteen of the murder cases involved the death of one person, three involved the death of one victim with at least one other individual injured, and three involved the deaths of two or three individuals. In cases involving multiple victims, all injuries or deaths occurred within a single violent episode. The cases were evenly divided between involving a single perpetrator (n=11) and involving at least two perpetrators (n=10). In all ten cases involving more than one offender, the individual interviewed either received as severe a sentence as the accomplice(s) or a more severe sentence.

In *Lifers* (2009, 44), Irwin introduced a three-category typology to classify "typical" homicides: "(1) homicides resulting from deviant-group activities, such as 'gangbanging' and drug trafficking, (2) homicides resulting from robberies or burglaries gone awry, and (3) homicides related to high pressure, emotional contexts, sequences, or relationships, such as in an ongoing spousal conflict." All of the homicides in the present study in which the offender admitted responsibility can be placed into one of these categories. Among the present group, the most common category was homicides related to emotional stress (n=7). Six cases would be classified in the "felony-murder" category as the original intent of the offender was to commit a robbery or burglary. Only one case would be classified as related to deviant-group activities. In addition to these three, two additional categories of habitual offenders (n=4) and claims of innocence or justified homicide (n=7) were added to account for all twenty-five men.

Homicides Related to High Pressure

A startling eight men (nearly one in three) were incarcerated for the murder of a former or current romantic partner. According to court records, two of the slain women were pregnant at the time of their deaths. The six men who admitted guilt described their relationships with the victim as strained, laden with conflict, and marked by accusations of infidelity and rejection. These offenses were described as impulsive, emotional reactions to stress. Walter, who had served thirty-six years for the murder of a romantic partner, and Karl, who had been incarcerated since the age of twenty-four for the murder of his former girlfriend, reported that they had been drinking and/or using drugs before the crime occurred. Three men (Michael, Matthew, and Karl) claimed that their wives or girlfriends had been unfaithful to them. Michael, who had been incarcerated for three decades, described the tumultuous relationship he had with his wife and his jealousy when he learned his wife was romantically involved with another man:

> Well, it was a roller coaster marriage, you know, that I'd come home [and] the furniture would be gone. She'd be gone and then she'd come back and, you know, just . . . a back forth roller coaster marriage. . . . Well, it's

a crime of passion. I snapped out. I was mentally off balance and it was a crime of passion. . . . I went to get her and bring her home. We had been out on a date, you know, a couple of nights before, went to dinner, had sex, and everything, you know, and I just went to pick her up and take her home. And she was with this [guy] and I snapped out. . . . No, it wasn't pre-meditated. I loved her.

Besides infidelity, two other sources of conflict included feelings of rejection and the threatened safety of a child. On the day of the incident, Gabriel, who was in his twenties at the time, had intended to commit suicide. As described below, he felt rejected by his estranged girlfriend when she refused to speak with him and decided to go to her place of employment to have a face-to-face conversation. The situation escalated quickly, and he shot his girlfriend and several of her coworkers:

On that day, I made the decision that, you know, this was going to be my last day on Earth. . . . I called my girlfriend at work. . . . She doesn't really have time to talk to me, and I don't tell her what my plans are, but she's like, "Look, I can't talk." . . . She hung up, I called her back. She hung up, I called her back. So my attitude was like if this is going to be my last day on Earth, you know, you're going to hear what I've got to say. [In order to avoid security], I scaled the fence, I'm on her job, and I went into the building and I saw her. . . . At that time I just snapped, I'm kind of like, you know, blaming . . . her for everything that I was feeling. So I took a gun out and from where I could stand, I shot her. . . . They said there were bullets all over the place and I remember hitting one of the guards. . . . I walked through the [building] and I saw a guy that I'd had an argument with six months earlier. . . . I shot in his office about three or four times and I shot him.

In a similar situation, Karl claimed to have been motivated to go to his former girlfriend's place of employment so that he could speak with her and resolve the argument that they had had earlier in the day. When she refused to speak with him, he became angry and killed her. This was not an isolated incident of violence in their relationship as court records indicate that Karl had admitted to being physically abusive toward her in the past. Alternatively, Thomas claimed that his estranged wife was suicidal and threatened to harm their child, and as a result, he felt that he had to act to protect the child. Twenty-one years after murdering his wife, he was resolute in his belief that he had few other options to resolve the situation: "This crime that I committed, I wouldn't have committed that crime if the situation hadn't been . . . as it was. Crimes of violence are committed for a reason because you have to . . . and this is what I get for it." As he was leaving his wife's apartment, court records indicate that he informed a passerby that she needed to call the police because he had committed murder.

While all six men accepted responsibility for the murders they committed, five disputed the conviction of first-degree murder and the subsequent LWOP sentence. Because the crimes were committed in the heat of passion, the men claimed that a lesser charge (e.g., second-degree murder) and a lighter sentence (e.g., a twenty-year sentence or LWP) more accurately reflected their culpability. Matthew asserted, "They said that it was premeditated and I coldly planned the whole thing which I didn't." Thomas was the only one who believed that life without parole was an appropriate sentence given his culpability, and as a result, he never appealed his sentence. (He had planned to apply for commutation after he had served thirty years but died in prison after serving twenty-three.) Alleging that he was "off-balance" after the crime and unable to make sound decisions, Michael turned down a plea-bargaining arrangement that could have resulted in a much lighter sentence. He described his meeting with an assistant prosecutor: "[He] said if you take this deal, you know, [in] fifteen years, we'll help you get out. . . . And he said . . . we go to trial, you know, my boss [the prosecutor] will get re-elected on you, so you should take this deal. . . . He said you're no threat and he said you're no threat to society, you'll never commit this crime again." Michael did not agree to the deal. At trial, he claimed the prosecutor "said I was the worst thing in the world. I was a sociopath." Another one of these men reported that he suffered "a mental breakdown" and was found incompetent to stand trial; he spent several years in a mental institution before he was deemed competent to be tried.

Unlike the above cases in which the primary victim was a former or current romantic partner, the final case that fits within the expressive violence category involved the homicide of an acquaintance. Claiming that the victim was mean-spirited and had threatened Victor's life previously, Victor, who had been incarcerated for twenty-six years, admitted to killing the acquaintance while he was under the influence of PCP. He reported that at the time of the offense he felt as though he "did the world a favor," though over time he grew to be remorseful and stated, "I'm sorry about it, real sorry."

Homicides Resulting from Robberies or Burglaries Gone Awry

According to these six men, homicide was an unintended result of a robbery or a burglary. Alan, Robert, and Adam each reported that they were under the influence of drugs or alcohol when they committed their crimes. Acquiring money or valuables was the motivation for the robbery or burglary, but in each case, the situation escalated resulting in homicide. Alan was forty-nine when he began serving life without parole and had been incarcerated for nineteen years. He was the only individual in the group who was serving life without parole for the murder of a blood relative. Unlike the strained relationships between intimate partners discussed above, Alan described his relationship with his female relative as devoid of conflict and reported that he felt closer to her than he did his mother. During the interview, he was unable to recall the incident clearly and could not provide a motive for the offense. Alan described it "as a strange incident" and stated that "it just happened." Court records indicated that he had a drug addiction and went to his relative's house to obtain money to purchase drugs, and when she refused his demand, he murdered her. Court transcripts also indicated that he called the police to report the crime and that he made statements expressing a need to be incarcerated so that he would not commit a similar offense in the future.

Henry, who was thirty-one when he entered prison and had served more than thirty years, reported that after drinking all day, he and a relative confronted an acquaintance. Henry demanded money from the acquaintance, and when he claimed not to have any, Henry brandished a gun. Henry reported that he regularly carried firearms because he "had an addiction to pistols and guns." He claimed that he and the victim were fighting over the weapon when the gun discharged, fatally injuring the victim. In a similar situation, Adam, who had served over three decades for a crime he committed in his early twenties, reported that after drinking for several hours and ingesting PCP, he and a friend went to an acquaintance's house to rob him. The situation escalated, and Adam admitted to killing him.

Noah, Nathan, and Joshua had planned to burglarize an unoccupied home. However, when surprised by the appearance of a homeowner, lethal violence ensued. Nathan, who was in his early twenties at the time, was not in the house when the murder occurred. He claimed to be in the vehicle waiting for his accomplice. Nathan and his accomplice refused to accept a reduced sentence in exchange for testifying against each other, and because the police were unable to identify the actual killer, both received life without parole. Noah and Joshua both admitted to killing the homeowner in their respective offenses. When I asked Noah, who was fifty-eight and had been incarcerated for twenty-seven years, how often he thought about the offense, he responded: "Always. It's something that I never will forget. I see it every time I close my eyes and go to sleep at night, I see that. It's something that I will never forget and that I will never be without. . . . Every avenue that's possible to humanly think about, I've done it. What if I have done this? What if I hadn't went there?"

Homicides Resulting from Deviant-Group Activities

Only one homicide fits within this category. George, one of the oldest and longest serving of the group, was incarcerated for the murder of an acquaintance. Involved in drug trafficking, he claimed to have killed the victim because he believed the victim was a police informant. While there were four accomplices charged for their involvement in the offense, George admitted that he was the actual killer.

Habitual Offenders

Four men (Francis, Anthony, Troy, and Samuel) were declared to be habitual offenders and received life without parole as a result. The triggering offense in two cases was burglary, and in the other two robbery was the precipitating offense. The motivation for each offense was to acquire money. Although he purported to own a successful business, Francis, who was fifty when he began serving life without parole, claimed to burglarize houses in order to fund his gambling addiction. Troy and Anthony reported that they committed robberies because they were frustrated that they could not find legitimate employment.

Claims of Innocence or Justified Homicide

The remaining seven men purported that they were not responsible for the murders they were incarcerated for or they were legally justified in their actions. A spectrum of alleged culpability exists in these cases, between the poles of complete innocence and justified homicide. On the far end of the spectrum, Ryan, who had been incarcerated for twenty-four years, claimed that he had no involvement in the murder and attempted murder for which he was imprisoned. John, who was sixty-five and had been incarcerated for thirty-five years, claimed that he was wrongfully incarcerated for his wife's murder. He reported that after ingesting drugs, he fell asleep; when he woke up, his wife had been killed. John claimed that "[if it] wasn't for drugs I wouldn't be in none of this mess." In a similar incident, Robert, who had served more than thirty years and was now sixty-seven years of age, claimed that he had come to the mid-Atlantic state to visit family, and after "drinking and partying" he "blacked out." He denied any involvement in the crime, stating "I know that I didn't do it." James, who at fifty-eight was the oldest of the men when he began serving life without parole, was adamant that he had no idea when he agreed to give an acquaintance a ride to a residence that the individual planned to commit an arson that resulted in three deaths. Daniel, who entered prison at the age of twenty-six and had served thirty-one years, claimed that he participated in a robbery with an accomplice (and later co-defendant) earlier in the day but that he was not present when the co-defendant and another individual invaded a home and killed the resident. He alleged: "I'm not saying I was a good guy. I committed robberies, but I never murdered nobody. Maggie, I even had the robbery victims come to the court in the murder case and testify on my behalf. They called me a gentleman bandit because I wasn't trying to hurt [them] . . . the only reason I started the robberies [was because my wife and I were getting evicted] and that's why I did it." According to Daniel, The Innocence Project had reviewed his case, but because any forensic evidence that was collected had been destroyed, preventing DNA testing, the organization was unable to provide assistance. While Charles, who had served thirty-two years and was now sixty-four years of age, admitted that he was responsible for killing his estranged wife and injuring her boyfriend, he claimed that he acted in self-defense. William, who was in his early forties when he began serving life without parole, also contended that he acted in self-defense when he killed an acquaintance. He reported that the individual was acting in a threatening manner toward him.

TURBULENT TRANSITIONS

Adjustment to incarceration has long been a topic of interest in corrections and is the focus of several classic studies of prison and prison life, including *The Society of Captives* (Sykes 1958), *Asylums* (Goffman 1961), *The Felon* (Irwin 1970), and *Psychological Survival* (Cohen and Taylor 1972). In particular, special attention has been paid to how long-term inmates adjust to confinement. This research indicates that the initial period of confinement is the most stressful period for inmates (MacKenzie and Goodstein 1985, 407; Zamble 1992, 417). To apply general strain theory (Agnew 2006), which explains crime as a reaction to negative emotion, stressors exist in prison as inmates have to cope both with the loss of positively valued stimuli, including heterosexual sex, family, food preferences, privacy, freedom, and with the presence of noxious stimuli such as violent inmates, a cramped cell, or unfair officers.

Compared to other inmate groups, LWOP inmates are in a unique situation as they adjust to permanent imprisonment and its accompanying stressors. In *Life without Parole,* Hassine (2009, 10–12), a first-time inmate serving life without parole, described his experience as he acclimated to prison life. Initially, he attempted to symbolically escape from prison: sleeping most of the day and later developing interests in painting and reading as a means of distraction. However, in time, Hassine accepted the reality of his present environment and channeled his energy into other pursuits such as using his legal training to assist inmates with their cases and to initiate litigation against the Pennsylvania Department of Corrections to improve conditions within its prisons. His experience is consistent with other accounts, which indicate that when long-term inmates, including LWOP inmates, begin serving their sentences, they experience denial, depression, and a hesitancy to adopt a routine (Coughlin 1990, 116; Unkovic and Albini 1969, 158;

Villaume 2005, 274; Welch 1987, 7). While they may have periods of apathy or hopelessness as the years pass, LWOP inmates eventually become involved in the prison community, and as has been contended by prison administrators, older inmates exert a calming influence on the institution and mentor younger inmates (Adams 1995, 484; Aday 1994b, 52; Yates and Gillespie 2000, 172). Self-interest is a motivating factor for LWOP inmates to develop a routine and acclimate to prison life as argued by Robert Johnson and Sandra McGunigall-Smith (2008, 332): "Lifers do not adjust well because prison life is easy; they adjust well because self-interest moves them to make the most of a very difficult situation—a life confined to the barren, demeaning, and often dangerous world of the prison."

Initial Reactions to Receiving Life without Parole

Despite the fact that it was anywhere from fifteen to twenty-nine years ago, the men had clear recollections of how they felt when they were sentenced to life without parole and in the initial days of incarceration. Denial and shock were commonly reported:

> It was like a dream. . . . For a long time, I thought I was dreaming and that I would wake up and not be here. It took me quite a few years to get used to it. (Matthew)

> I was really shocked. (Karl)

> In a blink of an eye, your whole life has changed right in front of you. (Noah)

> Well, when I was first sentenced, it was like two and a half years after the crime had been done. I already been in jail for that long, and at the time, I was in denial. This is not right, this is not fair. This shouldn't be happening. (Victor)

Others—including Michael, a first-time inmate—were surprised at how prisoners were treated. He explained: "Well, see, now if you would've talked to me back then thirty years ago, or a couple of years before that, and you told me that prison . . . is the way it is, and the life in prison is the way it is, I would've said you're lying. I wouldn't even believe you. I wouldn't even believe that you would treat human beings this way."

Along with disbelief, anger was a commonly reported feeling. James and Daniel, along with the other five men who professed their innocence, were angered over the injustice of being wrongly incarcerated. Three of the four habitual offenders (Francis, Anthony, and Samuel) felt it was unfair that they received the same sentence as those convicted of murder:

[I am] disgusted with the system . . . but it's not an anger or bitterness where I'm walking around in a cloud, and, you know, I don't want nobody to speak to me, talk to me, you know. I just say something's wrong with this system, you know, should I have been punished? Absolutely, but should I have received [this] punishment? No, because there's guys that committed murder, more than one, and they have parole eligibility. So, yeah, that crosses my mind. (Francis)

I'm angry about it now, sure. . . . You can understand why. (Anthony)

Yes. . . . I think about it all the time. . . . I think about the fact that I got life in prison without parole, so this is their intent for you to die here. . . . I really feel and I know for a fact that I don't deserve, you know what I mean, to be here until that, but my sentence says that. (Samuel)

Alternatively, the only person Gabriel was angry at was himself: "I felt that anything I got I deserved. . . . My whole thing was that I didn't blame anybody but myself for being in the position that I was in."

The eight first-time prisoners recalled having difficulty adjusting to confinement. One first-time inmate was a police officer. Once apprehending offenders, he was now the criminal. James and Ryan, both immigrants, learned to speak English in prison. An appropriate analogy offered by both Anthony and Troy was that imprisonment was as foreign and disorienting an experience as traveling to another country:

It's like, almost like I guess, going to another country. You know, like say for example you're an American and you suddenly went to China and life was just different, the culture is different, the food, everything. Well, that's the way it is here. (Anthony)

We have a society in here just like on the street. And, you know, it would be just like you being dropped off in some strange place that you didn't know. It's the same thing here. (Troy)

When newly incarcerated, Gabriel learned that his friendly nature, although acceptable on the streets, was disapproved of in prison:

You have, you know, certain perceptions of how you interact socially out in society; in prison, it can be a lot different and I didn't know that. . . . When I see people walk by . . . my habit was to say hello, hi, how you doing, but for some people, they just felt that's strange.

Others, however, experienced smoother adjustments to confined life; this subgroup tended to be those who had been incarcerated previously. Seventeen men had been jailed or imprisoned previously, and as a result, they experienced less uncertainty and anxiety about confinement:

I would say this was easier than the first time because once you come in you know that you have to act like them. (John)

I knew how it was. (Alan)

Unfortunately, I made a fine adjustment because this was not my first time, you know, and I had been incarcerated in [another state] as well as [the mid-Atlantic state], you know, more than once. So, you know, as you grow older, it's easier to adjust because you know the routine, you know the inmates, you know the games that are played by both officers and inmates so I had no problem adjusting. (Francis)

You know what to expect and . . . it's much smoother. (Anthony)

It's just like my home. I've been in and out of jail all my life. [I have] been serving time since 1952, so it's just no difference. You adjust yourself and go on about your business. (Thomas)

It really didn't bother me that much. It would probably bother me, you know, a whole lot if I hadn't already been in the federal system. (Robert)

However, none of the previously incarcerated had ever served such lengthy sentences before and they acknowledged that adjusting to a LWOP sentence was more arduous than a shorter sentence. For instance, Noah claimed that adapting to a LWOP sentence "was hard from the start because doing [a] two-year bit compared to a life bit is a whole lot different, and it's a whole lot harder and it gives you a lot to think about."

SUICIDAL IDEATION AND PRISON MISCONDUCT

Suicidal ideation and prison misconduct are two commonly used measures of adjustment to prison. Prior research indicates that both are frequently engaged in during the initial stages of incarceration, especially by young males (DeRosia 1998, 28–30, 34–35). Both indicators, but in particular prison misconduct, reveal that the men initially struggled to cope with confinement, but in time, they were able to acclimate to prison life.

Suicidal Ideation

Certain inmate populations are at a higher risk of committing suicide. These include male inmates, younger inmates, inmates convicted of murder, inmates with a history of mental illness, and inmates who had made previous attempts on their lives. Long-term inmates also comprise a disproportionate number of prison suicides (DeRosia 1998, 34–35; Mumola 2005, 5, 8; Salive et al. 1989, 366–367; Schimmel et al. 1989, 20, 22; T. White and Schimmel 1995, 53–55). For example, Salive et al. (1989, 367) found that, of the thirty-seven suicides that occurred in Maryland prisons in the period of 1979 to 1987, nine suicides were those of life-sentenced inmates. In fact, they had the highest suicide rate as compared to inmates serving shorter sentences.

While there is evidence of life-sentenced inmates committing suicide after serving several decades of confinement (Hassine 2011, xii; R. Johnson and McGunigall-Smith 2008, 341), the time period of greatest risk for long-term inmates appears to be early in the incarceration, from the first days of imprisonment to several years into the sentence (Flanagan 1980a, 152; Paluch 2004, 9; Schimmel et al. 1989, 22; Unkovic and Albini 1969, 160). Unpleasant life events, including the loss of a family member, marital difficulties, and conflict with other inmates, such as being labeled a snitch, were identified as potential triggering events (Schimmel et al. 1989, 22–23; T. White and Schimmel 1995, 56).

Consistent with the studies mentioned above, eight of the twenty-five men reported suicidal ideation in the early days of incarceration. While in jail awaiting trial for the murder of a female relative, Alan contemplated suicide to spare his family from hearing the details of the crime. He recalled: "I didn't want to take my family through, you know, the trial and whatever else that was supposed to be taking place, you know. They had the pictures, and to hear what happened, I didn't want them to hear that."

Suicidal ideation continued when newly incarcerated. For Gabriel, the self-loathing that had caused him to plan to commit suicide on the day he committed his offense intensified after he was imprisoned:

> When I committed my crime, I hated myself even more because I couldn't understand why I did [it] and, you know, that bothered me. I did something that I absolutely despised and my thing was I never cared for a man who put his hands on a woman, abused a woman, disrespected [her]. I didn't like that . . . if a guy put his hands on my sister, you know, I would walk from here to Alaska to ensure that that's not going to happen again. And then to commit a crime like that, you know, I just, I hated myself for that. So, you know, I just didn't even want to be here.

For others, pessimism over the prospects of serving the duration of their lives incarcerated caused them to consider suicide, as reflected in Thomas's statement: "When I got this sentence, and I didn't get the death sentence, [I considered suicide]. I didn't fight against the death sentence. One of my daughters did. She's the one that got up there on the stand and said, 'Don't kill my dad.' . . . Do I want to stay here for a hundred years? Knowing me, I'll probably live to be a hundred."

None of the men who contemplated suicide actually made an attempt, though Joshua, who had been incarcerated since the age of thirty for a murder that occurred in a botched burglary, came closest. According to him, when a correctional officer caught him near the outer fence of the institution as he was attempting to escape, the officer warned Joshua that if he touched the fence, then he would be shot. He remembered, "I honestly contemplated go[ing] ahead and hit[ting] the fence. [It] would be over in a minute."

For most, the contemplation of suicide faded after the initial stages of confinement. Other men, even if they had never seriously considered suicide, believed that suicidal ideation was a common thought among long-term inmates, though they may not admit it:

> I think anybody in a situation like this thinks about that . . . from time to time. (Anthony)
>
> Sometimes you wonder, is life better? (Adam)
>
> It's a thought that's always in your head that you can do this, but I've never thought about acting on it or I've never planned on it. . . . I don't want to do that. (Victor)

Various reasons were noted to explain why the men did not seriously entertain thoughts of suicide or act on them. These included their relationships with their families (e.g., Gabriel, Matthew, and Daniel), religious beliefs (e.g., Matthew, Alan, and Robert), the personal value placed on life (e.g., Ryan and Troy), hope of release (e.g., John, Troy, and Robert), and a desire to not give up (e.g., Victor and Nathan). Gabriel explained how a close relationship with his family deterred him from making an attempt on his life, and over time the desire to die dissipated:

> Earlier in my incarceration, it was like I wished I was dead but my responsibilities to the people that loved me, it was like I couldn't put them through that. But again you evolve. And that was a feeling that I've grown beyond. I wrote a poem "Day Nineteen" . . . and it talked about those feelings. Wishing you was dead but being a hostage to obligations. . . . Every once in a while I go back and read it, and it really kind of like makes me aware and thankful for how far I've come from wishing you was dead to thanking God that you're alive and appreciating the things that you are able to do.

Hope of release was also reported as a reason why suicide was not an option, as evident in the following statement from Robert: "As long as you [are] breathing, you got a chance that the laws change. You know what I'm saying? One day it's going to change in your favor. . . . It's just like gambling . . . the day that you don't gamble is your lucky day. So, now you're waiting all this time . . . and you're going to pick a certain day to commit suicide. That particular day, boom, they change the law in your favor. It's too late."

In 2006 and 2011, only Walter expressed the desire to end his life, but he claimed to lack the courage to do so. He commented, "I don't care if I die. I'd rather be dead than live. If I had the courage, I [would] commit suicide, but I don't have the courage and that's being honest. I always even tell the staff that." In 2011, Walter repeated the sentiment: "I'll probably wind up dying in here, you know, that's the only thing I look forward to. Yeah, I look forward to that. Like I always told the psychiatrist, if I had the courage, I would have committed suicide but I'm a coward. I said, I can't do that. I can't take my own life."

To reiterate, serious contemplation of suicide was not widely reported by the men, and of those who had considered it, it was primarily limited to the early phase of incarceration. Of the two measures of adjustment, prison misconduct was more widely engaged in by the group. However, as with suicidal ideation, misconduct was largely limited to the early years of incarceration. By the time of the interviews, only a few were still violating prison rules.

Prison Misconduct

There is special concern associated with the adjustment of LWOP inmates. In fact, one of the original arguments against adopting life without parole was that these inmates would have little incentive to be well-behaved in prison, as they have no hope of parole and little chance of obtaining release through another mechanism (Cheatwood 1988, 53; Stewart and Lieberman 1982, 16; Wright 1990, 564). In other words, there are not enough carrots or sticks to inspire good behavior. However, what was not considered in this line of reasoning was that their limited likelihood of release would serve as motivation for good conduct for it would be paramount to LWOP inmates to maintain the best quality of life possible. In fact, the bulk of research suggests that LWOP inmates are less likely to engage in misconduct than inmates who are serving lesser sentences (Cunningham, Reidy, and Sorensen 2005; Cunningham, Sorensen, and Reidy 2005; Cunningham and Sorensen 2006, 693; Sorensen and Wrinkle 1996).

For about one-fourth of the men, their serious offending ended with the crimes for which they were permanently incarcerated. They claimed that they had never engaged in any behaviors that would constitute major rule violations in prison, whether they were caught or not. Desistance from crime took longer for the remaining nineteen men. Six were the most disruptive in terms of the quantity and severity of the infractions committed. Joshua acknowledged his difficult nature when newly incarcerated, saying: "Well, I don't know if you like me too much right now, but back then you wouldn't have liked me at all."

As indicated by the accounts below, the majority of the group continued familiar patterns of behavior, such as violence and substance use, when they began serving their sentences:

> Basically, I done some of the same things that I had done in jail [as I had] on the streets as far as criminal activities, selling drugs in jail. (George)

> I've done [drugs] for three years before . . . I come to jail, I just kept that up for another five, ten years, so I was not really dealing with the issue. (John)

> The first five years nothing much changed except for the drinking because coming into jail nothing changed. I still had to drink. I still had that every day, so like I was still doing that, you know, so it wasn't no different than when I was in the street. I mean [the only difference was that I was] drinking the jailhouse liquor [instead of] street liquor. (Henry)

> I used to beat up one [inmate] a day. (Thomas)

> When I first came in here, I was always in fights and stabbings and everything. I didn't give a shit if I hurt you or not. (Walter)

In addition to acting violently and using drugs or alcohol, the men also gambled, attempted to escape, and rioted. While many of the men may have dreamt of escaping when newly incarcerated, and several tried, Nathan successfully escaped. His escape was motivated out of his frustration that after a year and a half with a clean disciplinary record, he failed to receive a lower custody status. Believing that he was being treated worse than he deserved, Nathan explained his mindset, "Look, if you want to treat me like an ass, I'm going to show you what an ass can act like. Two weeks later, I escaped." He escaped from a local hospital and was not recaptured until two months later. Nathan received an additional thirty-year sentence for the escape and for injuries an individual sustained during the incident. In 2011, Nathan reported that he regretted the escape because "it made things harder for me. In a sense, in the early years, it made things a little bit harder, you know, I got thirty more years. It made things a little tougher on my family. . . . I made a mistake and I feel that I deserve [to be punished] but I don't think I should spend the rest of my life in prison for it."

While four men (Daniel, Walter, William, and Joshua) reported physically assaulting staff members, the most commonly reported prohibited behavior was inmate-on-inmate violence. Seventeen men recalled that most of the fights had occurred during the early years of incarceration. Thomas attributed his willingness to use violence as a part of his constitution. He claimed, "I've been a violent person all of my life." In fact, several years prior to killing his wife, Thomas had been placed on probation for disfiguring a man's face. The vast majority of men, however, did not feel as though violence was a part of their natures; instead, they felt compelled to use violence because of the nature of the prison environment during this time period. For those who had been confined previously, they had learned to use violence as a means to ward off sexual victimization. Nathan described an incident that occurred when he was serving a jail term in which an inmate whistled at and made sexual advances toward him. In response, Nathan picked up a weapon "and wore his ass out. I never had a problem again ever." One interviewee recounted an even more disturbing incident. While confined in a state mental hospital as an adolescent, another patient threatened to rape him in the shower. Later that night, the interviewee, along with four others, raped him.

When newly incarcerated, the men found themselves in a predatory environment in which violence was commonplace. Troy, who at twenty-two was the youngest of the group when he began serving life without parole, described prison life during this time period with the following: "When I first came in, I mean it was more violent. Guys would seriously hurt each other. It's not like that now." Victor echoed this sentiment stating, "It was dog eat dog. It was [a] fight every day. It was a hustle every day. It was survival of the fittest." As has been noted in other studies (Bowker 1982, 64; Wikberg and Foster 1990, 11), the men felt they had little choice but to act aggressively:

> You can't be weak. You got to fight, and then once you get some respect, you're cool. (John)

> You did what you have to do. . . . I mean, it's just, I had to do something. (James)

> I was taught that when you come through the system, if anybody ever threatens you, you got to deal with it. (Troy)

> It was like you either had to fight or you were gone. (Victor)

In order to survive in prison, John and Henry developed tough violent alter egos:

> If I stayed the good Christian [John], you know, I would probably some-how end up being abused somehow, you know, but I got to stand up sometimes, you know, and that [was,] like, the [other] . . . person, you know, just to keep everybody in order so I'm lucky I can distinguish the two. (John)

> I put on this aura while I was here the first year or so, and I had this men-tality . . . I guess I could say it was intentionally. [Other inmates] would

really try to evaluate me first to see what type of mood I was in [and] whether it was okay to speak to me or not. And so I carried that the first five years, that's the way I carried [myself]. (Henry)

Mirroring his imposing demeanor, Henry reported, "I kept my body big and tight . . . just to intimidate people." These statements suggest that the men's use of violence was a preventative measure to ward off attacks.

Some acknowledged that they had committed potentially lethal acts of violence; Henry, Joshua, and William had each stabbed an inmate. Henry commented that, had it not been for a friend's intervention, he would have killed an inmate: "I had a couple pretty tough close fights where a guy could have lost his life because I was in that zone. You know, I stabbed a guy one time, and had it not been for a good buddy of mine, I probably would have killed him. Yeah, I probably would have killed him." Years after the incident, Henry reflected on the damage that committing serious violence had on his psyche: "I've been in situations where I've won the fight, but it does something to you mentally and spiritually because I got to a point a couple of times where I almost came close to doing what got me in here. That's not good. It's scary. It's very scary. To say, man, you almost killed that guy." Thomas reported supplying inmates with the weapons used to assault officers and inmates, selling them for ten dollars each. He claimed, "[I] used to make them for people. [It] didn't matter who it was . . . if they had the money. . . . Most of them wanted ice picks [because] they do the most internal damage."

The willingness to fight was reported by Gabriel and John to be just as effective as winning a violent confrontation. Even fights that the men lost were enough to avoid future conflict as reflected in the following statement by John: "See, you have to fight when you come to jail because there's always somebody that's going to try you, and once whoever those people are see that you are willing to fight, they'll move on and go someplace else. It doesn't mean that you have to win." Gabriel explained that most aggressive inmates were seeking easy victories and would be deterred from fighting an inmate who had established a reputation as being willing to use violence. For these inmates, then, initial displays of violence were rewarded as their reputations of violence discouraged other inmates from initiating conflict with them. The ability to avoid future conflict, in particular violence, would be especially beneficial for LWOP inmates. Since they stand to be incarcerated into advanced age, it would be important to establish a reputation early on as an inmate who was willing to fight.

As has been noted by Lee Bowker (1982, 65) and Doris MacKenzie (1987, 429), violence was also used to express anger and frustration. According to some men, violence provided an outlet for these feelings:

It fed something in me and that's when, you know, I really started realizing how angry I was because, you know, when the opportunity presented itself, I didn't shy away from it. (Gabriel)

I used to fight a lot, and I still get angry. How would you feel if you were doing all this time and was convicted for a crime that you didn't do? (Daniel)

When looking for an outlet to express anger, some reported that inmates of low status, such as snitches and child molesters, were easy targets. Walter reported, "I was taking most of my . . . anger out on snitches and child molesters. I was taking my, you know, rage out on them."

Snitches and child molesters were, and remain, social pariahs within the prison community and physically assaulting these inmates was reported by the men to be a common occurrence, especially in the 1970s and 1980s. According to their accounts, they would read newspapers to learn if any sex offenders would be incarcerated in the state in the near future. Once known or suspected sex offenders were assigned to his housing unit, Walter claimed they were treated as outcasts and were delivered an ultimatum. The inmates residing in the housing unit demanded that suspected sex offenders leave the unit or they would be physically assaulted. Walter recalled, "You just told them: 'Look go pack your stuff. You're not welcome in here. If you don't want to leave, you're going to get whipped.' . . . It was unity; everybody jumped them. . . . That's the way it went." Therefore, inmates may have assumed, and correctly so, that other inmates would be less likely to intervene on the behalf of a child molester or a snitch who was being attacked.

Noah and William reported two additional reasons for committing violence. Noah claimed that he was violent not out of self-preservation but because he hoped to die. He explained, "[I was] too much of a punk to commit suicide or hurt myself, so I thought the best way to go out [was] like a warrior and just . . . maybe in the process somebody might kill me. I mean inside my head that's the attitude I had." Therefore, he perceived "death by inmate" to be the most favorable means of escaping a LWOP sentence. Alternatively, William was paid to fight as part of an inmate gambling ring.

Despite the sanctions imposed for their misconduct, which ranged from the loss of privileges to being placed in administrative segregation (also known as "the hole"), these penalties did little to alter the behaviors of the most disruptive men—as Joshua's and Troy's experiences illustrate:

I was violent when I first come to jail, and I stayed violent for years. That's exactly where I wanted to be and that's what I did. I did whatever I wanted and I didn't give two shits if you sent me out for three years and locked me down. When I got done, I'd come back and do the same things all over again. It didn't matter. . . . I was pretty much isolated in a cell where I just got out one hour a day for damn near the whole 1980s. . . . I got caught with bowl cutters, hacksaw blades, knives, everything, you know, over the years. (Joshua)

All of your decisions are poor. To actually think they just gave you natural life, they just put you in jail. Most people would think that you would say, "Oh my God, I need to straighten up." No, you're already warped in your thinking, so when you come to jail, you think I'm going to continue the same thing. (Troy)

Part of the reason for continuing to engage in misconduct was the perception that, in Henry's words, there was "nothing left to lose." After all, the men reasoned that the death penalty was the only penalty worse than theirs that they could receive. Troy explained:

After I got back from the courts, I went in my cell and I cried and I made a commitment. I said, "I'm going to break every rule they got." As long as I don't kill nobody, they can't do nothing to me. And I went on a spree.

Institutional sanctions were not effective in deterring misconduct at first, but in time, even Joshua and Troy desisted. The men ultimately came to realize that they did have something to lose after all.

Some exceptions exist to the general trend that most serious rule violations occurred in the first years of incarceration. For instance, Walter escaped after serving close to twenty years. The reported catalyst for his escape was a negative commutation hearing. While on the outside, he lived in the West and in the South for several years before his capture. Walter received an additional five years for his escape. In contrast to Nathan, who also escaped, Walter did not regret his decision to escape, despite the fact that he felt he was mistreated by prison staff as a result.

In 2006 and again in 2011, most of the men were not engaging in any rule-breaking behavior. Of those who were, it tended to be minor violations, such as keeping an extra pair of socks in their cells.[1] However, there were a few who were involved in major violations. One reported being involved in the underground prison economy as he sold contraband to other inmates. At the second interview, John and Daniel reported they had each fought with another inmate in the previous five years. John got into a fistfight with another inmate over what he described as "stupid stuff," while Daniel's altercation was more serious. After catching an inmate stealing from him, Daniel "beat him up." According to Daniel, the other inmate retrieved a knife, and he explained, "so then I had to take the knife from him." During the fight,

Daniel was stabbed twice and kicked in the face. Although the stab wounds were minor and could be treated without stitches, Daniel reported that his "nose has been messed up ever since." He rejected the notion that there was any means of resolving this situation other than to use violence, claiming, "[When a friend on the outside] asked me, 'Why didn't I walk away?' You can't walk away." Daniel was transferred to the secure housing unit. Prior to the incident, he was preparing to be moved from his double cell to a single cell, a privilege for well-behaved inmates. In addition to losing his housing assignment, he also lost his job and his special visit privileges, called honor visits, for the year.

Based on John's and Daniel's experiences, it appears that situations continue to exist in which the men felt compelled to use violence. Similar to these two men, a couple of the others reported they would use violence to protect themselves. Joshua's statement represents this viewpoint: "I would never let somebody hurt me physically. If there was some way I could prevent it, I would. If it meant I would have to hurt that guy, I would still do that. See, today, I call that self-preservation. To me, I think that's okay. You're allowed to do that. Of course, you're not allowed to do that here, but you have to do it. You don't have a choice."

EXPLANATIONS FOR THEIR DESISTANCE FROM MISCONDUCT

An established reputation, maturation and aging, fatigue, a lower risk of victimization, and stakes in conformity were the most common explanations for the men's eventual roads to desistance. In addition to individual explanations, an institutional level factor that helped to explain the reduction of violence was the changing nature of the prison. The men claimed that the high level of violence that was present when they were newly incarcerated had diminished over time. For example, Henry stated that in the 1970s the institution in which he was currently incarcerated "was violent and just about everybody carried a knife." Gangs were not reported to be a problem at either prison.

Established Reputation as Willing to Use Violence

Once a reputation as being willing to use violence was established, the men believed there was a lower likelihood of subsequent physical confrontations. This tactic can be viewed as a defense through offense measure. Lee Bowker (1982, 64) explained the intended goal: "Prisoners who achieve notoriety as fighters are much less likely to be attacked than those who appear to fear overt conflict." Thus, an inmate may opt to fight in the short-term with the goal of being left alone in the later stages of the sentence.

Gabriel, Thomas, and Henry reported that they had succeeded in acquiring reputations as being violent and consequently they did not have to worry about being attacked:

> So, after a couple of fights, you know, word got out that I would fight, that I wasn't just a guy that said hi to people that, you know, I wasn't just a nice guy that I was also an angry convict, so after that, I really didn't have no physical confrontations. (Gabriel)

> See what happens is you boogered them up so bad that word gets around, you know, don't go there. . . . Nobody threatens me because they know if they threaten me, they're going to have to live up to it. (Thomas)

> Most of the inmates that had been with me for a while, they knew pretty much how I was and so like those who were coming to jail or just came to jail or had only been in jail for a short time [were warned] don't mess with him, he's crazy. (Henry)

According to Thomas, his reputation has remained intact despite his advancing age and deteriorating physical health. For instance, on his walk over to the building on the morning of his interview, he claimed to overhear one inmate say to another, "That's the meanest old White man I've ever seen in my life." Thomas, who had recently undergone quadruple bypass surgery, went on to comment, "I don't have to use violence because my reputation precedes me. . . . Ain't nobody going to jump on me, even at this age, even being as sick as I am."

Maturation and Aging

Maturation manifested itself in the men's behaviors and attitudes in several critical ways. John described aging as a settling down process. He explained, "Everybody's settled down, you know. Nobody is like they were when I first came here." The men felt that they were less impulsive and more often considered the ramifications of their actions as compared to when they were younger:

> As an older person . . . [I've learned] to stop and count to ten and look at a situation. (Gabriel)

> You look at both sides of the coin, you don't act so quickly. . . . It goes back to the mature department and sitting down and thinking about what you do before you do it. . . . We've got more sense. (Noah)

> I've learned from my mistakes. (Robert)

> You mellow out as you get older. (Walter)

When you're younger, you got, it's obviously a lot of negative behavior coming into prison, anti-social behavior and actions. As you get older, when you get a little more therapy and treatment and so forth, then you start to see why I am fighting? You just get away from that negative behavior and just try to do your time. (Adam)

The men also reported that they had acquired wisdom over the course of incarceration. Daniel commented, "You get older, you get wiser, you do better. . . . That's it . . . you think before you react more. Before I just reacted, you know what I mean, I didn't think."

Greater self-awareness was another identified indicator of maturation as the men attempted to limit interpersonal conflict from escalating into violent altercations. Gabriel explained, "I knew that certain situations could trigger that kind of reaction or response. . . . I've learned as an older inmate . . . to recognize what triggers those feelings and to kind of stop myself before, you know, I get there." Charles described a self-assessment that he performed to prevent him from losing his temper and responding with aggression. When a situation between him and another inmate seemed to be escalating into potential violence, he explained: "I have to ask . . . Why am I getting angry at this guy? Say, man, that's bullshit. It's just some stuff I'm carrying and I'm reflecting that back on him. And what this [person] is saying doesn't mean anything, right, it's just bullshit. And I'm off, I'm walking about my business."

The group also reported that they had learned that verbal aggression was just as successful—but not as risky—as physical aggression in expressing anger, defending status, or avoiding confrontation. For example, Adam explained, "What I didn't realize [when I was first incarcerated was] that usually in prison [the person] who yells loudest won the fight. It didn't have to get physical." Matthew agreed: "I still get angry sometimes, I just shout." Combined, these narratives demonstrate that the men as they aged were able to anticipate conflict and resolve it without resorting to violence.

In addition to the effects that maturation had on mental health, four men (Gabriel, William, Noah, and Joshua) felt that the physical limitations associated with aging—for example, loss of speed and strength—discouraged them from acting out. As Gabriel noted: "There's just physical limitations connected to that now. . . . You're not the guy you used to be, you know, whether you see that or not." Similarly, Joshua reported, "I'm just too old to do them kind of things anymore." Noah simply attributed his desistance to the general effects of aging: "I've got[ten] a lot grayer, a lot older, and it changes a person. I believe in that, that it really changes you."

Fatigue

Six men reported that they had grown tired of engaging in disciplinary infractions and the resulting sanctions:

> You either get tired of the life that you live and want to better yourself or you just keep on that same path. . . . It's the mental aspect of the thing. You know, you just get tired. For the most part, guys . . . get tired of being screw-ups. You know, guys get tired of being locked down all the time. Guys get tired of having no privileges. Guys get tired. It gets old. (Nathan)

> I understand now that I can't win the game, but, you know, before I thought that I could get away with it. And one thing, I didn't care. Now, I'm more concerned with how I live my life than I used to be. (Anthony)

> It's not exciting. It's not for me. I've made a decision to steer clear of that. (Victor)

> I tell people there is no such thing as rehabilitation. . . . I've done all of the programs and things in the world. Programs didn't change me. I got tired of what I was doing. (George)

> We can change, like I've changed, but the only reason I'm going to change is because I was just tired of getting knocked in the head, beaten in the head and everything by the guards. You get tired of it after a while. . . . I got sick of it. (Walter)

These statements indicate the increased feelings of "burning out" as the men moved through the life course, and the frustration and mental fatigue associated with misconduct.

Lower Risk of Victimization

Twelve men believed that keeping a low profile and avoiding disciplinary infractions helped them to function better in the prison by avoiding potential conflict with other inmates:

> The best way to avoid incidents, in reference to this game, [is] just don't play. You know what I mean, if you involve yourself then you got to anticipate consequences . . . that's how you avoid incidents, just don't participate . . . if you participate in these sort of games, there are repercussions that are inevitable. (Samuel)

> When I came to jail in the '60s, you know, people told me don't talk to nobody, don't take nothing from nobody, don't trust nobody, you know, because there's this group of people that come in and take this, take that, and then one night they're at your door saying it's time to pay back. (John)

Well, there's things that I don't do because these things create, you know, situations where that happens. I don't run a prison store because, I don't care who you are, somebody's not going to pay you, and, you know, you're going to have to get your money. . . . I don't deal with no institution contraband, whether it's drugs or stuff like that. I don't mess with homosexuals. . . . Things where [they] just create those kinds of situations. (Gabriel)

Mind your own business, and if you see something act like you don't because it's none of your business. (Robert)

Keeping a low profile meant not getting involved in another inmate's business, avoiding attracting a lot of attention, and avoiding risky situations (e.g., playing cards, getting involved in illegal misconduct, going to the gym, or wearing valuable items). The men believed that when inmates were involved in these activities, they assumed the risk of violence that might occur.

Stakes in Conformity

Seven men reported that they no longer engaged in illegal behaviors because it would negatively impact their quality of life. In particular, the men were fearful of losing their single cells, jobs, and honor visits. Robert chose not to engage in prohibited behaviors because it would make his confinement more difficult: "I look at it this way, I'm in their ballpark now. I have to play the game by their rules and regulations. I have a choice. I can make my bit harder, or I can make it easier."

The impact that stakes in conformity had on the men's behavior is apparent in an experience that Victor shared during his first interview. In 2006, he claimed that another inmate had recently stolen several beverages from his work locker. Victor admitted that two decades ago he would have responded with violence. He stated, "[If it was] back in the 1980s and he took six sodas from me, I would have worn his head out or had somebody do it for me if I couldn't have got to him. But, it ain't worth it." Victor elaborated further that he did not want to jeopardize his current quality of life by retaliating against the inmate. He stated:

What would tick me off before and get me in your face, I don't care about. It's not worth it. Somebody [stealing] something from me. . . . I know who took them. But you know what I've said to that man? Not one word. Because I look at it like if he's dirty enough to steal them sodas, I'm dirty enough not to say anything to him. Not that I'm scared of him. I ain't. You know, I work in the same place that he does [the gym]. I could pick one of those weights in there and just wear him out. But, I don't want to do that anymore.

Thus, while he reported being angry that his property was stolen, Victor no longer believed it was in his best interests to physically attack the inmate. Victor was active in the lifers group at Institution Two, and his involvement was a source of pride: "It gave me something to focus on. It gave me something to be proud of. It gave me something to center my life around." He also had regular communication with his family. Both of which would be jeopardized if he were to attack the suspected thief. Similar to Victor, Matthew was also concerned with maintaining the privileges he had earned. At the first interview, he expressed fear that even the smallest provocations would mean he would be moved from his single cell. Matthew explained his anxiety: "You break a rule, you keep breaking these rules, you'll end up getting moved and all that. And you're afraid that you'll mess up and get moved. . . . So you're constantly in fear of violating some of the rules that they continue to make."

At the time of the original interview, all but four men at Institution One had, with good behavior and participation in prison programming, acquired their own cells.[2] This afforded the men increased privacy, as they no longer had to share a small space with another person. As the men reported spending much time in their cells, a single cell represented a sanctuary from the stresses of prison life. Thomas believed that the possibility of losing privileges, such as a single cell, constituted a significant deterrent for older LWOP inmates to avoid getting into trouble: "They don't want to lose that, they know if they get in trouble, they're going to take that and they don't want to lose that."

Victor and Matthew maintained that they were well-behaved because they wanted to ensure they remained eligible for honor visits. During the first interview, Matthew explained how easily honor visits could be lost: "If you have an extra t-shirt or an extra pair of socks, they can take your honor visit from you . . . and bringing back a sandwich from the chow hall, they take your honor visit. I'm saying you're scared to death . . . and they more or less use that to control you." As discussed above, Victor was angry that someone had stolen from him. However, he did not retaliate against the alleged perpetrator in part because he did not want to risk his housing status or the opportunity to see his family: "It's bad that somebody did that, but I think I showed growth when I didn't go throw everything that I've worked for away, mess everything up that I'm able to do to help other people just because this guy did something wrong. . . . I'm not going to hurt myself because of [what] he did. He's going to get out in about five months, he's going home. If I went in there and got all crazy with him, I'd be the one suffering. My family would be the one suffering."

The potential costs of engaging in prison misconduct, loss of a single cell and loss of honor visits, were so great that the men refrained from engaging in illegal activities. Thus, Henry was incorrect in his original belief that he had nothing left to lose. He and the other older LWOP inmates lived meager existences, which meant that a preferred housing assignment, involvement in clubs and organizations, and visitation privileges were highly valued and carefully guarded. Thomas offered: "When somebody gets a natural life sentence . . . they come here and they want to make life the best they can for themselves. They want honor visits. They want visits. They want to be able to talk to their families on the phone whenever they want to. They want a nice cell with air conditioning, so they're going to abide by the rules and they're going to do the best they can." The men understood that serving a life sentence would be much more difficult without these privileges. Joshua offered, "As bad as it is here, I know that if I go off the deep end, it would get worse."

In addition to valued privileges, attachment to family constituted another stake in conformity and served as a deterrent to continued involvement in misbehavior for three men (Gabriel, Troy, and Joshua). Following his father's death, Troy reported that he "made a commitment after he passed away that I was going to make as much positive [association] to the family name as I had brought negative. That's my only concern. I really want to do that now." After thirteen years of confinement, Joshua reported that he reevaluated his behavior after his family member threatened to cease communication with him:

> I'd say about 1990 . . . my family had come to see me and they talk[ed] to me, they said, if you don't straighten up, that you're killing your mother, you know, and you're in jail and you're stabbing people and you're trying to escape and you're doing this and you're doing that. And I never gave that a whole lot of thought. I mean, I never really did. Now, it's almost shameful to think like that, but that's how I thought . . . if I don't change, they were just going to cut me off. So, I gave it some thought. And it was easy for me to swing myself around because I only had that one thing in mind. [A friend also told him,] "Look, [Joshua], if you don't like yourself," he said, "change. If you don't like who you are, change. If you don't like what you do, stop it." I mean, just to me at the time, it sounds stupid. How the hell could I stop being who I [had] been all of my life?

Joshua's statement highlights the difficulty entailed in personal growth but also demonstrates the potential for even the most disruptive prisoners to change.

Sentence commutation was an even greater opportunity that could be lost by engaging in misconduct. Michael did not want to decrease his already slim chances of being released by engaging in prison misconduct: "I got thirty years in. What good would it do me to get into a confrontation with an inmate or staff? That would stand out more than anything." Troy agreed that the hope of release was an important factor in ensuring that LWOP inmates behaved: "The funny thing about that is you always think you're going to get out. . . . If you ever take that hope away, okay, then I think you have some real dangerous people. . . . It was always still in my mind I might get out. You got to hold [on to] that. . . . I think then you start victimizing people. Because I mean what do you have to lose? Once you lost that hope, you're dead. So if I'm already dead, what am I going to lose?" As can be seen in their statements, the men did not want to engage in any behaviors that could provide the pardon board with additional reasons to deny their petitions for sentence commutation.

AWAKENING

As the men moved away from misconduct, their gaze turned inward. They took stock of their lives including the decisions that they had made that led to permanent incarceration. They considered how they could be active agents in cultivating meaning and purpose in their lives instead of drifting through life repeating the same destructive patterns of behavior. Most believed that they could be released and set out to prove that they would be good candidates for commutation. In *Lifers* (2009, 66), John Irwin described the awakening of life-sentenced inmates as beginning when "lifers fully appreciate that there has been something fundamentally wrong with their former behavior. They realize that *their* actions have brought them to this disastrous end. They come to sincerely regret that they have taken a life of another human being. They further realize that there may be something fundamentally deranged in their personality or character. And they conclude that they better do something about it." Troy described his awakening:

> When I first came in, I didn't care. It wasn't even a concern if I was ever going to get out of jail and I did everything that I wanted to do and got involved in all of the stuff that I shouldn't have got involved in. And you go through a process. At points, in between, you know, I'd wake up and it's like what are you doing? I mean, do you really want to stay here because you're doing the things that could keep you here. . . . It would have been in the last fifteen years I'll say, it's like this is not what was meant for me. You know, I need to do something to change who I am so I can make sure [when] the day comes when I'm released that I can get out and function in society. It's a—I don't know—it's a process that you go through.

Awakening is a transcending moment in an inmate's life. According to Troy, afterward, the individual cannot regress into previous harmful behaviors or antisocial attitudes: "We done walked into the light. You can't come back into the darkness. It's unacceptable to do that because you know what you've done and you know what you've done to other people. You can't go back that way. We say this: Everybody has to reach that point by themselves."

As Troy pointed out, awakening is an individualized process that happens earlier for some than others, and for others it never occurs at all. Central to awakening is the acceptance of responsibility for the crimes committed, and the men felt that it served as an important benchmark in their personal development. Adam stated: "It's my fault. I put myself in this place. And I accept responsibility and a lot of them can't accept that. So I think that's what's helped me." A few of the men (Matthew, Alan, and Thomas) had accepted responsibility for their actions soon after the commission of the crime, as they reported their actions to the police or to others. For the rest, it took time to acknowledge their culpability. Henry commented, "For a lot of years, I pointed fingers as to who put me in prison." In a similar vein, Troy remarked:

> I'm like . . . this is what I asked for. Okay, I played the cards and this was the hand that I was dealt. I can't sit around now crying. . . . My anthem is Michael Jackson's "Man in the Mirror." That's what I believe in now. I'm the one that set this whole thing in effect and it took me time to get to that point because I blamed the judge, the lawyer, the police. I blamed everybody, but one day I came to realize only one person put this thing into effect, okay, and that's the person that should be in charge of it. And once I accepted that, the time is, like, secondary.

Victor, convicted of the murder of an acquaintance, claimed that he no longer made excuses for his actions: "I [used to] make all kinds of excuses. Well, he was that and he was going to do this, he did this, and he did that. But . . . that's no excuse for me [now]." Joshua admitted that it took him over ten years to admit to himself that he had killed the homeowner in a botched burglary.

Most men avoided self-pity and had taken ownership of the poor decisions that resulted in life imprisonment:

> I have grown to know what I did, know what I did wrong, know how I affected other people. (Victor)

> I accept that these are the consequences for what it is that I've done. . . . I'm the offender not the offended. (Gabriel)

> I put myself in this position and . . . if I would have dealt with myself differently I wouldn't be in this position. (George)

Even those who claimed to be innocent of the crime for which they were incarcerated (e.g., Daniel) or claimed that taking someone's life was not an intended part of the crime (e.g., Noah) acknowledged the consequences of their actions:

I know that I put myself in this position by doing the robberies. I put myself in the position to be accused by hanging around the wrong people. (Daniel)

It was an accident. It was never meant to happen. I'll tell the world that, but it happened. So I got to deal with it. I'm not happy about it. I'm not pleased . . . that's a part of me that hurts. (Noah)

The men expressed guilt and shame for their actions and were remorseful that they were responsible for taking another's life:

It is not easy. It is not easy at all. . . . It wears you down. It tears at you. I don't care how tough a guy [might] think he is, it tears at you. (Henry)

You go through a period of shame that you could let yourself slip so low in society. (Adam)

Serving time for the murder of an acquaintance, Henry learned more about the victim at trial and realized that the individual did not deserve to be killed. He remarked, "I didn't know this guy real good, I learned about him through the trial. . . . I learned that he was like my Dad." Henry found it difficult to come to terms with how little value he placed on life, either another's or his own: "That's what I cared about somebody else's life? That's what I cared about my life?" As he was raised to believe that "you don't prey on the weak," Henry was ashamed that he had acted in a way that ran counter-current to his upbringing: "This whole thing went against everything . . . it broke every rule of my upbringing."

The men expressed sympathy for the families of their victims. Victor remarked: "Another hard part is thinking about the families that I influenced on the streets in a negative way that my crime affected. That's a hard part of my life. That's not a nice section of my life." Adam described how his actions led to a "cancer" in his victim's family: "They're still frozen in time and it's like a cancer eating away, and . . . eventually the mother did die just a couple of years back, but she was just consumed." In addition to considering the effects of their crimes on the victims' families, the men had also considered the ramifications that their behavior had on their own families:

There's a rippling effect to my actions which has hurt a number of people, and I see that and hear that through my family. (Adam)

[My] victims are in the [following] order: the victims of who I perpetrated my crime on, their family and friends, then my family and friends, and then me. (George)

Most men reported that they did not think about the offense as much as they had at earlier points in their sentence. Although they wished they had never committed the crime, they realized they could do nothing now to correct the situation as much as they wished they could. Henry's statement reflected this belief: "I can't change that. . . . I really wish that could have been different, but, you know, there's nothing I can do about it now." However, he noted that even after forfeiting his life as punishment for the crime, "I'm pretty sure I will have to pay for [it in the afterlife]." The men did not forget the crimes they had committed, but because they could not alter the past, they instead wanted to focus on how they could avoid making such costly mistakes in the future. Noah remarked: "It's something that if a person forget where he's been or where he has come from he won't know where he's going. So that's how I feel about that. You don't forget what has happened in the past because you try not to repeat that again. That's what I'm trying to say. I wouldn't want to do that again to nobody. And I wouldn't want that to happen again to nobody." After accepting responsibility for their actions, the men felt that self-forgiveness and atonement were the next phases of personal development. Though they were mindful of the gravity of their crimes, some men were able to forgive themselves. Victor explained: "I have personally, and I'm not trying to make light of anything here because I know what I did, but I have gone past that, and I have forgiven myself. Some people don't forgive themselves and they can't live."

Gabriel's experience illustrated the slow process of self-forgiveness. He claimed that earlier in his sentence, he would think about the murder of his girlfriend and the shooting of her coworkers "all the time" because he "wanted to punish myself for what it is I had done." His thoughts would also frequently center on his girlfriend's family. He stated: "I think one of the things, you know, that was, like, heavy on my mind was, you know, my victim and her family because, you know, her family were people that were really good to me. I felt real bad." Over time, he was able to realize that his behavior was inhibiting personal growth and development. He explained: "[I am remorseful], but I don't think you can function out of a place of remorse for twenty-seven years and be healthy and safe." In 2011, after being incarcerated for almost three decades, Gabriel believed that he was finally worthy of consideration for release and for the first time was submitting a commutation application:

> I finally feel comfortable . . . because people have been asking about that process [for] a long time, but at first I wanted to do at least twenty years because, you know, I thought that anything less than twenty years would be an insult to my victims, but even after twenty years, I wasn't comfortable with the process. Now, I finally reached the point, you know, where

I'm more comfortable. . . . Twenty-five years was good, but I wasn't at where I am today. And I think the biggest aspect is forgiveness and it's been a process that at least [has] taken twenty-five years. . . . After twenty-seven years, I feel worthy of asking for, and when I say worthy I understand, you know, that it may not happen . . . but, hey, I'm worthy of the consideration. And that's what I'm comfortable with right now.

Four men (Henry, Robert, Nathan, and Victor) specifically mentioned a desire to want to help others in order to make amends for their involvement in the death of another. This notion is reflected by Victor's and Robert's statements:

I think I would like to be able to try to make some amends in that area there if not with the direct family then with people that's around them in some way. Just try to do something—you can never make up for what you did—but you can be a difference in some way. (Victor)

I know what I did was wrong but there's nothing I can do to bring that man's life back to his family and loved ones, so maybe I can make up for it by helping someone else. Help save a life. (Robert)

After arriving at a point where they wanted to make changes in their thought processes and behaviors, the men set about actualizing these desires. As Irwin explained, "once awakened, the lifers begin transforming themselves by participating in rehabilitative programs" (2009, 78). In addition to participating in programming, the men found purpose and fulfillment through working and assisting others.

CONCLUSION

An examination into the homicides committed by the group reveal that most were not well-planned offenses. Instead, it seems they were impulsive reactions to a situation in which the individual felt threatened in some manner. Their crimes are consistent with Irwin's notion of "typical homicides." Irwin argues that most homicides, "though tragic and blameworthy, [are] much more ordinary and understandable" (Irwin 2009, 43). While this does not excuse the serious crimes these men committed, it does suggest that they were not depraved killers. None of them was a serial killer who professed to enjoy hurting others. Instead, these were young men who made exceedingly poor decisions. A sizeable number were under the influence of drugs or alcohol, which further impaired their judgment. Some immediately accepted responsibility for their offenses; they reported the offense or turned themselves in to police. Most of them expressed deep remorse for the harm their actions caused.

As can be seen from the indicators of suicidal ideation and prison misconduct, the group's adjustment to life imprisonment was difficult, especially for
those who had not been incarcerated previously. The men were more likely
to engage in contemplation of suicide and serious misconduct, especially violence, in the initial stages of incarceration. Although it took time for most
men to desist from prison misconduct, and a handful continued to engage in
misconduct or remained committed to using violence under special circumstances, desistance did occur for most.

The present group of older LWOP inmates provides evidence of a decline
in criminality similar to that reported among older inmates and older people more generally. Age is one of the most consistent factors associated with
prison misconduct. This group's experience conforms with prior research on
prison misconduct that suggests that older inmates commit few serious disciplinary infractions (McShane and Williams 1990, 199–200). In explaining
their desistance, the men provided reasons that are similar to those discussed
when explaining the low levels of criminality among older people in general. In *Crime and Victimization of the Elderly,* Ezzat A. Fattah and Vincent F.
Sacco (1989) offered several explanations for the decline in criminality among
the aged. First, they proposed "the burn-out hypothesis" in that older people
"become more settled, less adventurous, less rebellious and less eager to defy
authority or to fight the system" (13). The burn-out hypothesis explains the
decline in offending for some of the men, as they reported having grown tired
of engaging in institutional misconduct and incurring sanctions. Second, Fattah and Sacco observed that age was accompanied by a decrease in strength
and agility, thus discouraging older inmates from engaging in institutional
misconduct, especially violence (14). The men attributed their desistance in
part to the effects that maturation and aging had on their minds and bodies.
This is reminiscent of Gottfredson and Hirschi's explanation that a decline in
offending is universal "due to the inexorable aging of the organism" (1990,
141). Third, Fattah and Sacco (1989, 15) contended that older people have
stronger inhibitions against engaging in crime as they "have more to lose if
caught, punished and stigmatized, and are, therefore, less willing to take risks.
It is well known that growing maturity, stability and responsibilities bring
about increased caution and prudence." The men reported that, as they aged,
they no longer engaged in illegal activities because of their greater stakes in
conformity. Due to the length of time they will be incarcerated, the men
were less likely to engage in rule violations because the potential ramifications of disciplinary violations will have a greater impact on the quality of
their lives in the institution. Prison becomes home for LWOP inmates (R.
Johnson 2002, 105). Misconduct would jeopardize their privileges, their ability to communicate with family members, and their (already slim) chances of

release. Life-course theory provides an additional theoretical framework for explaining the decreased offending of respondents. As the men acquired stakes in conformity, they were placed on a trajectory that steered them away from their previous violent and disruptive pasts (Sampson and Laub 1993).

The men's desistance from crime and their awakening appear to be linked and, for some, could even be causal. After being incarcerated for a couple of years, most of the men underwent personal transformations as they decided to better themselves and to help others. Instead of drinking and using drugs, fighting, and becoming entrenched in the prison subculture, the men earned degrees, founded self-help organizations, and mentored younger inmates. As a result, the men developed purpose and meaning in their lives and found that their mental health improved.

CHAPTER 3

The Pains of Permanent
Imprisonment

THE TWENTY-FIVE MEN FEATURED in this book are survivors of a life spent incarcerated. They experienced firsthand the changes that occurred in prison as a result of the mass expansion of the US penal system. In 1991 (the last year in which the men could have entered prison and still be eligible for this study), they were a small fraction of the approximate 830,000 sentenced prisoners in the country (Beck and Gilliard 1995, 1). Over the past twenty years, the number of sentenced prisoners has doubled to 1,537,415 (Carson and Sabol 2012, 1).

The rise in the prison population and the increase in the LWOP population, in particular, reflect the shift in correctional aims that has taken place. When rehabilitation was eclipsed as the dominant sentencing philosophy, a new era of "tough on crime" policies was ushered in during the 1980s and 1990s. The men acknowledged that the changes in prison operation were spurred by the hardening of attitudes related to crime and the treatment of offenders:

> There's really no reprieve with the attitude of the American public right at this time. And that's understandable, you know, different periods of penal systems, you know, you have some that go pro-education, you know, work towards rehabilitation, help that person get out and turn his life around and be a productive person in society. And then you go to where the pendulum swings back to where everything is just punishment and, you know, we're coming through that time. (Adam)

> Well, you know, I mean, you read in the newspaper all the time, like every time, something goes on here where they want to give us a little something else. You read in the newspaper where the public talks about they're there to do their time. Treat them like animals. Don't give them anything. (Nathan)

Nathan, who had been incarcerated for thirty-four years, cautioned that the harsh treatment of inmates could have a criminogenic effect. To illustrate his point, he used the following analogy: "You take a dog. You put a dog in a cage. You keep that dog in that cage for six months. You stick him with a stick every day. You squirt him with a hose. You throw him a little piece of meat. You agitate him for six months. You open up that door. What's he going to try to do? He's going to try and bite you."

Six men maintained that the actual experience of imprisonment stands in stark contrast to the public perception of it. Gabriel, one of the youngest men in the group, stated: "I'm not looking for this to become Club Med. I think that [this is] the general perception that a lot of people push out there in society. . . . I'm going to get enough people angry about the situation and I'm going to get what it is that I want out of it. But, it's not a reality, you know, prison is not a Club Med, you know, at this particular institution, they don't have cable . . . [or] conjugal visits." Almost all of the men agreed that through the decades of incarceration, it had become increasingly difficult to serve time:

> All of the changes have been negative. . . . Twenty years and they continue to take from us and take from us. I don't know what they're going to do next. . . . It's getting worse all the time. The funny thing is that it scares you, what are they going to do next? Are they going to lock you in a room and feed you? Slide your food under the door on a tray and lock you down? I think that's what it's going to come to. (Matthew)

> The environment and the conditions have gotten harsher than what it was [when] I came in here. I think that's one of the things that [is] bothering me as an old man. (Anthony)

According to the men at Institution One, the new warden was responsible for making policies even stricter. One commented, "[This warden] ended up being one of the worst people that we've ever had. We've never had nobody this bad, ever." In almost all facets of prison life, the men felt that the rules had become increasingly restrictive. One specific example referenced was the termination of the prison furlough program. The longest-serving men recalled how, earlier in their sentences, they were eligible for furloughs (i.e., temporary leaves from prison) to visit their families. For LWOP inmates, the prison furloughs held special significance as explained by Matthew, who had been incarcerated since the age of forty-five for the murder of his wife: "Yeah, you could go home for the weekend. So, if I never get out, at least I'll get to go home for the weekend. And they turned around and closed the door on that after . . . a few years." The men could not recall the specific reason as to why the program ended. According to John, who had spent more than half of his life confined, "somebody did something." They were not sure if a furloughed inmate in the mid-Atlantic state had committed a crime while on release or the program was ended because of a well-publicized incident in another jurisdiction, such as the Willie Horton case (as discussed in Chapter 1).

Other changes occurred that the men perceived as increasing the difficulty of imprisonment. The men recalled that at one time there was a rich array of programs for inmates to participate in. Robert, who was sixty-seven years of age and had been incarcerated for over thirty years, described the change: "Back in the day, I mean they had programs here, all kinds of programs. [They] used to have Jaycees, Toastmasters, I mean all kinds of stuff. Just over the years, they just take it all away. They used to have nighttime educational programs. They're almost non-existent anymore. . . . The problem is they just don't want it. I mean this is the only prison I've ever been in that doesn't have a lifers organization. I mean we had it years ago, but because they didn't like our thoughts or our ideas about things, they just did away with it." As a result of the abolition of Pell grants for inmate higher education (per the Violent Crime Control and Law Enforcement Act of 1994 § 20411) and the disqualification of life-sentenced inmates from participating in certain programs, their efforts at self-improvement were impaired. The curtailment of social clubs and organizations increased the monotony of prison life. While Institution Two had a lifers group, the three men there agreed that there had also been a general decline in prison programming.

The reduction in prison programming is both a reflection of the changing sentiments toward offenders and a casualty of the prison boom that the United States has undergone in recent decades. John Irwin (2005, 74) described the modern American prison as a warehouse with fewer opportunities for inmates to participate in educational and vocational programs and social clubs and organizations than before. The men I spoke with agreed with this characterization of prison:

> Prison is just a waste of time. It's a warehouse where people are given time and the punishment aspect of prison is served to a certain extent, but, you know, you come here and you sit. You have an institution here, I don't know, there's 2,800 people in here, somewhere around that number, and you have about 400 jobs. So you have . . . 2,400 people who are doing absolutely nothing, you know. There's a push to get people involved in education, you know, so they say, but the reality is that there's a thousand-person waiting list, you know. There are no job skills taught here, you know. They have the garment shop, but you go there, and you make institutional uniforms that suits the need of the institution but, you know, how many guys are really going to leave here and [pursue that kind of job]? (Gabriel)

There's nothing for me to do but lie around. (Walter)

You're cattle and you're in our cattle stall and you're just here. We're warehousing you. That's what it is. It's almost a warehouse project. (Victor)

The prison warehouse would be unpleasant for any inmate as it means more time confined in one's cell, less opportunity to participate in prison programming or have a job while incarcerated, and less chance of rehabilitation. For a LWOP inmate, it would be especially difficult because of the length of time spent in the environment with little chance of release. However, the men adapted and found means to cope in a bleak environment.

In *The Society of Captives* (1958, 65–78), Gresham Sykes described "the pains of imprisonment" as the deprivation of liberty, goods and services, heterosexual relationships, autonomy, and security. Over fifty years later, three of these pains (i.e., deprivation of liberty, autonomy, and goods and services) were mentioned by the group, while deprivation of heterosexual relationships and security were not commonly identified as hardships associated with life without parole.

Deprivations of Liberty, Autonomy, and Privacy

The abstract notion of liberty was expressed in simple activities that were no longer available to the men, such as dining at a restaurant, riding a motorcycle, or traveling:

I would like to be able to go out to dinner, have a real meal, sit down and have a conversation with real people, you know, because it just don't happen here. Everything is regimental. It's a rush to eat, get over to chow. (Michael)

What brings the lonely feelings is that there are certain experiences that you kind of like remember from the street that you miss and, you know, like I love riding motorcycles and so, like, I can sit in my room sometimes and you can hear a bike on the highway and so it's like, you know, just in that moment, I might just sit in my room for thirty minutes just listening, you know, I missed that, you know, and I enjoy it because as I said memories are good and sort of a great distraction, you know, from this sometimes. (Gabriel)

Freedom was gone. My freedom was gone. There was things I loved to do, places I liked to go. I couldn't do. I couldn't go to no more. It was just like it's over with. (Noah)

I can't travel the world or anything. (Charles)

Nathan contended that humans are capable of adapting to even the bleakest of environments; however, he claimed that he was not equipped to cope with the loss of freedom:

> The physical things that you have in a place like this aren't what is hard at least not for me. When they put me in prison, they turned that key and they locked me up. You can take everything in the world you want away from me. You can take all of the material things that I have. You can take them from me and I can learn to adapt to that. I'm not ever going to learn to adapt to not being free. You know, being able to get up and go where I want to go when I want, go to bed when I want, walk as far as I want to walk in a straight line without somebody having to unlock a gate or telling me I can't do it, go down to the corner and buy a piece of pizza, things like that, seeing my daughter, my grandkids grow up. They've hurt me worse with that than anything they could ever take away from me. We're human beings and it's nature for us to adapt to things, you know, take your TV away, a couple of months you get used to not watching TV. They don't let you get out of your cell, couple of months you get used to not getting out of your cell. To being locked away and never having your freedom again, you never get used to that. Never.

Robert regretted that he did not appreciate his freedom when he was living out in society: "While I was on the street, I was taking everything for granted. It never crossed my mind that I could lose my freedom. I never realized how really sweet it is."

While the men tried to find ways to exert control over their lives, they found the lack of autonomy in prison to be difficult. Daniel, fifty-seven years of age, provided a particularly effective illustration of the combined losses of freedom, privacy, and autonomy:

> This place, just the pressures, Margaret, you're constantly being told what to do. . . . You're actually really told when to use the bathroom if you don't want to do it in front of your cellmate. You got to go defecate or something, you got to wait until he's out of the room or you have to put up a sheet and the cell's not as big as this room. So, you know, you're living in a toilet.

Privacy extended into ownership of possession. Because of the limited number of personal possessions he owned, Karl, who had been incarcerated for over thirty years, was reluctant to share his items with others because "it's mine . . . it's important to me." Walter, the longest-serving member of the group, described the prison staff's treatment of his possessions during searches as invasive and likened it to rape: "They go to your area, they shake your area down. I mean, they tear it up, some parts of it. It's like being raped." Henry, who had been incarcerated for over three decades, noted that his property had been damaged in searches, which was especially bothersome because of the limited number of personal possessions that he owned.

As a privilege for good behavior, most of the men at Institution One were in single cells. According to the men, a single cell was one of the few sources of privacy available to them. Several made the case that a single cell is critical for LWOP inmates; Henry explained, "It means a lot . . . if you're doing a life bit, a single cell is very important." In specific terms, the men spoke of their single cells as a refuge from the turmoil in prison and a place in which they could exercise personal autonomy through the arrangement of possessions, as reflected in the following statements:

> I go from seven-thirty in the morning to nine at night. Having my own cell, when I go back, shut down and just do absolutely nothing. I don't have to say anything. So the down time is really, really appreciated. (Gabriel)

> You could put everything exactly the way that you want everything. (Joshua)

Prior to the follow-up interview, three men at Institution One (George, James, and Walter) had been moved into a special needs unit for inmates with physical health issues. Walter was especially displeased that he had been moved from a single cell into an open barracks-style housing assignment; the lack of privacy and noise were reported to be the most vexing aspects of living in the special unit. Walter claimed to need sleeping pills so that he could rest at night. While single cells were not available at Institution Two, all three men incarcerated there reported that they wished they could have their own cells.

DEPRIVATION OF GOODS AND SERVICES

The lack of appetizing food options was a commonly mentioned source of frustration. Victor and Adam commented that the meals were not nutritious as they were high in starch, for example, rice and potatoes were frequently served. Adam, fifty-nine years of age, claimed that this was a misguided strategy by the department of corrections (DOC): "They normally want to feed inmates heavily, a starch program. Because if you've got an inmate that is satisfied, belly full, usually he's not complaining or creating a lot of problems. The downside of that . . . is with a lot of heavy starch, it's more readily for a lot of inmates to come in at one hundred sixty [pounds] and shoot up over two hundred pounds with the starch. Over the long period, it also leads to diabetes, hypertension, and a few other chronic problems." While the practice of feeding inmates a diet heavy in starch might have short-term advantages (e.g., better-behaved inmates), in the long run the DOC could be spending more on health care because of obesity-related medical issues.

The men described several ways in which they coped with the lack of appetizing food. They reported looking forward to group fund-raisers in which they could purchase meals prepared on the outside, for example, subs and chicken dinners; however, food sales were infrequent and expensive. The annual honor visit provided another opportunity to enjoy homemade food. One advantage to needing medical attention at an outside hospital was the opportunity to eat better food. While recovering from knee replacement surgery, Joshua, who entered prison at the age of thirty and was now sixty-four, reported that he took advantage of the chance to order from a menu: "They give you a menu. You can order all your own meals. Boy, I ate like a king. As good as you can for a hospital, right. I was always eating." Day-to-day, the men purchased groceries at the prison commissary to supplement the food served in the kitchen. However, some mentioned that the inflated commissary prices deterred them from purchasing healthier food and instead encouraged them to buy junk food. According to Adam, "A lot of them are being forced to buy cheaper items, which is your junk food, you know, like your little cookies, your [Little] Debbies, and stuff like that."

An illegal means in which inmates could compensate for the deprivation of appetizing food was to pay prison staff to smuggle in outside food (e.g., pizza and Chinese food). One individual admitted to paying a staff member to bring outside food into the institution. Others also reported engaging in prohibited activities in an effort to ease the hardship of confinement. For example, John admitted that, because he was serving a LWOP sentence, he was more likely to acquire prohibited items to ensure that his sentence was as comfortable as possible: "I'm doing life. I'd be a fool to say, 'Well, that's against the rules. I'm not going to do that.' From my place, you know, if I want something, I'm not going to deprive myself of nothing." Although refraining from institutional misconduct reaped certain benefits, such as a more desirable housing assignment, work assignment, and special visiting privileges, the men reported that there were desired commodities that they would never be eligible to receive even if they had good disciplinary records. And for some, the opportunity to enjoy the luxury was worth the risk of punishment.

Two pains of imprisonment not frequently raised by the group were deprivation of heterosexual relationships or security.

DEPRIVATION OF HETEROSEXUAL RELATIONSHIPS

The deprivation of heterosexual relationships was not widely discussed by the men. The lack of mention could reflect the fact that the men had grown accustomed to living without this type of relationship. It appeared that there were other aspects of free society that they missed more than sexual intercourse as can be seen in Alan's rankings of what he missed the most from the outside: "There are three things that I've come to miss the most: church . . . a Sealy posture-pedic mattress, and making love. Those are the three . . . that I miss the most in that order." Alternatively, it could be the case that they were reluctant to discuss this topic with a female interviewer who was several decades younger than them.

When the topic of sex was broached, the men's statements centered on the themes of missing interaction with women, a lack of intimacy, and feelings of sexual frustration. The following comment from Joshua reflected his desire to interact with women: "I've not had a girl other than my sisters come and see me for me, shit, I don't know. I'd like that once in a while." Michael, who had served thirty years for the murder of his estranged wife, missed all forms of physical contact with a romantic partner. He stated: "[I miss] not just the intimacy of the sexual contact but just that intimacy of just having somebody to hold a hand, you know, you don't have that [here]." Nathan was the only one who discussed feeling sexually frustrated claiming that he felt that way "all the time after being locked up for thirty-three years."

Deprivation of Security

Consistent with previous research on long-term and life-sentenced inmates (Flanagan 1981, 212; R. Johnson and Dobrzanska 2005, 36; MacKenzie and Goodstein 1985, 407), most of the men were not fearful of being violently victimized. John explained why it was especially important for a LWOP inmate to be unafraid: "I'm doing life, I can't be afraid. I mean . . . I worry, but I'm not scared. . . . You know, if I'm scared, then I'm weak and then people are going to take advantage of me, know what I mean, I just don't let [that] happen."

They attributed their lack of fear to the length of time they had been incarcerated, the severity of the offense for which they were convicted, the reputations that they had established of a willingness to use violence, and in Joshua's words, how they "carried" themselves. While, overall, the men reported few interpersonal issues in their lives, they were not entirely without conflict. Threats of physical violence were interpreted by the men as being a ubiquitous feature of prison life. Some men in 2006 and 2011 reported that other inmates had made threats toward them. For example, Matthew commented, "You hear [threats] everyday. . . . [For example,] 'I'm going to kick your ass.'" However, the men reported that they were not bothered by the threats and accepted them as part of the environment.

The men felt compelled to use violence when newly incarcerated. As a result of some of their encounters, they sustained serious injuries. In the early period of incarceration, four men (George, Daniel, Nathan, and Adam) had been stabbed, and John and Adam had been struck in the face and head, respectively, with a sock containing heavy objects (e.g., rocks). The men were not random targets of violence. George and Daniel blamed their involvement in illegal activities for their attacks. When he was transferred to a prison in another state, Nathan claimed that he was stabbed in the chest because he refused to join a White supremacist gang. Given the high level of violence in prison when he was newly incarcerated and the length of time he had served, in 2006, John felt he was fortunate to have sustained only one serious injury: "Out of the thirty-one years, I had my cheekbone broken once and that's a pretty good record. I didn't get stabbed or nothing."

While other research has noted that older inmates are susceptible to victimization (Kerbs and Jolley 2007), physical victimization in their later years was not commonly reported by the men. Matthew, Daniel, and James were the exceptions. When he was sixty-one years of age, Matthew claimed that his cellmate attacked him because of his snoring: "Well, I was incarcerated with a younger guy, and I snore a lot. I snore . . . and he thought it was something that I could turn off and on. . . . And he severely beat me one night, and I got blind in one eye" (for a greater discussion of the injury he sustained see Chapter 4, Medical Staff). In the intervening years between interviews, Daniel had been stabbed while he was defending his property. James, the oldest member of the group, reported a variety of abuses. He claimed that a former cellmate repeatedly made sexual advances toward him at night. James was able to prevent rape from occurring by alerting the correctional officer; when the officer came to the cell, the aggressor would pretend he was sleeping. More recently, James reported that he was verbally and physically assaulted by other inmates as they would curse at him and slap him.

According to the men, one of the most vulnerable groups of inmates, regardless of age, was snitches. Daniel remarked, "They got a phrase here: 'Snitches get stitches,' and anybody can give them to you. So once you're labeled, you [are] a mark, like you got an 'X' on your back." Three men (James, Daniel, and Robert) had each been labeled a snitch by other inmates. For all three, no physical violence transpired as a result of being labeled as an informant, and in 2011, none were still considered to be snitches. However, in 2006, Robert had been confined in the administrative segregation area for over ten years because it was unsafe for him to be housed in the general population. According to him, he was coerced by other inmates on his tier into hiding alcohol in his cell. Robert complied with the inmates' request but later reported the contraband to a correctional officer. Even though the incident occurred over a decade ago, he was concerned for his safety if he returned to the general population. At our first interview, he explained:

They know who I am, but I don't know who they are. . . . I don't know if they got something against me or not . . . so like I'm just a target standing out in the front of four or five hundred people, and at any time, anybody could come up and run something up in me. . . . Everything [could] look normal, but it's not because all of a sudden a blanket goes over your head. You don't see nothing and you're stabbed up four or five times. So you don't know who's stabbing you because you can't see nothing. Put a blanket over your head, everything goes black. You know, nobody's saying nothing, so you can't recognize no voices.

In 2011 Robert reported that he had been living in the general population for two years and his previous apprehension about retaliation was unfounded. He explained, "I found out after I got out of there, a lot of those guys are gone, so there's only maybe two or three." While he was no longer concerned about the potential for victimization as a result of being labeled a snitch, he felt that he remained in a "dangerous situation." Robert sleepwalked. When he had his own cell in administrative segregation, the sleep disturbance was not as severe; however, he claimed that he had recently begun to experience night terrors in addition to sleepwalking. He was concerned that during an episode his cellmate would mistakenly believe that Robert was attempting to attack him and respond with violence:

Before, when I was back there, I didn't have no problem of hollering, fighting, kicking, punching, all of this in my sleep. I was just sleepwalking, but now, with[in] the last year, being out here, I've done started screaming, fighting, kicking, punching. I kicked my TV, crushed my radio . . . plus I'm rolling out of the bed. . . . [A new cellmate] might think I'm there to harm them. They don't know that I'm sleeping . . . they could haul off and hit me, stab me, anything. It's not their fault. You know what I mean? And it's sure not my fault because I have no control over nothing.

As a result of the potential for victimization, Robert had requested to be moved to a single cell. He claimed that he was willing to return to a restricted area, such as the protective custody or secure housing unit, even though it would diminish his quality of life as he would not be able to work or participate in programming. According to him, "the warden, the deputy warden, the doctors, [and] mental health" had denied his request.

In order to avoid victimization, prisoners have reported they refrained from engaging in prohibited behaviors, avoided certain areas of the prison, stayed in their cells, and threatened or used violence to ward off victimization (McCorkle 2004, 207). Similar to the prisoners surveyed in the McCorkle study, John and Michael avoided the gym because they felt that it was a location where violence was more likely to occur. Four men (Michael, Alan,

William, and Victor) felt they had to be watchful for signs of danger. For example, William, who was forty-two when he entered prison, commented, "The only step I have is to keep my eyes open. . . . I just have to be careful." Michael compared living in prison to driving, for both require defensive tactics. He explained, "Well, it's like anything in the world out there, you know, if you're going to go out on the road and drive, you know, you got to drive defensively." Some of the men reported making verbal threats to prevent physical victimization. John described an incident in which an inmate had threatened to take his property, and in response, John delivered a tirade of verbal threats. He described the encounter: "I said, 'I'll tell you what I'm going to do, you take the TV, you take the radio, take the commissary, take anything you want, I got no problem with this.' And then I said a lot of cuss words, and I said, 'You will go to sleep. You will have your back towards me. You will be in the commissary buying, you will be in the food line, I'll cut your throat.'" As a result of these threats, John reported that the inmate left without incident.

The possession of weapons was infrequently reported, especially as the men aged. Four men reported that they used to carry weapons at earlier points in their prison sentences, but no longer did so. Only Thomas, who was sixty-eight years of age and had been incarcerated for twenty-one years, admitted that he had a weapon in his cell: "I have one close by. I don't have it on me, but I do have it in my room. But I can get it in a few seconds. I haven't had to use it yet." Overall, the men reported little fear of victimization, and few reported experiencing a physical victimization in recent years. Even the men who reported sustaining severe injuries (primarily when they were young men) were unperturbed by the experiences and claimed they had not led to greater fear of or worry about physical assaults.

MISSING FAMILY, LOW PROBABILITY OF RELEASE, AND INSTITUTIONAL THOUGHTLESSNESS

The three most commonly reported painful aspects of life imprisonment were not mentioned by Sykes (1958). These are missing family, institutional thoughtlessness, and indeterminacy. Sixteen men in at least one interview indicated that the separation from family was the most difficult aspect of life imprisonment. Over half the group reported that the lack of sensitivity for older inmates and the low likelihood of release compounded the hardship of doing time.

Prolonged absence from family constitutes one of the greatest penalties of a LWOP sentence. Most relationships undoubtedly suffer from the limitations of confinement, yet for LWOP inmates, separation is likely permanent and significantly impedes the stability of a family and other social support networks. Over the course of decades-long incarceration, major changes can affect the family. Many of the men had relatives, most commonly parents and siblings, who had died since they were incarcerated. While their families grew with the births of grandchildren or great-grandchildren, these additions were not enough to offset the loss that the men felt when the relatives with whom they were close to prior to imprisonment died.

Visits

While exceptions exist (see Jackson et al. 1997, 82; Zamble 1992, 415), most research indicates that long-term inmates, including life-sentenced inmates, are generally unable to sustain meaningful contact with loved ones over the course of incarceration (Cohen and Taylor 1972, 67; Flanagan 1981, 210; McGinnis 1990, 119; Sapsford 1978, 136; Wikberg and Foster 1990, 12). Overall, the subjects of this book and their outside contacts proved no exception. At our first interview, more than half reported that the level of communication with their family had diminished over time. When newly incarcerated, the men remembered communicating more often with their families. Thomas's statement illustrated this point: "When I first got here, I had two visits every week. At Christmas time, I got thirty Christmas cards." Most families were unable to sustain a high level of communication, and a gradual decline occurred in both the number of people with whom they communicated and the frequency of communication. Karl and Victor quoted the adage "out of sight, out of mind" to explain the decline.

Visiting policies permitted ninety minutes of visitation each week in either one ninety-minute block or two forty-five minute increments. In 2006, two men (John and Charles) received the maximum amount of visitation time available each week. They were outliers, as only one-fourth of the group reported receiving at least one visit a month. The men who enjoyed regular contact with their families acknowledged that they were blessed compared to their counterparts who had little contact with their families:

> I have some contact with the outside world and these other guys don't. You know, you got to feel sorry for them because it's rough. . . . I'm blessed because I got a family. (John)

> I know that I'm very, very fortunate, you know, when measured against other guys. (Gabriel)

Ryan, Nathan, Joshua, and Victor received visits less frequently, around three or four a year. The rest of the group received visits sporadically such as two visits a year, and even less often for Thomas, Troy, Henry, and Robert who averaged a visit every two years.

In 2011, almost half the men reported a further decline in the number of visits they received. Nine reported that they received less visits than they had five years ago, while seven reported no change. Matthew and Troy continued to have a low number of visits each year (e.g., three or four), yet both estimated that they received more visits than they had five years ago. Only Robert reported an appreciable increase in the number of visits he received. At the original interview, he reported that he was estranged from his family and did not receive visits. However, five years later, his situation had changed. According to Robert, he had defended a friend, from harassment by other inmates. He explained: "[My friend] went to his visit and started telling his family what I had done, you know, to help him, and now his people accept me like part of the family. And they come and see me just about every other week. You know, so they told the [pardons] board that don't worry about [Robert] not having any place to live when he gets out because he can stay with us for as long as I want to." Robert credited these new relationships with an increase in his well-being: "I feel really blessed today, really blessed. I think my health is better. My communication with others is better, whether they're in here or whether it's on the street. . . . My whole life has been turned upside down for the better."

Most men were pleased to communicate with their family. For example, Ryan, who had been incarcerated for twenty-four years, claimed, "[A visit] is the best time that I spend in jail, being with my family." Regular communication with family reminded the men that they were cared about and helped boost their morale. Karl remarked, "It's nice [at] mail call to hear your name being called." Robert reported, "You might be feeling down and they tell you something, you know, that really lifts you up." When feeling defeated, Gabriel found that communication with his family provided him with the necessary boost to keep going:

> That, kind of like, obligates me to do things in a different way than, you know, in the past when I, kind of like, felt selfishly. I didn't have that same, kind of like, obligation to work from. When some things are happening and you're kind of like leaning toward . . . giving up what it is that you have, and then you get that message, and it's like hey I can't disappoint them again. And so sometimes when you don't have the strength to do it for yourself you have to, kind of like, you know, do it for somebody else and I know that's what my case has been.

The possible loss of visits, especially honor visits, proved a deterrent from engaging in rule-breaking behavior. The informal social control that the family could exert remained powerful, despite the separation. The ultimatum delivered by Joshua's family—that they would sever all communication with him if he continued to engage in disciplinary misconduct—was the catalyst he needed to change his behavior.

For the men with little or no communication with their family, they described feeling forgotten and unloved. In 2006, Robert described the loneliness he felt when he did not receive any birthday or holiday cards: "It seems like everybody on your tier gets Christmas cards, birthday cards, Thanksgiving [cards], you know, but you can't because you don't have nobody. On your birthday or Christmas, you don't get no Christmas cards. So you feel like nobody out there even knows you exist." No one likes to feel so insignificant as not to matter or even be remembered. For LWOP inmates, this is a real fear as they remain permanently separated from their loved ones and are unable to participate in daily family life.

While visits were generally welcomed and eagerly anticipated, there were negative aspects associated with them. As described by the men, both parties, the inmate and the visitors, avoided discussing painful or sensitive topics so as to not worry or burden the other. Self-censorship had the undesirable consequence of making visits superficial. Gabriel explained:

> Visits aren't real, you know. When I say they're not real, it's like they come and pretend everything is okay on the outside, and I come and pretend everything is okay here, so you have this, kind of like, pretentious existence. And I'm not saying that the love that, you know, we have for each other, that's not real. I'm just saying, you hide each other's lives, and I just think that my mother and my father aren't telling me everything that goes on, and I understand why. I respect it. I don't necessarily agree with it, but I understand. . . . They feel as though [I go] through enough in there . . . but, you know, for the same reasons that, you know, that I won't tell them [because] . . . I think that I'm protecting them, or. . . . I don't want my mom or my pop worrying, just like they don't want me worrying. So, there's certain, I guess, facets of real life experiences that you don't share.

When more meaningful conversations occurred, six men felt helpless to aid their family members in the struggles that they faced, such as caring for a sick relative, making burial arrangements for a deceased loved one, or providing financial assistance. This was probably the reason Gabriel's family chose not to discuss family issues with him.

The men were largely incapable of assisting with financial issues and other family problems. Troy, incarcerated at the age of twenty-two and now fifty-five years of age, remarked, "There are a lot of problems that they have that I can't resolve nor can I participate in." Adam regretted his inability to assist his siblings in caring for their ailing father: "One of the most trying times that I had was when my father took ill. . . . My baby sister took my pop down to her place because she had a little cottage and there would be times, you know, you call to see how dad's doing and everything and [she would say,] 'Why'd you have to mess up, you know, being in jail and so forth like that? We need you out here to help us with dad and so forth.' Man, I tell you that, the reality of that, really hits home."

A logical inference would be that negative feelings generated through communication—artificiality, powerlessness, guilt, and resentment—had the potential to further splinter social networks. Visits could cease altogether if they were not considered meaningful by either party. The men maintained that they preferred an honest dialogue with their family members and would prefer to be aware of a negative situation than have it concealed from them. During his 2011 interview, Noah, who had served twenty-seven years, reported that he was upset with his siblings because they did not inform him that a prolonged illness had preceded their mother's death. He responded, "Let me worry. I can handle the worry. . . . It feels like you are shunned because nobody wants to tell you what was really happening." Thus it appears that the grief over the death of a loved one could be exacerbated when information was hidden from them.

When visits ended, the men found it difficult to say goodbye to loved ones. Victor, a father of nine, commented, "They get to leave. That's the hard part." Some men admitted to crying or getting choked up when their visits were ending and recalled how painful it was to say good-bye to their children, especially when their children were younger. The end of a visit served as a reminder of the loss of freedom. Alan, who had served almost twenty years for the murder of a relative, elaborated: "One thing that I don't like about the visiting room is when the visit is over, I see them walking out and that brings back . . . that I can't leave. . . . That has the tendency to bother me and I guess I got to get over it." Nathan reported that he preferred letters and phone calls to visits because "the personal contact, sometimes it makes me a little emotional . . . [because] it reminds me too much of the outside."

Honor Visits

In addition to regular visits, honor visits were another means by which the men were able to see and interact with loved ones. In 2006, Matthew described why honor visits were special: "You get to embrace your family, sit there without an officer for two or three hours. You can talk to them and you don't have that wall in between. You can bring food in. It's a relaxed atmosphere." Honor visits were reserved for those prisoners who did not accrue any disciplinary write-ups in the previous year. As they were a reward for good behavior, honor visits had special perks not associated with regular visits. They took place at outdoor picnic tables during warm weather months. More visitors were permitted at honor visits than at regular visits. Unlike normal visits, where physical contact between the inmate and his visitors was limited to the beginning and end of the visit, inmates were allowed greater physical contact with their loved ones during an honor visit (e.g., holding a grandchild). One other unique feature of the honor visit was that visitors were allowed to bring food into the institution. Most men looked forward to their honor visits because of the chance to eat food specially prepared for them and the relaxed quiet atmosphere in which they could visit with their loved ones. At the first interview, they remarked that the effort that went into earning an honor visit was worth it. Victor commented: "We work all year long for [an] honor visit. . . . And you don't mind once you're out there how much you had to do to get there. It don't matter how much work I have to do . . . because my family can come . . . and you know it's worth it." For some men, because of their or their relatives' dislike of regular visits, honor visits were the only time in which they saw their family members.

During the follow-up interviews, I learned of major changes that had taken place to the honor visit policies at Institution One, which decreased the ability of the men to have these visits. Charles, sixty-four years of age, reported that he no longer had honor visits because "they're not really honor visits anymore." Instead of two honor visits a year, inmates were now permitted only one each year. The duration of the visit was shortened from three hours to one and one-half hours. Alan commented, "It's really not enough time to eat and then chit chat." The amount of outside food permitted had been reduced as now families were only allowed to bring a single cooler of food into the prison. All of these changes detracted from the visit, but the one that caused the greatest hardship was that honor visits now took place on Wednesdays, instead of on the weekends. Almost all of the men reported that this change had caused them greater difficulty in scheduling visits. Alan stated: "Not too many people can come for an hour and a half on a Wednesday." Most of their family members had to miss work, and with the reduced length of the visit some of the men now felt that the honor visit was no longer worth the effort. Charles commented, "I'm not going to put my people through that. . . . They take off work, come down here [and because of the security procedures] you might get an hour if you're lucky." Gabriel reported that, because he was eligible for only one honor visit each year (of up to five visitors), he could not include all of the relatives who would like to be at the visit. The men were not aware of any particular reason for the change in the policy and frequently cited the modifications to honor visits as further evidence of the increasingly restrictive prison policies during the new warden's tenure. John wondered, "We had to be good for a year to get it. Now, why [does the warden] want to put a damper on it?" Nathan felt that the changes were expressly designed to deter visits from family; whether intended or not, this was the reported effect.

Fathers and Husbands

Only four men (Alan, Troy, Samuel, and Robert) did not have children, either biological or step-children. At the time of the second interview, all of the men with children had become grandfathers, and several were great-grandfathers. When the men began serving their sentences, though, their children were young. Victor was already incarcerated when one of his children was born, meaning that he had "never seen him outside of prison."

The men recalled that when they were newly incarcerated, the welfare of their children was a constant concern. Matthew recalled that his daughter "was about eighteen months old. . . . She was a baby, and I was concerned about her." Charles regretted that he was unable to care for his two young daughters: "My mom was taking care of them. I'm like damn, man, I'm not, and I'm supposed to be doing that." Victor recalled feeling guilty that his children did not have access to services that could help them cope with having an incarcerated parent: "When I got locked up, we had groups in here that I got to express myself in and I could get some help. My children didn't have that. I'm really, really sorry about some of the things they had to go through. . . . They couldn't afford no psychologists or therapists or to go to any groups like that. And they had to suffer through without any help. And I'm responsible for that. I don't like that."

Regret was a commonly expressed emotion. Five men reported that it was difficult being absent from important milestones in the lives of their children and grandchildren. Francis, who had five children and eleven grand-children, provided specific examples of the life events he had missed: "That's been difficult . . . missing not seeing their graduations . . . not seeing them married, not being able to walk them down the aisle." Some of the men worried that they had been poor fathers. Because of his almost twenty-year separation from his family, Francis believed that as a father he "did a very poor job on the youngest kids." George, a father of four, reported that he told his children, "I failed as a parent, and I said, but that don't make you a failure." Despite his absence, he attempted to maintain his parental role stating, "I function in the family unit not as an absent father." Although he was tempted to deceive his children when they were younger about his where-abouts, he felt it was important to be honest with them in the hopes that they would avoid making similar mistakes. George explained: "When they used to come and visit me when they was little, they didn't know what this was, and I never told them it was a military school or this was where daddy works. This is jail, and as time went on, they were able to understand the concept of prison and what leads to prison." As they grew older, he and his children were able to maintain honest communication. Through letter exchanges, they discussed difficult issues such as the criminal lifestyle he was immersed in that ultimately led to his incarceration for first-degree murder. Despite the fact that his contact with his children was reduced, George's expectations of them had not diminished as he stated: "I've always accentuated or demanded that they do well." His children had done well for themselves. His pride in his children was readily apparent as he detailed their accomplishments, and there was a lot to be proud of. All of his children were college graduates and three had earned advanced degrees.

None of the men wanted his children to inherit the addictions that had dogged him or for them to make similar mistakes as he once had. George described a conversation with his sons in which he cautioned them to avoid following in his footsteps, "Criminal behavior is not genetically passed on. I said that it's a learned behavior." Francis, a self-identified gambling addict, was ashamed to admit that when his children were young he had taken them to horse races and placed bets for them. He was concerned that his behavior had contributed to two of his children developing gambling addictions. Victor was upset that his incarceration could have contributed to his daughter's alcoholism.

In addition to their roles as fathers, the men's ability to be husbands was severely compromised by life imprisonment. As has been observed in previous research, the spousal relationship is especially vulnerable to long-term separation (Reed and Glamser 1979, 356). In the words of one English inmate serving a life sentence (Sapsford 1978, 142): "How do you expect a marriage to last when the man only sees his wife for eighteen hours a year?" While the men in this study had the option of seeing their spouses more frequently than this particular English inmate, the end result was the same. It would be difficult for any marriage to survive when one partner was to be incarcerated for the rest of his life.[1] The unmarried men of the group felt that marriage could not withstand permanent imprisonment:

> If you got a life sentence, your wife is gone . . . in all of the years that I've been here and in jails, every guy that's got over two years, he can forget his wife. She'll jump at the first nice guy that comes along, you know, and it's nature. . . . You don't have no true blue woman that's going to stay by her husband that's doing LWOP, I mean, come on, be realistic. (Thomas)

> I've seen guys . . . maybe about the first three or four years, their girl or maybe wife will maybe come see them like every week . . . make sure they got money for [toiletries] and maybe get mail like maybe three times a week. Then, after a while, the mail will cut down to maybe two letters a week, then one a week, then one every other week, you know, and after a while, the mail starts slowing down longer and longer and

longer. After a while, you might start getting one letter a month, you know, and you know, maybe one day you might be getting that "Dear John" letter. . . . Then the guy he just breaks down. That's what changes a lot of people. (Robert)

Consistent with their peers' predictions, divorce was virtually universal for the men who were married at the time of prison admission. Of the seven who were married when they entered prison, only George remained married in 2006. Although George had told his wife that marriage "didn't mean for jail or worse" and that he "didn't expect my wife to put her life on hold because I got a life sentence," his wife remained committed to him. George's wife died in 2010 after a lengthy illness. Shortly after his wife's passing, the warden asked a mental health staff member to evaluate George to determine if he was in distress. George asked the staff member, "What you think I'm trying to catch up with my wife? . . . I don't know how they expected me to react." During our interview, George expressed that he would have reacted differently if his wife's death had been unexpected, but the fact that he and his family had had time to prepare for it allowed him to cope better with the loss.

Adam and Anthony were active in initiating their divorces and explained their reasoning:

I guess it was about a year after my incarceration. I realized that [with a] life without [parole sentence,] appeals could take a long time. . . . I tried to look at things from, you know, a business standpoint. My life's over. My wife was twenty-four at the time. You're still young, you can start your life over and I didn't want her to, you know, wait until the appeals and stuff like that. So, I kind of pushed her for going for a divorce. (Adam)

I'm the one that filed for the divorce because she had stopped seeing me and communicating, wouldn't answer my letters or anything. So I said why be married? (Anthony)

Francis believed that his wife had ended their marriage because she had grown tired of his repeated incarcerations. A LWOP sentence proved to be the breaking point, he explained: "All the other times I was in prison, you know, I mean, she was right there with me, you know, come and visit, bring the kids. . . . She's been through so much, and she thought that, you know, this is the last straw." In contrast, Daniel and Walter claimed to have received no warning or explanation as to why their wives filed for divorce.

The individual's relationship with his wife directly affected his relationship with his children. George's wife's commitment to him contributed to his ability to have close relationships with his children. Francis and Daniel remained on good terms with their former spouses, which helped them maintain contact with their children. In contrast, for Anthony, Henry, and Adam, divorce not only meant an end to their relationships with their wives, it also meant an estrangement from their children:

> I don't even communicate with them anymore. I've been cut off. . . . I have no idea [why] really. . . . My ex-wife has poisoned the children's mind against me. . . . She's not supportive. (Anthony)

> Sometimes, I regret [encouraging the divorce] . . . because when she did move on, the guy she married didn't want us to have any contact between me and my son because he was afraid that she might have been on the rebound. If I ever got my appeal, [she] would come back to me instead of staying with him. So, that's the only thing I regret there. (Adam)

> [The mother of his children was on a] hate mission [and told them that] your daddy don't love you. He really don't. If he did, he would be here. (Henry)

More than one-fourth of the men reported an estrangement from at least one of their children. I usually learned early on in the interview whether they were estranged. One of the first questions I asked was how many grandchildren they had. An early indicator of estrangement occurred when the interviewee could not answer the question definitively. Typical responses included: "Twelve that I know of" (Anthony); "Last I heard it was three" (Henry); and "I have no contact, so I really don't know" (Adam).

The reasons for the estrangement varied. As mentioned above, divorce or a bitter end to a relationship increased the likelihood of estrangement. Thomas and William had little contact with their families, and their relationships with their children were no exception. According to the men, some of their children were resentful that they had been incarcerated for most of their lives. For instance, John alleged that his daughter felt he had "abandoned" her. As a result, she no longer wished to speak with him. He stated: "She ain't been down in years [to see me]." Estrangement also occurred as a result of disapproval of a relative's romantic relationship. Walter's daughter was in an interracial relationship. He admitted to being "prejudiced" and consequently "cut[ting] her off." In the same vein, Francis was not accepting of his grandchild's same-sex relationship. He claimed, "If I was home, they would not be welcome in my home, you know, I'm just that strongly against that." I was surprised by both Walter's and Francis's reactions as I expected that they would be more tolerant of their relatives' lifestyle choices because they would want to maintain as much communication as they possibly could with family members. However, it appeared that voicing their disapproval was one means by which they acted as the patriarch of their families, a role they did not often have a chance to engage in.

In addition to taking issue with his grandchild's same-sex relationship, Francis admitted, "There's a couple of daughters that I might see every two or three years and I think it's fair to say we're estranged." The source of the tension was a common one in families: money. More specifically, two of his daughters failed to repay a loan that Francis had given them. According to him, one daughter "comes about every two years and I hate to see her name on the visiting list because when she comes, and I see it, I know she wants something. She only comes when she wants something." Francis explained that the common pattern in their interaction was to avoid any discussion of money until the end of the visit and then his daughter would broach the subject, saying: "'Well, dad, you're in prison. You don't know if you're going to get out, and we don't see what you need this money for. . . . You don't need this money and we have a need, and I think if we ask you for it, you'd have gave it. And plus by the time you get out, which might [be] ten years or eleven, we'll have it back.'" While Francis used to acquiesce to their demands, in more recent visits he had declined saying, "I'm your father, I'm not a bank . . . somewhere along the line it just has to stop."

Most of the men appeared to be bothered by the estrangement from their children. To them it represented failure in their roles as fathers. It also meant that they had lost a connection to the outside world, as well as missing the opportunity to be involved in their children's or grandchildren's lives. In addition to the commonly expressed feelings of regret and guilt, during his 2011 interview, Henry expressed anger at his children for their refusal to visit him. He described a conversation that his son had with another relative about their estranged relationship: "I don't want to go down there. I don't even know that chump [Henry]. And really I don't want to know him." Henry recalled his reaction, "That hurt. That hurt, but I can understand why. But at the same time, I didn't understand why because when they were babies I took care of them." While Henry provided financial support to his children, he admitted that he spent little time with them: "I didn't spend a lot of time with them. The street took up all my time then. . . . Looking back, you know, I should have spent more time with them. But to me at the time, by me being young, I thought as long as I'm dishing out money to them, that's all that's necessary." Henry was angry with his children that they would not consider reconciling with him. He reported that he had asked a family member to relay the following message to his children: "All I'm asking for is forty-five minutes of their time for one visit. And after that one visit, if you are not satisfied as to how that visit goes or what I have to say, not to defend myself but to give you my point of view. . . . I'm not going to say nothing negative about their mother. . . . [I] had problems. . . . just explain why I did what I did. And if [they] didn't like [it], don't bother about ever coming back." However, not all of the men reported being upset with the estrangement from their children. Joshua claimed to not harbor any resentment or other ill feelings toward his estranged son. He stated: "I don't communicate with [my son], I haven't seen him since I've been here. . . . I mean, my daughter tells me about [him]. . . . [He does] well without me, and I'm glad at it. That's good enough." It appeared, though, that he would welcome any attempt his son made at reestablishing communication.

Challenges to Maintaining Contact

Many of the obstacles faced by other inmates when keeping in touch with their families also exist for LWOP inmates (Aday 2003, 123–124); however, for this population of inmates, there is no release date for their families to anxiously anticipate. As discussed above, estrangement was a relatively common experience for the men and would contribute to the decline in communication. Overall, one-half of the group reported an estrangement from one or more family members. In addition to their children, the men reported being estranged from a parent or a sibling—and for a few, their entire families. Nathan's father visited him one time at the beginning of his incarceration, but they had had little communication in the years prior to his father's death. In addition to his father, Nathan was also estranged from his sister, stating, "It's not a really good relationship. You know, she's done a couple of bad things since I've been in prison." Six men were estranged from at least one sibling. While in Nathan's case it appeared that he expressed disapproval of her actions, the opposite was true with Joshua's and Adam's. Both had sisters who stopped communicating with them when they were convicted of murder:

> I've got a sister that never spoke to me since I've come to jail. I've tried to open channels of communication with her even when she was sick. . . . She don't talk to me. Sometimes I call home and talk to my mom, and she'll answer the phone. She'll accept the charges by pushing the button but she won't talk. She'll hand the phone off to my mom, so I've never spoken to her and I've not tried to speak to her in the last ten years. You know, it's her choice and, you know, I accept it. That's how she feels. (Joshua)

> I have four sisters, three of which I'm real close to. One couldn't accept the fact that I was incarcerated, so we don't have any contact whatsoever. (Adam)

As of 2011, only Troy had reestablished communication with an estranged relative. He reported that his sister had stopped speaking to him because of the crime he committed. Recently, he had apologized to her, which then led to their reconciliation.

While money was a tense subject between Francis and two of his daughters, it was also an issue between Charles and Alan and their respective sisters. Charles believed that the reason his sister no longer communicated with him was because he had refused to lend her money. He was emphatic in his claim that he was in greater need of the small amount of money he possessed than she was: "She's just upset about the money but I don't have the money, I need the money." Alternatively, Alan had written and asked his older sister for a loan of five hundred dollars. He had had no contact with his sister since his request and decided that he would wait for his sister to initiate communication with him before he attempted to contact her again.

Even more extreme, Robert, William, Henry, and Walter reported that they were estranged from their entire families. Robert and William were uncertain why their families were no longer in contact. Both reported that they had attempted to reestablish communication with their families by writing letters, but the letters went unanswered. William commented, "I don't have anybody now." Walter and Henry were aware of the reason for the estrangement. Walter indicated that his family members were angry with him because he had made no effort to contact them when he escaped. Unlike Robert and William, he expressed no desire to communicate with his family: "I just don't want to bother with people, period." Henry was estranged from his extended family. He was angry with them for failing to inform him that his mother had died. He described the incident: "Family didn't even tell me nothing. I had to find out through the chaplain. . . . If my family had any love at all, you know what I'm saying, why couldn't you take the time out and . . . go down there and let me know that my mom had passed?" As a result, Henry concluded, "Yeah, I have family, but I don't care much about them. . . . I don't hate them, but I have dislike for them, a lot more dislike, than what I thought I would."

As the men have grown older, so too have their family members. Advanced age and the failing health of relatives had also led to diminished communication, for these impaired the ability of relatives to visit, converse on the phone, or write letters. At the time of our interview in 2006, Ryan and Matthew expressed concern and sadness over a relative's deteriorating health. While Ryan's mother had visited him regularly during the eighteen years he had been incarcerated, she had recently become ill and returned to her native country. Ryan lamented, "I don't know, maybe I'm not going to see my mom no more." Matthew's brother was gravely ill. He estimated that the likelihood of seeing his brother again was low: "I'll probably never get to see him again.

He's got cancer. He's terminally ill." Over half the group reported that at least one relative was in too poor of health to visit. Henry relayed a conversation his father had with him at their final visit: "'Boy, I just wanted to come and see you but I probably won't make this trip no more. . . . I don't feel up to it. You take care of yourself.'"

The death of a relative also served to reduce communication with the outside world. More than half the men reported that family members—most often parents and siblings—who used to visit regularly were now deceased. When newly incarcerated, it was painful for Nathan, then twenty-three years of age, to realize that many of his family members would die while he was incarcerated: "Everybody was pretty much alive when I came to prison. . . . The only care I had was the fact that I knew that while I was going to be here, you know, these people were going to start dying." His prediction was accurate: Almost all of the men identified a relative who had died while they were imprisoned. The loss of family members continued to mount over the course of incarceration; at the follow-up interview, nine men reported a loved one's death in the period between 2006 and 2011. Some had multiple relatives die in that time frame. For example, John's mother and father died, both of whom had visited him each week. Both of Noah's parents and a sister died, and two of Joshua's sisters died.

The death of a relative was described as one of the most difficult aspects of serving a LWOP sentence. Even Thomas, who claimed that visits were unimportant to him, described the deaths of his parents and siblings as the worst part of life imprisonment: "The hardest part was losing my family the way that I did, all of my family, you know. My brother died. My sister died. My mother died. All while I was in prison. . . . I'm the only surviving member of the family. You know, it's kind of lonely at the bottom if there's nobody there." Troy regretted that his prolonged incarceration had caused him to never form close bonds with his family: "[The hardest part] was always the passing of my parents. You know, being incarcerated, I've been incarcerated for a third of my life, and it made me never really know my parents. You know, to this day, I still have brothers and sisters, [but] I tell people well I really don't have brothers and sisters because I don't know them." Troy underestimated the amount of time he has been incarcerated; in actuality, he had spent more than half his life incarcerated. His parents were a tenuous lifeline to the outside world, and when they died, the connection was severed.

The cost of communication also precluded the men from seeing, speaking, or writing to their families as often as they would have liked. While it was easier to remain in contact with loved ones through letters and phone calls than visits, these were not without their own challenges. Daniel and Robert stated that the price of stationery and stamps prohibited them from sending more mail. In addition, prison life was dull with little changing from one day to the next. According to five men, the monotony of prison life made it hard to communicate because there was little positive to write or speak about. Matthew explained: "I'm not that good at corresponding by mail. I write, but like I said, there's nothing to write about, it's just the same old thing. I don't even want to talk about it, you know. Nothing happens in here, same old stuff over and over again. If you have anything to say, it's negative. There's not too much good to say about the place." As he was terminally ill, Thomas had even fewer bright spots in his life to share in a letter. He described the bleak tone of any letters he would write: "What are you going to say? What can you say. . . . The doctors are telling you, 'You're going to die. You'd be lucky to make it to Thanksgiving.'"

The reported high cost of making collect phone calls discouraged most using the phone. Estimates of the cost of a fifteen-minute collect call ranged from five to fifty-five dollars depending on the location. The men contended that they and their loved ones were, in Charles's words, being "ripped of" by the prison administration and the phone company. Despite the fact that some outside contacts encouraged the men to call, they refused to do so because they could not help pay for the cost of the collect call:

Why would you want to put that burden on your family? (Francis)

I don't like making phone calls and have problem creating bills so I just, you know, I don't call. (Gabriel)

I can't call them because it costs too much money. (Victor)

I can't give no input onto the bill. (Henry)

Charles alleged that, even with the rising price of gas, it remained cheaper for his family to visit than to make phone calls. A policy change at Institution One, which, according to the men, only allowed relatives with a specific phone company the ability to accept collect calls from the prison, further decreased communication by phone. Charles and Alan reported that they each had family members who were unwilling to change phone companies, and as a result, they were no longer able to communicate with them by phone.

Visits generated additional expenses such as the costs of childcare, tolls, gas, and lodging and the loss of income because of missed work. Regular visits were difficult for those relatives who did not live in close proximity to the institution. Almost all of the men had relatives who were living out of state, while James and Ryan had immediate family who lived out of the country. An additional impediment to regular visits was the out-of-state transfer that most men had experienced at least once in the course of serving their sentences.

For instance, while serving life without parole, George had been transferred to prisons as far away as Florida and California.

Restrictions placed on visitor eligibility also reduced visits. Daniel and James each had a son who was unable to visit because of his own criminal record. Most of the men described with frustration specific incidents in which a mistake or oversight on the part of prison administration occurred and their visitors either were not permitted to enter the institution or were harmed. As an example, Michael was upset that his brother, who had respiratory problems, was forced to wait outside in inclement weather for a long period of time as prison officials verified his identity.

For the men at Institution One, a topic of universal dissatisfaction was the visiting room. The layout of the room consisted of two concentric rectangles of benches. Inmates sat on the inner benches, while their visitors sat on the outside. A wall, which the men estimated to be about forty inches high, separated the two rows of benches. (In 2011, the men reported that the wall had been lowered by several inches.) They felt that the wall diminished the quality of visits because it increased the noise in the room as visitors and inmates had to speak in loud voices to hear each other. Matthew explained, "Yeah, you're separated, it's a wall in between. . . . You got fifty inmates in there. You got fifty visitors and they're trying to out shout each other." As a result of the raised voices, and combined with the close proximity of adjacent inmates and visitors, the environment was not conducive to discussing personal or sensitive matters. The men also alleged that the poor acoustics in the room exacerbated the trouble of maintaining a conversation, especially for those inmates and visitors who were hearing impaired. For instance, James claimed that he could hear little during visits, which led to a decline in the quality of the few visits he received. The noise was an even greater issue on the weekends and holidays when the visiting room was more crowded. The men were disappointed that the visits, already a challenge to take place, were diminished by the poor environment in which they occurred. John noted, "You wish you could have a better visit with them. . . . You want [no-contact] visits, you know, just so it'll be quiet or peaceful and you don't have to yell and scream."[2]

Conditions in the visiting room were reported to be especially problematic for younger and older visitors. John contended that the wall made it difficult to interact with young children: "A lot of family is little and you can just like barely see their faces over the wall." Because of an incident that occurred in which his niece fell off a wooden bench in the visitor room, Troy commented, "I refuse to let my people come and visit me here." The wooden benches posed a challenge for older visitors too. Michael described that his visits were truncated because of the uncomfortable nature of the wood benches: "I don't expect, you know, people, you know, my age or older to come sit on a piece of wood out there like that, you know, for forty-five minutes."

Because of the hardship on visitors, it is not surprising that six men were aware of at least one family member who was reluctant to visit. The two most commonly reported reasons were security procedures and poor treatment by the officers, as reflected in the statements below:

> I know that it hurts them when they come in here. . . . They got to go through the hassles of being patted down [and] being wand[ed] down. Take your jewelry off. Leave your purse out here. Take your shoes off. They got to go through a hassle to get in here. (Charles)

> I just don't feel they should be punished for what I've done wrong. You know, when they come in here, they got to take their shoes off. They got to be patted down. They got to hear some of the negative comments from officers that don't want to be bothered with inmates getting visits. (Adam)

> I don't get a whole lot of visits because none of my families like coming down here because the guards are so rude. (Joshua)

Joshua went on to recount an incident in which his sister was refused entrance to the visit because the officer considered her shirt to be too revealing: "My sister is almost seventy years old and they were telling her that she wasn't properly dressed."

Five men alleged that visitors were treated no better than inmates. Victor described the stigma that families of the incarcerated bore: "They do suffer bad. Humiliation to have to come over here. Humiliation to have to accept my phone calls. I don't know [what] the postman would think seeing letters coming from a prison, you know, there's all kinds of ways they get humiliated." For Adam, the reported negative treatment of his relatives had caused him to cease having visits: "I don't want any visits. . . . I cut a lot of the visits off because . . . I just don't feel they should be punished for what I've done wrong. . . . Sometimes our families are punished for us and it's not right, so I refuse to put my family through that." Michael added, "People in free society committed no crime are treated like an inmate." Three men (Matthew, Charles, and Daniel) maintained that the burdens placed on visitors were intentional:

> They don't want you contacting your family. . . . They do everything they can to keep your family away from here. . . . They're punishing your family. They're punishing your family because you're in here. (Matthew)

> I think they're trying to discourage as many people from coming down. (Charles)

Another explanation for the diminished contact is that the inmates may desire minimal communication. Prior research has shown that long-term inmates may decide to end or severely curtail communication with their outside contacts (Farber 1944, 176; Flanagan 1982b, 119; Welch 1987, 8). Inmates may choose to cauterize their relationships with the outside world as a proactive self-protective mechanism because they are fearful that ultimately their families will do so. For the inmates who adopted this practice, the termination of relationships improved their ability to function in prison as it reduced their worry about family issues or disappointment when they no longer received visits (Flanagan 1982b, 119; Welch 1987, 8). For instance, one life-sentenced inmate claimed that "he makes his visitors stay away for stretches, 'because I want to be prepared for when the day comes I don't get no visitors at all'" (Welch 1987, 8).

In applying this to the present group of older LWOP inmates, none of the men reported severing ties with family members as a means of easing the hardship of doing time. Thomas, Troy, and Walter were the closest to adopting this sentiment as they had asked their families to stop visiting them. However, it should be noted that all three had experienced higher levels of communication at earlier points in their incarceration and continued to maintain contact with their families through phone calls or letters. As mentioned earlier, Troy had requested that his family members no longer visit him because of an accident in which his niece fell off the wooden bench during a visit. Thomas claimed that, compared to other inmates, he was not as reliant on visits to keep his morale up: "They enjoy that sort of thing. . . . It doesn't affect me like that. I don't need it. They have to have that phone call. They have to have that visit or they'll go crazy. . . . but that doesn't affect me. . . . I told them all not to come back. . . . This place is terrible, a big old stone castle, you know cold, impersonal, why would you want to come down here?" His lack of emotional affect continued even as his health began to fail. Thomas described an incident in which he abruptly ended a visit with his daughter when she became overly emotional: "My daughter came down to see me when I was up in the infirmary, [when] I was real sick one time. . . . The only reason she came down was because . . . she thought I was going to die. And she cried the whole time she was here, and I cut her visit short. I told the guard to let her go. . . . Matter of fact, I've never had a visit outside of the infirmary since I've been there. This visit with you is the first time." Walter was not interested in having visits as they brought up reminders of the loss of freedom: "I just don't want any visits. They're going home, I'm not. You know, they're going out there and eating [a] pork chop and I can't eat a pork chop." Thus, there were a few men whose behavior was consistent with the sentiment to limit relationships as described in previous research, but the vast majority of the men were pleased to communicate with their family.

Strong Relationships with Family and a Professed
Satisfaction with Communication

Despite the limited contact most men had with their family members, the two major sentiments they expressed when discussing their families were that they had good relationships with them and they were satisfied with the frequency of communication. They expressed gratitude that their family members continued to offer them emotional and financial support. In fact, six men believed their relationships had actually improved since incarceration. For John's family, confinement alleviated the stress of not knowing where he was: "They never knew where I was when I was on the streets." Troy and Victor felt that over time they were able to be more honest with their families about their motivations to engage in crime. Nathan's and Joshua's families were pleased with the pro-social changes they had made in their lives. According to Nathan, "Believe it or not, for the most part [my relationship with my family] probably has gotten better because, you know, they knew how I was before I came here and when I first got here and they see the changes. You know, they see the improvements that I've made in my life."

When asked why they had better relationships with their families than other inmates, the men reported that they had closer relationships with them prior to incarceration and treated them better:

> The inmates, I hear them. They come over to chapel. They use the phone. . . . The girl that's sleeping with them, having their babies, [and] sending them money, they talk to them like they're animals. Holler, scream at them, you know. Demand this. Demand that. (Michael)

> A lot of us have burned our bridges behind us right. I think in all probability it was probably the way you treated them. (Francis)

> Some people don't have no contact. . . . I think they burned bridges. . . . I think they just turned their family away because you hear a lot of inmates cursing their family on the phone cause they don't bring them drugs or something and they burn bridges. People get tired. (Daniel)

> It depends on how tight you are with your family before you come to prison. (Robert)

> Some believe that people owe them something, and my feeling is, like, you're fifty something years old. You think your mother is supposed to get you a pair of sneakers? . . . Any money she's giving you is coming from her Social Security [or] whatever income she has. (George)

Given the obstacles to communication outlined above, it makes intuitive sense that men with poor relationships with their families prior to incarceration or those who mistreated their families or romantic partners while incarcerated would have less communication with them. For example, Troy did not have close relationships with his siblings because he had been incarcerated for over half his life and had never developed close ties with them.

Most men purported to be satisfied with the level of communication they had with their relatives. It is important to remember that the decline in communication through the years was gradual; as a result, the men grew accustomed to the separation from their family members and the increased length of time between communications. Henry explained, "I was twenty-eight years old [when I was arrested] on this bit. I'm sixty-three now. You know, so I've been away from family for quite a few years. I'm not saying that I don't love them or care for them because I do, but it's not that type of command no more."

As the most frequently cited pain of permanent imprisonment, the separation from the family bothered them, yet at the same time, the men reported that they were used to the distance. Several emphasized that they could have more communication with their families if they wanted to, but they chose not to. The prolonged absence from day-to-day family life also appeared to soften the grief when a relative died. Joshua explained, "This might probably sound callous the way that I'm thinking, is that I've been apart from them for so many years, you know, and I mean I think about them, even now I think about them. But I don't know if my bereavement is as much as it would be normally if I was out with them every day." In addition, thirteen men understood that their family members had busy lives that impeded their abilities to communicate regularly:

> My baby sister and I are the closest. . . . It is kind of tough to catch her, you know, when she's off from work. She's got her own family she raised . . . so she's pretty busy. (Adam)

> If I request them, they'll come, but my thing is . . . there's things that they could be doing. That they need to. What are we going to sit down there and talk about for forty-five [minutes]? (Troy)

However, a couple of the men were dissatisfied with the level of contact they had with their families. For example, Alan was frank in his dissatisfaction with the lack of communication he received, and it caused him mental anguish: "Sometimes I think nobody loves me." Victor remarked: "It's hard, you know, but I can't be mad if they don't come. I can't lecture them when they do come, you know, about not being here because, again, I want to take their feelings into consideration. They did come. They are here. It took them three months, or four months, or six months, but they're here."

As described above, the demands of maintaining a relationship with a LWOP inmate are daunting. However, those who were able to keep in contact with their families described the benefits as increased morale and as an incentive to be better behaved. Overall, the men reported a decline in the frequency of communication with their families over the course of incarceration. This trend persisted in the time period between interviews. Virtually all had experienced the death of a relative or had a family member who was in poor physical health, which impeded communication. Lastly, most men claimed to be satisfied with the level of communication with their loved ones even though it had diminished.

A few men reported positive developments in their social networks. Robert had grown close with another inmate's family and enjoyed regular visits for the first time in his incarceration. In 2006 Troy reported that he was estranged from a sister, but by 2011 they had reestablished communication. In the time between the interviews, Noah learned that he had several half-siblings. Noah had resumed communication with a cousin whom he had not spoken with in eight years and had presumed was dead. In 2011 Daniel was the only respondent who reported that he was currently in a romantic relationship. According to him, he had reconnected with a friend from school a couple of years prior and a romantic relationship had developed. Daniel felt as though he was "falling in love." He expressed the pain of being away from her: "[It's] very difficult. I hug my pillow and start crying."

INSTITUTIONAL THOUGHTLESSNESS

Although they entered prison as young men, at some point in the course of their confinement the men had grown old. Advanced age and poor physical health compounded the hardships of prison life. For example, Alan admitted that, as a side effect of a blood pressure medication, he had become incontinent. He explained, "Taking all those pills, I was urinating about twenty, twenty-five times a day. I couldn't hold it. I started urinating in the bed. I said this has to stop." While incontinence would be difficult to deal it with in any environment, in prison the inmate could be faced with ridicule from insensitive inmates or prison staff.

Developed by Elaine Crawley (2005, 350), the term "institutional thoughtlessness" has been used to describe "the ways in which prison regimes (routines, rules, time-tables, etcetera) simply roll on with little reference to the needs and sensibilities of the old." As examples of institutional thoughtlessness the men cited the failure of prison staff (1) to ensure that older inmates received a lower bunk assignment, (2) to ensure that the temperature in housing units was comfortable for older inmates during cold weather months, (3) to provide older inmates with adequate clothing during inclement weather, and (4) to make accommodations for older inmates so that they could participate in prison programs and have the necessary time to eat and shower.

Bunk Assignment

The group felt that housing officers were insensitive to the needs of older inmates when making bunk assignments. Matthew explained the situation in his housing unit: "I got guys in my building that have been in my building for ten years, guys that are sixty, seventy years old that are still on the top bunk. They move some young guy in twenty years old, give him the bottom bunk. It's crazy, it's crazy. No respect." The men were aware of older inmates who had fallen as they climbed in and out of their bunks, some of whom sustained broken bones in the fall. Despite two shoulder replacements, Victor claimed that he would rather have slept on the floor of his cell and incurred a disciplinary write-up for doing so than attempt to climb in and out of a top bunk:

> It's awkward . . . because the ladder is straight up and down. . . . Once I had my shoulders operated on, I said, I'm not going on the top bunk. I said I'll put my mattress on the floor. And I meant it. No, I'm not going on the top bunk. . . . I'll be sleeping on the floor. Lock me up if you want. I'm just not going. I shouldn't have to go, not when they have twenty-five-year-old men down there on the bottom bunk. No, I'm not going to go there. I've done my tour of duty on the top bunks. . . . And I wouldn't want to get up and climb around on that bunk and somehow [lose my balance and fall].

Cold Temperatures

The men also felt that prison staff failed to consider older people's sensitivity to cold temperatures. About one-fourth of the men reported that it was too cold in their housing unit. According to John, the air conditioning in his building was not shut off until mid-October. As a result, "all of the old guys, you know, now we're freezing because you know it's damp outside and this happens every year." In addition to the discomfort, the men claimed that the cold had negative ramifications for their health. For example, Anthony felt that it exacerbated his arthritis because the cold "seeps into our bones."

The men claimed that the prison staff members were not understanding of the situation, including the men's attempts to make the environment more comfortable. Alan received a disciplinary write-up when he blocked the air vent in his cell. Walter contended that the prison should provide older inmates with sweatshirts so that they would be more comfortable instead of making them buy clothing: "Now they don't want to give us sweatshirts, they said we got to buy our own. They're supposed to furnish this stuff to us. . . . And we don't work, but if you get any money on the books, then you got to pay for ourselves. Our people send us that money for commissary for what we need, and I'm not spending my money when they're supposed to clothe me, they ain't clothing me. People on the outside don't understand that. They think we're getting clothed, but we're not." According to Walter, a sweatshirt was approximately twenty dollars at the prison store.

The men were displeased that they did not receive better protective gear to keep them warm in cold weather. Michael felt that older inmates were especially affected by the inadequate clothing they wore in inclement weather: "Things that I didn't mind when I was younger, I was still flexible, but, you know, standing out in the rain or out in the snow or out in the cold without proper clothing, it's rough on me now." George felt it was unfair that inmates had to pay a four-dollar co-pay to treat illnesses that he alleged were a direct result of the lack of proper attire: "They don't give you rain wear. You have to walk a distance of at least two city blocks to go eat, but during the process, if you have to stand out in [bad] weather and . . . you get sick, you have to go to medical [and] you got to pay four dollars when they force you to get sick." Instead of continuing in his daily routines despite the bad weather, Matthew opted to stay in his housing area: "When it's real cold, it's raining and snowing, when it's pouring down rain, I just stay [in], I have some food to eat. That's why I say [that an inmate needs] a thousand dollars a year to live off of, so you have something to snack on instead of going over."

A Lack of Accommodation in the Prison Schedule

According to the men, staff regarded the prison schedule as invariable and would not make allowances for inmates with special needs, including older inmates. For example, Joshua claimed to be healthy enough to work a full day as a math tutor; however, he was only permitted to work in the afternoon because it took him too long to get ready in the morning and the prison would not permit him a special accommodation to start working at a later time: "Well, I could work all day long [but] . . . medical has me on half days because in the morning getting up and getting started is way too much trouble. I got to [do] an hour of stretching and stuff, you know, just to get started, so that's why I'm only on half days."

Prison rules were also inflexible to the needs of older inmates. According to Robert, neither inmates nor visitors were permitted to use the bathroom during visits. If either needed to, then the visit would be forced to end. He expressed concern that because of his frequent need to urinate (a side effect of a prescribed medication), he would not be able to enjoy a full visit: "They had me on a water pill, take one of them things, boy, you'll have to run to the bathroom twenty times within a half hour. You can't even sleep. . . . I heard that in a visit when you're in the visiting room if you or your visitor had to go to the bathroom, your visit is terminated."

The men felt that there was little they could do to remedy the situation. The men reported receiving disciplinary write-ups when they attempted to make the situation more comfortable. Some were afraid they would be punished if they filed a grievance. For example, Matthew complained that it was damp in his single cell, but he was unwilling to report the problem because he was fearful he might be transferred: "Yeah, it's damp in here. . . . It's a very bad environment for older people. . . . They need to do something, but I don't want to complain about it because I don't want to get moved out of there." As the men had been or were fearful that they would be punished if they tried to improve the situation, they reported that they were forced to rely on sympathetic correctional officers to help them circumvent institutional thoughtlessness. For example, Robert described the request he makes to correctional officers to receive additional time to consume his meals: "I can't eat in five minutes or ten minutes, and if I do, my system brings it back up and I get sick. So every time I go to chow hall and have a different officer working, I have to tell them. . . . I need more time eating, so no matter where I'm sitting, when you call the first row, let me go get my tray first." In addition to receiving more time at meals, Daniel reported that some officers provided extra time for older inmates to accomplish other daily activities: "You got a few guards that try to make sure, they look out for the older guys and see that they . . . open their doors first so they can get in the shower first, go to the commissary first, or let them get in the front of the line because you got to walk almost a mile to go to chow, so they let them get a head start . . . but the majority of them . . . they don't have no compassion." However, despite the need of Robert's and Daniel's requests, correctional officers were not required to abide by them. And sometimes, even formal medical requests were not followed by correctional officers. In 2006 George commented that, due to his chronic back pain, he was supposed to receive a cell assignment on the first floor; however, he received a second-floor assignment instead. Joshua was frustrated that the prison would not permit him to have a sleeve prescribed by his doctor for his knee and instead provided him with an inferior, cheaper substitute:

> [The doctor] wanted me to have a strap, a sleeve [to help keep his knee straight while he slept]. . . . Two weeks go by, I don't get it, so I sent over a slip and I'm asking why I didn't get this because the doctor had ordered it. And they told me that they're disallowing these sleeves, this particular type, because of the Velcro on it. So I go back and see the doctor, I say they didn't give me the sleeve for my leg because of the Velcro. He said, "But that's what [I] ordered. That's what I wanted you to have. That's what you need." . . . He ordered it again. Then, a couple of days ago, they brought me over a regular old sleeve . . . basically a knee warmer. It doesn't prevent me from bending my leg. . . . so I didn't accept it. I told them, "I don't want it. This isn't what the doctor ordered. This isn't what I needed."

THE UNCERTAINTY OF RELEASE

In 1944 Maurice Farber noted that inmates with an "indefiniteness of knowledge as to when [they] will get out" (1944, 172–173) experienced higher levels of suffering than inmates who knew when their sentences would end. Most other sentences carry a maximum release date, so inmates have a sense of how much time they can expect to serve, but no definitive release date exists for LWOP inmates. James Paluch Jr., a LWOP inmate incarcerated in Pennsylvania, described the sentence as "riding on a wheel [because it is] a punishment in perpetual motion that continues until the prisoner's life expires" (2004, 15). The lack of certainty regarding release was identified by ten men as being one of the most trying issues associated with life imprisonment.

The prospects of release were bleak as conveyed by Victor: "We don't have a life beyond right here, right now . . . we can't plan for I got twenty-four more months, I got three more years, . . . we're not playing in that ball park. Our ball park is inside of a dome and you can't see the sky from here. We are locked in, you know. We're locked into knowing according to right now we got to die here, we got to be taken out horizontally, feet up, and it took a while for all of us [to realize it]." Noah described how difficult it was to accept that even after serving a decade in prison he was no closer to release: "The period that was most difficult for me was after the [first] ten years. After I started realizing, after ten years, I'm still stuck in this hell hole and I'm not going nowhere. That's when it really smacked me in my face . . . after ten years went by, I said damn, I'm not going nowhere." Similar sentiments were expressed by other men:

> If you buy into the idea that you're not getting out of jail, you know, there's no light at the end of the road. That might be the hardest part. Knowing that all the things that you had out there on the street, if you had anything, you don't have much of a chance of getting back to any of that now. I guess that would have to be it. (Joshua)

> Just knowing that you're not getting out. That's the hardest part. Knowing that you're not getting out. (Walter)

> Not knowing if you'll ever get out. (George)

> Knowing that you might not ever get out. See when you're young you don't even think about things like that. (Anthony)

The men reported that it was difficult to witness the release of other inmates, as it served as a reminder that their release was unlikely. For example,

Karl admitted, "I think one of the hardest things for me is seeing other guys leave." In addition, they expressed frustration that the positive changes that they had made in their lives while incarcerated did little to improve their chances of release. In 2006 Adam explained:

> No matter how much you look at yourself, you make changes in your life, you try to stay positive, continually doing positive things, you're never getting out. Realistically, looking at the [mid-Atlantic state], they've had one guy in their history who has ever [had a sentence of] life without parole . . . commuted to life with parole that I know of. And that's not a very good [record], it's not very encouraging put it that way. You look across the country, you're seeing life means life without parole.

Almost all of the men maintained that, as a result of the prosocial changes they had made while incarcerated, they were no longer the same individuals as when they committed their crimes. It was difficult for them to accept the fact that the value of their lives was reduced to a single incident that happened several decades ago. The thought of serving this sentence for another couple of decades led some to despair, as reflected in Noah's statement: "I'm not doing this for another twenty-five years. I can't do this no more."

A central struggle in the life of a LWOP inmate is the juxtaposition between the theoretical possibility of release and the slim chance of actual release. The fact that release is technically possible through executive clemency provides some men with a mirage of hope that they will one day leave prison. Some men's hope of release grew when Francis, a non-violent habitual offender, was released from prison. Hope of release is a fundamental motivator to keep going and work toward release. While the hope of release is misplaced, it has a profound effect on inmate behavior.

For LWOP inmates, no concrete answers exist to important questions: Will I ever be released? How much time do I have left? Am I going to die in here? How will it happen? Unless major changes were to occur in sentencing and correctional practices, for most of the men release will never occur and they will die in prison. As the men have aged, they are more likely to acknowledge the fact that they could die in prison. According to Anthony: "When you're old, you start thinking about that because you could die any day." Robert described his realization that he was serving a death sentence: "It dawns on you that, man, you know what, man? You've got the death penalty. Really, you got the death penalty. It's not that you have a set date . . . but there's a slow death penalty because, see, you are sentenced to natural life that means till the rest of your life. And when it starts seeping in . . . man, you know, chances are I'm going to die here."

CONCLUSION

To reiterate, the men described prison life in bleak terms. The men claimed that, instead of improving over time, the experience of doing time had worsened, for the rules had become increasingly stricter and there were fewer rehabilitative programs. The men acknowledged the deprivations of liberty, autonomy, goods, and services advanced by Sykes (1958). They found that the limits on their freedom, the lack of personal-decision making, and the unpalatable food were all trying aspects of imprisonment. However, Sykes's other pains of imprisonment—deprivation of heterosexual relationships and security—were not widely reported. Only three men specifically mentioned the lack of intimacy. Additionally, even though some had experienced serious injuries over the years, fear of violence was uncommon.

For the group, the three greatest pains of permanent imprisonment were separation from family, institutional thoughtlessness, and the low likelihood of release. The men missed their families and regretted that they had been absent from important events in their family members' lives. The challenges to maintaining contact, especially with the poor health and advancing age of some relatives, contributed to a decline in communication over the course of confinement. However, despite the decline, the men claimed to be satisfied with their relationships and felt that they could have greater contact with their families if they wanted. In addition, the men felt that greater sensitivity and understanding should be extended to older inmates in order to ease the hardship of growing old in prison. The uncertainty of release was another difficult feature of life without parole. They struggled with not knowing if they would ever be released and what they could do in the present to improve their chances of release.

CHAPTER 4

Coping with Permanent Incarceration

IN CHAPTER 3, THE men described the pains of permanent imprisonment. In this chapter, the coping strategies the men have devised to endure a LWOP sentence are examined. The men were more likely to rely on internal resources such as religion and maintaining a positive attitude to cope with problems instead of relying on external sources of support, for example, family members, other inmates, or prison staff.

RELIANCE ON SELF

Permanent incarceration was, in Charles's words, "a mental game" that the men had to learn to play—and a solitary one, as Charles claimed "the only thing I have is me." Henry, incarcerated for thirty-one years, described a conversation he had with short-term inmates regarding the process of dealing with a LWOP sentence: "A lot [of] them guys used to say, 'Well, man, I couldn't do a life bit, I don't know how you handle that.' And I [would] say, 'Well, look man, I'm telling you, man, it's a day-to-day thing. You don't get no guide or rule book as to how to do this bit.'" Henry's statement reinforces the men's contention that they had to find within themselves the necessary resources to cope with life imprisonment. He added: "The real deal is the guy that got the natural life sentence, the guy that's been down for a while and knows what he's dealing with, he knows he's by his lonely. . . . You only can depend on you." The men claimed that there was no single strategy adopted by LWOP inmates to cope with the length of time incarcerated:

> Everybody's sentence is different. Everybody does their time in a different way. You know, no two inmates can say they served the same kind of sentence. . . . I serve my time my way. He serves his time his way. (Thomas)

> Everybody has a different way of dealing with everyday problems, so what works for me might not work for the next guy. (Robert)

While the experience was felt to be individualized, there was commonality in how they negotiated a LWOP sentence. They shared the strategies—complete with personal mantras and adages—that they employed to remain mentally tough.

Find Meaning in Life

In their study of fifteen life-sentenced males, Robert Johnson and Ania Dobrzanska concluded (2005, 8) that lifers "are not pawns of the prison routine or of their own round of daily life but rather are active agents in their daily adjustment." Similar to their finding, each of the men interviewed here felt it was important to be proactive in shaping the course of his life, as reflected in Thomas's reiteration of a common prison axiom: "Do your own time, and [don't let] the time do you." The men felt it was detrimental to dwell on the length of time they had been incarcerated or would be incarcerated, as reflected in Troy's observation: "It's a form of punishment, you know, to sit there and mark those days. You know, those are days that you're not going to get back. So why are you keeping track of them? My reality now is let me do the best I can for right now, . . . do whatever I can do to better myself and let it go. And when that day is done, it's done, I got to move on." Instead of ruminating on how much time they had been incarcerated, the men were motivated to find meaning in their lives. George, who had spent about half his life incarcerated for murder, explained: "Even in jail, you have purpose but you got to define it. [When you die,] you will be evaluated by the good and the bad, it doesn't say the location. . . . [Even in prison, there's a] positive chance of getting some positive results." Ever since he began his sentence in the late 1970s, George stated with pride, he had "been a thorn in the department's side." Over the last four decades, he had campaigned to improve the conditions of the prison and had filed litigation against the prison in the areas of compliance with the Americans with Disabilities Act, legal assistance to inmates, and access to religious services. He wrote to the DOC to launch an investigation into prison health care and advocated for the development of a prison hospice program similar to the well-known program at Louisiana's Angola State Prison. In 2011, at the age of seventy-two, George was working on a project that documented wasteful spending by the DOC.

There were other avenues by which the men found purpose in their lives: bettering themselves, working, pursuing creative outlets, and assisting other inmates. In addition to giving their lives meaning, these activities also helped to ease the difficulty of serving a prison sentence, for they provided the men with structure to their days and a source of pride or accomplishment. Troy, who was the youngest when he began serving life without parole, shared his personal motto: "Keep on moving. Get involved in the things that you're involved in. Do what you can do and live the best that you can." In 2006, Nathan, the second-youngest when he entered prison, explained his motivation to work and take college classes:"I've been in jail going on thirty years. . . . I've worked twenty-five of the thirty, some type of job or another . . . to keep busy, to educate myself. I mean, I'm sixteen credits short of an associate's science degree from Ohio University . . . something that I wanted to do. You know to keep busy, better myself, you know I've never been one to believe [I should] just give up and sit down."

The men were motivated to pursue activities that led to personal enrichment, as can be seen in the following comments:

> I really stopped and looked at what's going on around me and what benefits I can get from what's here, you know, and what I can do with it to better myself, and I've taken advantage of that. (Nathan)

> And I chose very early on in my incarceration to, even though society says we want you to stay in prison for the rest of your life, I didn't want my life to end right there, you know, I wanted it to count for something. So, I started doing some positive things for myself. (Adam)

> I think it's very important because you're never too old to learn. I mean, you learn from the cradle to the grave. (Anthony)

In addition to intrinsic reasons, six men reported extrinsic reasons for working or participating in programming. Ryan, Walter, Joshua, and Adam reported they had been involved in activities so that they could retain their preferential housing assignment, while Anthony, Walter, and Noah felt that participation would improve their chances of release.

Earlier in their sentences, the men actively participated in educational programs, and to a lesser extent, vocational training. More than one-third of the group received their GED and/or high school diploma while serving life without parole. Noah, who had been incarcerated since the age of thirty, described how he felt to be a high school graduate: "Proud wasn't the word. I'd have to create a new word for that because it took me all these years to finally sit down and get it." He was especially pleased that his mother lived long enough to celebrate his accomplishment. Ryan and Robert reported that they were working on their GEDs. Even though he believed that his age hindered his ability to learn (as he stated, he was "too old for this stuff . . . too old to learn"), Ryan reported in 2011 that he was preparing to take the GED exam. George and Anthony had earned their paralegal certificates, and George had also earned a computer technology certificate, while incarcerated. Eight other men reported taking general interest classes (e.g., computers). Seven men had completed college correspondence courses, and Adam had earned a bachelor's degree. He hoped to earn a master's degree in pastoral counseling.

In contrast to education programs, the majority of men had not received any vocational training while incarcerated. Seven men reported participating in a vocational training program, including carpet-laying, custodial maintenance, basic house wiring, plumbing, blueprint reading, carpentry, air conditioning, auto mechanics, and electrical programming, while serving life without parole. Victor was the only one at the second interview who was currently enrolled in a vocational course. He enjoyed the small engine repair course and was doing well in it: "I love it. I've got about a ninety-two percent average. . . . I take it serious."

Institutional reasons were primarily offered by the men to explain their low participation in programming in recent years. More than one-third of the group claimed that there were few programs offered for prisoners to enroll in, especially for those who came to prison with high school or college degrees or for those who had been incarcerated for several decades and had already completed most programs. The men reported that because of the ineligibility of inmates to receive Pell grants and the termination of a partnership between the prison and a local community college, it was more difficult to take college courses than it had been previously.

In addition, Henry, Anthony, Troy, and Karl alleged that age bias on the part of staff or in institutional policies decreased the opportunity for older LWOP inmates to participate in programs. For example, according to Anthony, a sixty-two-year-old habitual offender, when he expressed interest in participating in a computer class, a prison staff member replied, "What does an older inmate want to learn about computers for?" Similarly, Karl had signed up for a course on heating, ventilation, and air conditioning but doubted that he would be selected because "lifers can't participate." In response to the perceived unfair treatment, Anthony claimed that older inmates were considering filing a discrimination suit against the prison because "we have a right to be educated." Most men agreed with Anthony that educational opportunities were just as important to older inmates as they were to younger inmates. Victor contended that age restrictions on programming should not exist because inmates of all ages could benefit from involvement: "Anytime you can better yourself. Get a better grip on who you are or what's going on in life. Yeah, absolutely, age shouldn't be a cut off."

Contrary to these sentiments, there was a minority of men who felt there was little practical value, either in the subject matter or in future benefits, for older inmates to participate in programs. For example, George, an advocate of inmate education, was critical of the course offerings and asked "What is the practical value of . . . college courses like European Civilization?" Other men maintained that, because older LWOP inmates would not be released from prison, completing courses would be of little use to them. The following comment made by Walter in 2006, the only one without a high school diploma (or equivalent) and who also had not worked toward earning a degree while incarcerated, underscored this point: "Most lifers today, the older ones that know better, they're never going to take the programs. What good is it for us to do them? They tell us that it'll make you a better person in prison. Why do you need to be any better for? We should make your time, make your jobs harder in here, you know, instead of making it easy for you." Five years later, he expressed a similar opinion: "And then they want you to have a GED and all this, I'm not getting a GED. I already went to ninth grade in school and I'm sixty-eight years old. What's a GED going to do me? If I ever got out, I ain't going to work. [I'll] draw on Social Security."

Charles, Troy, and Joshua were reluctant to enroll in vocational courses specifically because they believed it would be more beneficial for younger inmates to participate than older LWOP inmates who have little chance of using the skills if ever released:

> No, I don't get into anything like that because I know I'm not going to put it to use. You know, if I were getting out, I'd do it. Put somebody else in there . . . who's going to get out of here. . . . To me, I think it's a waste of time to let [long-term inmates] do it. They might not even have engines as they know it twenty-five years from now. I think they ought to put somebody in there who's getting ready to get out in a year or two. (Joshua)

> Why get into that vocation when you're not going to be able to use it? . . . You're taking a position away from some younger guy that probably could do that job and needs that skill. (Troy)

As such, a handful of men believed that it was appropriate for prison administration to place age and/or sentence restrictions on inmate eligibility for programming.

Work

At the first interview, fifteen men reported having work assignments within the institutions, and despite worsening health, twelve men had work assignments at the time of the second interview. They worked in a variety of areas including the garment shop, kitchen, environmental crew, gym, recreation department, greenhouse, and chaplain's office. Most of the men reported that they enjoyed their work assignments because it helped to provide structure in their days and helped to make time go by faster. In 2006, Noah claimed that he had maintained a work assignment for the entire twenty-two years he had been incarcerated because it provided a distraction from thinking about his sentence:

"When you sit and think about it, it hurts real bad, but if you keep doing some-thing . . . it makes it more bearable." Thomas agreed, stating that "while you're doing it, it seems like forever, but after it's done, you wonder where it went to. . . . It doesn't seem like I've been here twenty-two years. . . . When you're out working, I mean weeks and months go by like nothing."

A work assignment was also a source of pride for the men. Victor, who at one time worked in the kitchen, described his work philosophy: "When I did my baking in there, I baked everything I did, I did it as if my children were going to sit down and eat with me. The pots and the pans that I used, I would take them and clean them separately. . . . They weren't clean enough for me." The money earned from a work assignment gave the men the funds to pur-chase items at the commissary, and for some, such as Henry and William, this was the only source of financial support they had. For example, Henry stated: "I don't have people I can call on the streets and say, 'Yo, I need twenty dollars.' I don't have nobody like that."

Creative Outlets

Artistic expression was another activity that promoted self-discovery. Gabriel, who was in his late twenties when he entered prison and was now in his mid-fifties, enjoyed writing poetry. He felt it helped him process his feel-ings: "I'm not really a person who talks a lot about things, so I just like to look at [it], like, write it down then go over it, you know, what it is that I've writ-ten." Four men (Matthew, Daniel, Troy, and Nathan) pursued art in the forms of painting and drawing. Matthew, one of the oldest of the group, discovered his talent while incarcerated: "I never knew I had any talent. I couldn't even draw stick people." The focus of their paintings and drawings were telling as they reflected the men's nostalgia and a longing to leave the confines of the prison. Matthew and Troy both painted natural landscapes, and Matthew also painted buildings and cars from the 1950s. He explained how painting allowed him to temporarily escape from his present environment: "I love painting. It's like not being in here. You get caught up in what you're doing, and it's like not being here. I feel like when I'm painting, I feel like I'm there. . . . It completely takes your mind up. It's a gift from God." Thomas, who was sixty-eight years of age in 2006, had been keeping journals detailing his experiences while incarcerated; however, shortly before our interview, he destroyed the journals out of concern that someone else would read them. He stated: "It's nobody's business what's in them."

Helping Others

Another means by which the men found purpose in their lives was assist-ing other inmates. Many of the men had made positive contributions to the prison. The men were responsible for starting self-help groups (e.g., Gamblers

Anonymous) and serving in leadership roles in (now defunct) organizations (e.g., Toastmasters and Jaycees). Victor was active in the lifers group at Institution Two. Almost half the men facilitated programs addressing anti-violence, pre-release, and alcoholism and taught educational and vocational classes related to auto body, computers, and gardening. Five men were tutors in the education department. John, Troy, and Nathan had been HIV peer counselors. John and Nathan enjoyed working as peer counselors and were disappointed that the program had ended:

> You know because after I did my little talk, people would come up and [say] "I appreciate that. I didn't know this." . . . You got through to somebody. I like to see a smile on somebody's face, so that would take me away from everything. Instead of doing nothing, you're keeping [active]. (John)

> I mean I liked that because I taught people to do things, you know, I sort of got good feedback from that. (Nathan)

The men also provided less formal assistance to other inmates. One-third of the men spoke of the fulfillment they found in mentoring younger inmates, as Henry and Robert explained:

> I try and do things to help them [so] they won't come back. [Some have gotten out and written to express how much I helped them] and that kind of like motivates me. I think maybe I'm doing something right. It helps me in a way. I probably won't get out. (Henry)

> I have so much that's been given to me, far as knowledge and wisdom wise, and I would like to take and share it instead of keeping it bottled up. I like to use it and try and help somebody that really needs some help. (Robert)

While all of the men wanted to be released, some felt that even if they remained incarcerated their lives had mattered because of the work they performed in prison:

> I'm optimistic. I'm hoping and I expect something good to eventually happen, and if it doesn't, I've done some things in here that I can be proud of that I've accomplished and I've helped my family out wherever I can. . . . I've tried [to make the most of it] and that's really benefited me in enabling me to do all the time that I've done. And I've met a lot of great people, community people and everything and through the church and through the greenhouse. My life has been enriching for this place. (Adam)

> And I look at it, I might not never get out of jail but I get [the] self-fulfillment of being able to make a contribution even in this environment. (George)

If God has it in store for me, then it's going to happen. If not, then I still have work to do. And my thing is I'm going to do what it is that I'm supposed to do whether I'm on one side of the fence or another. (Gabriel)

Keep the Faith

More than half the men cited their religion or spirituality as helping them to cope with their sentences.[1] Most men claimed that they were religious or spiritual prior to serving life without parole; however, they admitted that they were not adhering to religious teachings in their everyday lives. For example, Michael, who in 2006 had served thirty years for the murder of his estranged wife, stated: "We went to church on Sunday. I could give the Lord an hour that day, you know, two hours, but . . . then I was gone, I was doing what [I] wanted to do, you know. Today, now I got guidelines from the Lord that I follow you know this is it. This is what I want to do." Contrary to the common perception that inmates "find God" while incarcerated, Alan, who was sixty-nine years of age, was the only individual who reported that he had become religious while incarcerated. Early on in his sentence, he had intended to commit suicide. However, when his cellmate invited him to attend a scripture reading group, he went and maintained "from that moment on I have been at peace. That was sometime [in] September, 1991."

Other research has also found religion to be an important coping mechanism for aging (Koenig 1995, 226) and life-sentenced inmates (Abramsky 2004, para. 24; R. Johnson and Dobrzanska 2005, 36). In *Lifers,* Irwin explained why religion is particularly appealing to life-sentenced inmates: "It offers meaning and purpose to their unsatisfying past and present lives, a method of expiation, and perhaps a future life after the one they are living now, which has been damaged and diminished profoundly by imprisonment" (2009, 68). In the present group, five men felt that their religion provided them with a model of how they should conduct their lives, for example, to be a good person and to help others:

> I believe in and acknowledge it, the higher power. I believe in, you know, the power of the higher power, and it keeps me in line. (Gabriel)

> [With] the Muslims, there's a certain conduct that we try to have that some of the other people don't try and have. (Francis)

> My faith is based on helping people and doing everything, but it's still basically doing the right thing. (John)

Four men credited their religious beliefs as exerting a calming effect on their lives:

> [Religion has been] a very big part of my life. It keeps me anchored, and trying to look for the good and not the bad. And I mean when you

become discouraged, you learn to pull your boots up by the boot straps and go on. (Adam)

I [don't] like the idea of being here, but no matter what happens in the process of my being here, this is my refuge. I just go to my Bible and read. (Samuel)

When I get tight and frustrated or something's not going right, and I feel like I'm on that last straw, see I can read [the] Bible. (Henry)

I think it's something that you can turn to when there's no one else to turn to, you can turn to the Lord. You can pray. You can lay [down] your head [and] pray. You can get down on your knees and pray. . . . Talking to God, it's a relief. It's a relief from frustration. You can tell God how you feel. (Matthew)

The men also felt that their religious beliefs provided them with the strength to confront personal issues, such as loneliness (e.g., Matthew) and addiction (e.g., Henry), and medical problems, for example, back pain (e.g., Nathan). Adam, who had been incarcerated for thirty-two years for the murder of an acquaintance, explained how his faith was instrumental in acquiring greater self-awareness and fostering a desire for self-improvement:

What helped me a lot was I made a personal relationship with the Lord. My faith has played a big part in my doing time. But, that just kind of just opened the door for me to start looking at myself, you know, why did I do what I did? You know, what am I going to do to change myself? And I started working on some core issues that led me to doing some of the crimes that I was doing on the outside. And when you do that, it kind of helps you out a lot as a person to grow and move on.

Six men felt that their incarceration was part of a divine plan. Gabriel, who had spent nearly half his life incarcerated for the murder of his girl-friend, explained, "God has a plan for all of us. And what it is that I'm doing now is connected to that plan, and you know, that keeps me going." The notion that "there is a reason for everything" was particularly important to the men who professed their innocence. Robert, who began serving life without parole at the age of thirty-three, claimed that being wrongfully incarcerated was God's way of saving him from alcoholism: "If you really look at it, the fact that I am here . . . it was meant for me to come to jail. It was meant for me to be in this situation because I know that deep down in my heart, if I hadn't come to jail, I would've been dead years ago [from drinking]."

During the interview, several men who claimed innocence recited the Bible verse: "The truth will set you free." Daniel, who had served thirty-one

years for a murder that he claimed he did not commit, likened his situation to
that of Jesus Christ when he stated: "They crucified Jesus Christ, and he didn't
do the crime either." Other men maintained that they will be released if it was
God's will. Anthony, a sixty-two-year-old habitual offender, explained, "Well,
it gives me faith that someday I will get out, you know, and faith in God, faith
in the, you know, promises that I believe he made to me." Even if the men
were never released from prison, religious salvation promised the men a better
existence after their deaths. Henry was comforted by the belief that "even a
sinner like you . . . even you can be saved. I find it so unbelievable, but I just
keep enduring in this thing." Religion was commonly cited as a reason why
the men were not fearful of dying.

In addition to the fortitude that religion provided the men, it also produced several other tangible benefits. It helped Daniel to feel connected to
his son and daughter as the three would pray at the common times of noon
and midnight. Religious expression (e.g., attending religious services, reading
religious texts, and praying or meditating) helped provide the men with a way
to pass time. Victor, a Protestant, had the following personal goal: "I try to read
the Bible every year . . . and that's five chapters a day." Participation in Bible or
Koran study groups helped the men socialize with others who shared similar
beliefs. Religious activities also helped the men identify a purpose in prison.
John, a Catholic, found fulfillment in ministering to sick and dying inmates.

Keep Expectations Low and Make the Best of It

Nearly fifty years ago, "the philosophy of minimum expectation" was
described by Charles Unkovic and Joseph Albini (1969, 159) as a strategy
utilized by life-sentenced inmates to manage expectations while incarcerated:
"The lifer fixes in his mind a far-off discharge date and expects nothing to
happen that will make his life easier in any way before then. Any occurrence
in his favor is a welcome surprise; if nothing happens, he is not depressed
because he was not expecting anything anyway." Timothy J. Flanagan (1982b,
122–123) expanded on the philosophy of minimum expectation: "This fatalis-
tic perspective assumes that life can be expected to deal no favorable developments during the prison term, hence the prisoner sets the likely release date
as a time boundary and fights off depression by expecting nothing positive in
the interim."

For the five men in the present group who endorsed this belief, they
felt that, if they did not expect anything positive to occur while incarcerated,
then they would not be disappointed. Nathan described how his optimism
had faltered over the thirty-four years he had been incarcerated: "I used to
be a very optimistic person years ago, and now I've a very pessimistic person
because in this environment, in this situation, most things never turn out the

way you expect them. So what's the sense [in getting your hopes up]?" Similar to Nathan, Gabriel had also readjusted his expectations, specifically in his interactions with other inmates and prison staff, as a self-protective measure. He stated: "I've lowered my expectations, so that you're not as disappointed when someone doesn't perform at the level that you expect them to. And it just creates less problems for me." The men were not expecting conditions in the prison to improve, and they struggled when I asked them what could be done to make their lives better. The lack of optimism was evident in the following responses:

> You know, it's hard doing time if, once I get this operation over, I get back on the compound, I'll be in a single cell in an air-conditioned building, I'll be back on my job in an air-conditioned [area] making enough money to buy my [toiletries] and provide things to eat and take care of my needs. You know, that's the best it can get. That's the best you can hope for in a place like this. (Thomas)

> My life here is never going to be really like better. . . . There's nothing here for me. I just try to stay in line, . . . do my job and don't get into trouble. (Ryan)

> There is a lot that I wish we had available . . . but it's never going to happen here. (Noah)

> I wish things were different, but I don't look for things to get different. (Joshua)

While Michael felt that it was beneficial for LWOP inmates to keep their expectations low, he also found it important to express gratitude when a positive event occurs: "Expect the worst, all the time, you know, don't look for anything special, but then when something good comes your way, that's a blessing. Be thankful for it."

Similar to Michael, several of the men found it beneficial to express gratitude. To some, this meant a concerted effort to count their blessings and focus on what they had in their lives instead of thinking about all that was missing from them. Alan maintained, "I'm too blessed to be stressed and too anointed to be disappointed." The men focused on simple comforts to be thankful for. Noah, who entered prison at the age of thirty and had been incarcerated for twenty-seven years, was grateful to be alive: "[Everyday] I stay above ground is a holiday. That's how I look at it." This is similar to other research on life-sentenced inmates that found that prisoners tried to enjoy small luxuries while they had them because the luxuries could be short-lived (R. Johnson and Dobrzanska 2005, 8–9).

Victor tried to make the best of his situation. He summed up his out-look as: "What do you do? You make the best of it. If you're given a lemon, make lemonade. That's my life." Though he hoped to be released, he was satisfied with the life he had made for himself: "I don't want to be here, but I want to be, I want to be, satisfied with the life I had. I don't want this life, but with what I have to choose from, I'm satisfied with what I've got. Would I like parole? Yeah. Would I like to get out and be a father, a grandfather, a brother? Yeah. But, with what I have in here, I think I'm doing fairly well." In a similar vein, Noah remarked, "This is the world we are living in, this is all we have, so we are going to make the best as we can for ourselves." Perhaps because they doubted that their lives would ever improve so long as they remained incarcerated, a sizeable number of men retained hope of release.

Have Hope

Almost all of the men expected to be released from prison. As such, hope of release profoundly affected their attitudes and behavior. The perceived chance of release was a powerful incentive for the men to participate in pro-gramming and to avoid misconduct. Hope of release also helped the men to retain a positive outlook and provided them with the motivation to keep enduring. Victor asked, "What would I be like if I said no [hope of release]? Why would I be going through all of this? . . . It's about being positive . . . if I wasn't sure about it, I'd be laying back not doing anything." Nathan explained how his confidence in his chances of commutation insulated him from adopt-ing a defeatist attitude: "Everybody was telling me this was the end [of] your life, you know, that you were done. No, I made up my mind you're not going to beat me and I've still got that attitude today. . . . It probably was a good thing because there's guys that are here that have been here as long as I have, and they walk around with their head hung down all of the time, woe is me, woe is me. You know, you can't get no place like that." Other studies have also found hope of release among life-sentenced inmates (Stewart and Lieberman 1982, 15; Welch 1987, 7) and found it to be a powerful factor in attitude, moti-vation, and behavior of life-sentenced inmates (R. Johnson and Dobrzanska, 2005, 37; Rasch 1981, 430). However, one downside of a hope of release was the disappointment and frustration the men experienced when their commu-tation applications were rejected.

Similar to other samples of long-term inmates (Flanagan 1980a, 153; Richards 1978, 166), the men interviewed here preferred to rely on them-selves to cope with issues instead of seeking assistance from outside contacts, other inmates, or prison staff members. The men felt reluctant to rely on external sources of support for various reasons.

RELUCTANCE TO RELY ON OTHERS

Relatives provided the men with an opportunity to reminisce about their lives prior to incarceration and encouraged the men to retain a positive outlook and to better themselves. Daniel's daughter was hopeful about his chances of release and told him: "You ain't going to die [in prison]. We're going to get [you] out." Karl, a fifty-five-year-old father of five, reported that he was motivated to earn a college degree because four of his children had done so. The men found conversations with family members to be an escape from the banality of prison life. Daniel stated that the communication he had with his girlfriend, his daughter, and his son "take[s] me away from here." In addition to emotional support, some of the men relied on their relatives for financial support, assistance, and advocacy. The money that their families sent allowed them to purchase food and supplies at the prison commissary. Their outside contacts also helped them to locate documents and to conduct research related to their legal cases. Relatives acted as their advocates and called the DOC or the prison to ensure they received proper medical care (e.g., Nathan, Karl, and John), to inquire about the status of their commutation applications (e.g., Samuel), or to voice frustration over the visiting policies (e.g., Matthew). Several of the men maintained that the involvement of outside contacts was, in Joshua's words, "how you get things done here." The men who were able to rely on their family members and friends for assistance knew that they were fortunate. John stated: "I'm blessed. I got family, friends that will make calls." The men were more comfortable discussing personal or sensitive topics, such as death and dying, with their relatives than with their friends in prison, and family members were also entrusted to carry out the men's burial wishes.

At the same time, there were drawbacks to relying on outside support networks. John reported feeling powerless as he was dependent upon his family to make calls for him. He expressed, "I can't force them to make those calls. Hey, I can ask you, [and say] please do it. But if I were out there, I [could] go out there and do what I have to do." In addition, the men expressed concern that they were adding to their family members' burdens. Most reported that their relatives were busy with their own lives; consequently, some felt it was unfair to increase their worries or concerns. For example, Gabriel was reluctant to discuss personal issues with his parents because he did not want them to worry (see Chapter 3 Separation from Loved Ones).

Reliance on family for emotional or financial support could be detrimental if communication with them diminished or ended, for any of the reasons outlined in Chapter 3 (e.g., if a relative grows ill, dies, or chooses to end the relationship). For instance, Victor's brother had promised him he would carry out Victor's burial wishes. In 2011, Victor was worried about what would happen if his brother died before him and the responsibility fell to his brother's wife: "I don't know what will happen if he were to die before me. I don't know if his wife, and I love her and she's good people, but I don't think she would have my best interest [at] heart. I mean I'm not her brother, and she treats me just like I am family, but in the back of my mind, I know that's because she's married to my brother. . . . That's a little worrisome."

RELIANCE ON ANOTHER INMATE

When newly incarcerated, the men relied on the friendships they developed with the "old-timers" to help them acclimate to prison life. Adam recounted the advice that a friend imparted to him: "Even though you're serving life without parole, most people think their life is over with, but you can still make your life count for something in here. You can either continue doing a lot of negative stuff, bury yourself real deep in the institution, where you'll never see daylight or you can try to do something meaningful."

Over the decades of incarceration, the men themselves had become the old-timers in the prison. Most of the group entered prison around the same time. Over the years, they had spent more time with the other members of their prison cohort than with their families. The proximity, combined with the length of time the men had been incarcerated, helped to cultivate close relationships between long-term inmates. Adam offered the following example: "My next-door neighbor . . . and I have been doing this time for quite some time. We were never really close early on, but I think we've become more close because of the proximity of our living conditions. We're in the same building, same tier, right next to each other." The men valued the opportunity to speak with others who had also "been down" for many years. Henry explained the therapeutic importance of speaking with a longtime friend: "You got two lifers who have been down for twenty-five, twenty, thirty years and they've been through some of the stuff that, you know, I mean a lot of stuff, and then seen the changes in the prison in the three decades. And to get together and to talk about the changes and to talk about how it used to be and talk about where we think it's going from here and just giving our opinions on how we feel about things today, it's a real, kind of like, it's like a support mechanism. . . . It's a support mechanism among ourselves."

Most of the men agreed that the few close friendships they had developed helped to ease the difficulty of serving a LWOP sentence, in particular for the men who were estranged from their families (e.g., Robert). One of the most commonly mentioned benefits of friendships was that they provided the men with someone to socialize with and to receive emotional support from:

> This is the lowest of the low, so I don't care how strong you think you are. You need somebody to go to, to cry on their shoulder . . . and it's good that I have friends like that. (Henry)

You must have that. You need that. You need to be able to confide in somebody without, you know, without worrying about them using it against you . . . but, yeah, you need to have contact with people. Talk about things. (Victor)

They reminisced with, confided in, and shared personal problems with their friends. Friends were able to offer empathy during difficult times. Karl provided the following example: "When you're facing a crisis at home and you can't talk to that person. . . . You can always go to somebody on your tier. . . . They've been through the same thing. [When a friend's mother passed away], I let him know that I lost my mother too, and I know what he's going through . . . and that got him to open up and deal with it because he had a hard time dealing with it like I did."

Friends could also be counted on to provide an honest assessment of a situation, as reflected in the following statements:

There have been times that you need somebody that you can go to that you can talk to that you don't need to worry. There are times that [a friend and I] talk to each other in a way that most people think we're having problems, but we know what we're doing. (Troy)

You can stray from the path and, you know, a friend will tell you what it is that you need to hear, rather than what it is that you want to hear. When you don't have a friend, the only person that you have to listen to is yourself, and I don't think that's very helpful. (Gabriel)

However, even among friends, there were some topics that were too personal to share. Death and dying was not commonly discussed nor were the circumstances surrounding their offenses or sentences. In 2006, Francis, a sixty-eight-year-old habitual offender, reported that he ended a friendship when he learned that the individual had been convicted of a sex offense.

Friends offered other forms of support and assistance. Henry credited a friend with helping him confront his alcoholism when his friend encouraged him to attend his first Alcoholics Anonymous meeting. Alan and Henry reported that their friends helped to keep them out of trouble. When Henry was fighting another inmate, for example, Henry's friend intervened and deescalated the situation. As Henry recalled: "Had it not been for a good buddy of mine, I probably would have killed him." While friends can prevent aggressive behavior, they can also ward off victimization. The men recalled that when violence was a more common occurrence at the institution, friends provided protection. Victor remembered that he and a friend would "watch each other's back" and defend each other in fights. As the men have aged and their physical health has worsened, they depend on their friends to care for them when they are ill or are recuperating from surgery. Joshua, who had several surgeries on his legs, explained the help that a friend offered him when he was battling an infection in his leg: "He took care of me [when I was sick]. He did all the cleaning [and] got all my meals. Waited in line, [and] brought me my meals when I couldn't get out of bed. [He] sat there and I ate and he took the tray."

When confronted with more serious medical situations, friends were counted on to alert the prison staff that help was needed. Joshua provided a specific example. He and several other friends noticed that a member of their group had started to act strangely and they encouraged the correctional officers to send him to the prison infirmary:

> He wasn't acting right. He wasn't talking right. His memory was leaving him. He wouldn't always go through the doorway, sometimes he'd hit the side walls. He always complained that his eyes were going bad. Too much light, you know, and stuff like that. Finally, we went to the guards and said look you got to do something with this guy. You got to send him to medical. Call medical and tell them that you're sending him over. There's something wrong with him. So they finally, he did it. They sent him over [and] took him to the hospital for a brain operation and all of that. Matter of fact, he had a seizure just by luck just an hour [or] so [after] we told them to get him out of here. He hadn't had a seizure before, so he had his first seizure right there in medical so they knew exactly what they were dealing with.

Another benefit of friendship was to distract the men from the bleakness of prison life. Henry claimed that this was especially important for newly incarcerated LWOP inmates. He explained: "When you go up on them cells and you have that idle time, that's the most worst time for a guy that's just been given a fresh life bit. . . . His preference is to be around other people to try to keep his mind off what's really he's doing. So to avoid that you really want to be around other people just to keep your mind almost happy [so that you're not] in that cell by yourself . . . thinking." Spending time with friends, for example, talking, trading commissary items, or playing games, all relieved boredom. Ryan, Daniel, and Adam valued friendship for the levity that it brought to their lives. Daniel explained why he enjoyed his interactions with a friend: "No matter how bad it is, he always puts humor into it. It's a bad situation but you can't go around moping all the time and have a pity party and stress yourself out. . . . We have some fun times in here as bad as the situation is." In another example of trying to infuse humor in bleak circumstances, Karl shared that he and his friends used the name "Casper," as in the friendly ghost, as a code for loneliness. He reported that after one of them has experienced a bout of loneliness, "They'll say, 'Casper came to see me.'" According to him, this has the effect of "mak[ing] it a little fun."

While forming relationships with other inmates had its advantages, the men reported several drawbacks to establishing close ties. About one-fourth of the group was distrustful of other inmates, and as a result, some men were hesitant to form friendships. Noah was emphatic that "a friend is nothing a person needs in jail." Robert and Adam maintained that it was important to be judicious in the information they chose to share with other inmates:

> I'm not going to let anybody in completely. . . . I'm just not going to give them the opportunity to [take advantage of me]. (Robert)

> In here you are careful on who you become close friends [with]. I have a number of acquaintances, but no one I would say [is] real close. . . . I would say no real intimate friends, someone that I could really confide [in]. . . . They might consider me a good friend to them but I don't look at it, I don't reciprocate, that way. . . . I just think it's healthier for an inmate not to have a lot of close friends. (Adam)

Along with Adam, five other men described their relationships with other inmates as "acquaintances" or "associates." When I asked Daniel to explain the difference between friends and associates, he responded, "[You] can't trust people. . . . You got associates, but you can't confide [in them]. I just can't because they're not reliable."

The men explained how attachments to other inmates could prove to be detrimental. Friends could be demanding. If their demands were not met, they could become vindictive. John knew firsthand the consequences; he described an incident in which he refused to share his supply of marijuana with an associate: "[It was] Christmas morning, and my family was in the visiting room, and [my associate] had wrote a letter, and they snatched me up and took me to the hole . . . so because of that they ruined my mom and pop's Christmas. I did forty-two days in the hole." Friends could also take information that they were entrusted with and use it to curry favor with the officers. John tried to distance himself from other inmates "because as long as they don't know you, they really can't put no bones on you, say nothing bad about you." Speaking from experience, Noah claimed that he lost his job after a friend reported him to the prison administration. He commented: "A friend could do you [dirty]. With a friend, you have a tendency of saying things that only friends are supposed to know and they can take that and hurt you with it in here." Henry had a similar experience with an associate. He described an incident that occurred in which he was upset and an associate offered him marijuana. The next day, he was called for a drug test. In regards to the timing of the drug test, he stated: "Strange, huh? Associates, associates, you know what I mean."

As noted by Troy, Walter, Thomas, and Noah, a further downside to developing a personal attachment with another inmate was that it could become emotionally or physically taxing:

> Friends are [a] pain in the neck for the most part because when you have a friend then you are responsible for him, you know, when something happens to him, he's expecting you to bail him out, help him out, you know. (Thomas)

> [Developing a friendship,] it's good and bad. It's good that you have somebody to talk to and express some things. . . . Then again, it can be bad because you stop thinking about what you're going through and start thinking about what they're going through. . . . That's his [burden]. Let me deal with mine because this life sentence is a hell of a burden and I need to carry this on these shoulders. I don't need to carry his too. (Noah)

> I don't want to know. I just don't want to hear them cry. I have enough problems of my own. I don't want to hear their problems. (Walter)

Alternatively, Alan tried to not burden a friend with his problems when he knew his friend was "too stressed out over other things." He explained: "I have enough trouble carrying my burden. Why should I give you my burden when I know that you have a burden also? I try to shoulder my own."

An abrupt end to the friendship, as a result of transfer, release, or death, was another reason for the reluctance to form attachments, as suggested by Thomas:

> As far as making friends in here, it's hard to really accept because you make a friend, he dies, he gets out, you know, [is transferred] to the SHU [secure housing unit]. . . . It's hard to make friends in jail. . . . It's not wise to really get too friendly.

Some men, such as Thomas, did not want to become dependent on a person who might not be around in the future. Inmates were frequently transferred to another building or another institution, sometimes with little advanced warning, as explained by Matthew: "You get attached to someone, and the next thing you know, they're moved to the back of the building or to another tier or to another prison." Release also brought an end to, or at the very least a major change in, the friendship. Anthony described the conflicting feelings he experienced when a friend is released: "When they leave, it's like losing a family member . . . and it's really mixed emotions." Although the men reported that they were pleased that their friends were being released, they were also sad that their friends would no longer be at the institution and were jealous for they remained incarcerated. Karl claimed, "I think one of the hardest things for me is seeing other guys leave." Joshua reported that he had remained in touch with several of his friends who were released from prison. He described what their lives were like: "Some of my very close friends have left. I've talked to a whole bunch of them, all the time. Every one of them by the way is doing very good. Not one of them [was] violating parole. They got boats, cars, [and] girlfriends. They all go fishing together. They all [are] helping out each other [and] going to church. They're doing all kinds of different things and they're all doing good."[2]

The death of a friend was also a painful experience. Most of the men could name one friend, though some could name more, who had died. Deaths, especially those that were thought to be unexpected, were difficult for the men because they lost an important member of their social network and had to adjust to prison life without the friend's presence. Henry explained, "Death, it's difficult. . . . I remember when we use to kick it on the tier together, and just the other day we were kicking it, and now this guy is dead." The loss of a friend also served to remind the men not only of their own mortality but also of the strong probability that they will also die in prison. Nathan reported that, after he "heard about one of my friends being real sick or passing away," he was more likely to think about his own death.

RELIANCE ON STAFF

Correctional Officers

Most of the men claimed to have non-contentious relationships with the senior correctional officers, and some reported that the officers treated older inmates with respect, for example, addressing them as "Mr." As the proximity and length of association had helped to engender friendships between long-term inmates, the men felt as though an understanding had been developed between them and the veteran correctional officers. Troy, who entered prison at twenty-two and had served thirty-four years, summarized the mutually beneficial informal agreement between the two parties: "The older officers always made us understand this: If you don't cause no problems for me, I won't cause any problems for you. And that's the way we moved." The length of interaction between the men and the veteran correctional officers also helped to secure an understanding of how each other operated. Troy added: "It's like any relationship. . . . We've known each other so long that you can see. I can tell who you are because I've been with you. And that's the way they treat me."

Despite the length of their association, custodial staff members were not seen as viable sources of support for the men. The men reported that it was important to maintain social distance from the officers. For example, Gabriel commented: "You stay in your place; I'll stay in my place." The established boundary and the power differential between the two groups were reflected in the following statements:

They're the police and I'm the inmate. (John)

Obviously, you're wearing a blue shirt and I'm wearing this white thread and that alone says that we're not on equal footing. (Charles)

Nathan stated that while there were a couple of correctional officers with whom he had established a good rapport, he quickly qualified his statement with: "We've built as good of a rapport as you can build in a place [where there] are two different factions."

As compared to the senior correctional officers, younger correctional officers were held in low esteem. The men compared the styles of current correctional officers with those in previous decades. Generally, they concluded that the correctional officers of today were less compassionate and professional than correctional officers in earlier periods of their incarcerations. Walter, who had served thirty-six years, explained: "The guards back in the day . . . the guards were way different [in the fifties] than the guards were in the seventies. And the guards in the seventies are way different than the guards today. The guards back in the seventies did more . . . counseling, they cared a little more than what the guards do today. Today, the guards just come in, talk come out of their mouth anyway they want and we have to put up with that."

Many of the correctional officers who had supervised the men during the early period of their sentence had retired, and the men were unimpressed with the caliber of the newer officers. Walter observed: "All of the officers that was here when I first came are gone. All of them are gone. Now some of their sons are working here and their fathers told them about me. And they'll ask about me and they'll say my dad speaks highly of you. Stuff like that. So they give you respect. Some of the officers, the newer ones, the foreigners, I don't get along with at all. I told them, 'Go back to your own goddamn country. Get the hell out of America.' . . . They get mad at me. Most of them are Africans. I don't care."

Of the prison custodial staff, the men reported the most problems with young correctional officers. They felt this class of correctional officer was immature, unsympathetic, disrespectful, unprofessional, and lazy. George, who was one of the oldest and longest-serving members of the group, was the most critical of the new correctional officers. He claimed that the officers hired in this particular mid-Atlantic state lacked the qualifications to be hired in neighboring states, because this state accepted lower test scores and age requirements. As a result, he claimed that they were of a lesser quality. Additionally, George felt that the younger officers were frustrated with their inability to become police officers, which led to their poor performance as correctional officers: "Now they have a uniform and a badge, they couldn't get into law enforcement. This was the closest they could get . . . that's why you have a lot of problems."

An additional complaint levied against the younger officers was that they were overly concerned with impressing the senior officers with their toughness and were not interested in cultivating mutually respectful relationships with the inmates, as highlighted in Nathan's and Gabriel's statement:

> I'll respect you. I expect the same in return. I'm not talking about, I'm not asking you to kiss my ass. . . . It's just that, if I treat you with respect, I expect to be treated with respect, you know. I don't cuss at you, I don't disrespect you, I don't scream and holler at you, I don't expect for you to do that to me and I'm not going to accept it. And, you know, that's just the way I am. (Nathan)

> I think the younger less mature officers are a problem, the ones that present the most challenge, because, you know, they have this feeling that they have to prove something and want acceptance from the older officers and respect from them. They don't necessarily feel that they need respect from the inmates. (Gabriel)

Many of the men felt that because of their ages, their good behavior, and the length of time they had been incarcerated, they should be treated better by the younger officers. For example, as Walter argued when cell searchers were conducted:

> You got too much dumb stuff going around. The guards—I don't know where they get these guards from—but they're ignorant. They think they're so tough. . . . They come around and tore all our stuff up in our cells. [I told one of the officers,] "I'm old enough to be your grandfather, who are you talking to?" That kind of stuff, it irritates you. It does irritate you listening to fools like that. You know, I could smack them. . . . And you're supposed to stand there and just take it. They throw your pictures, your personal belongings, on the floor. They don't care.

Alan recommended sensitivity training for new officers: "When they hire the new officers, at least they could train them. I don't know what they're teaching them, but the majority of them act as though they're not mature. . . . Even though I'm an inmate, I'm still human." Henry provided an example of the perceived unprofessionalism of the younger officers: "What I can't respect is the fact when this twenty-year-old officer comes in . . . you dive in with another young inmate, and you all listening to the rap songs, you know Tupac and Biggie, and . . . your conversations are about bitches and hoes, that's what they call it, so your conversations are about that so [then you come to me and] it's the same type of conversation. I'm telling you, 'Hey, man, I ain't with that. . . . Don't relate to me like you relate to him'. . . . I'm not going to be in that conversation with that, you know, type of talk." As a result of these experiences, the men found it difficult to respect the authority of younger correctional officers.

The perceived unprofessionalism extended to how the younger officers treated the men's families (see Chapter 3, Separation from Loved Ones). As an example, John reported that because of a relative's hearing loss, she required a special chair to sit in during visits and provided the prison staff with a doctor's note explaining the need for the accommodation. Yet, John claimed it was an ongoing battle to provide her with a chair: "[They] give [her] a hard time. We've been through this. I need a chair for her." Some of the men, such as Adam, were reluctant to have visits because of the perceived ill treatment of their relatives. He commented: "I chose not to put my family or friends through the nonsense that they got to go through out here especially when you got some of the newer and younger guards coming on. Sometimes they punish your family."

The negative assessment of the officers and other staff members was one of the major reasons why the men felt that they could not rely on them as sources of support. In particular, the men reported that they would be unlikely to seek the assistance of prison staff because they were unresponsive to the men's needs. According to Michael, "They come in and do their count, they'll take counts and then they disappear. They're not on the job. You got to fend for yourself." Robert felt that some of the prison staff "either don't have time or aren't willing to take time" to assist an inmate. As an example, Robert claimed that when inmates learned of a mass shooting (e.g., school shooting), the staff were unhelpful in providing inmates with information: "He can't get information on who was shot, who was injured, and when he go to the counselor to get some help with that, the counselor brush him off. You know what I mean? He can't call nobody to find out information. Everybody he try and talk to don't have time for him. They ain't trying to hear his problem. All they say is, man, I got problems of my own."

Another dimension of unresponsiveness that was frequently mentioned by the men was the inability of the correctional officers to intervene when they observed other inmates, oftentimes younger inmates, mistreating older inmates. A frequently mentioned example was that it was common for younger inmates to cut to the front of line at meal times. According to the men, correctional officers observed this behavior, but in Gabriel's words, "you wait for the officer to say something, and he says absolutely nothing." As the officers could not be relied on to help control the environment, the men reported that they were forced to intervene. After becoming increasingly frustrated with the line cutting at meals, Gabriel made an announcement to the 130 inmates in the chow hall that this behavior sent the message that "your time is more important than anybody else's time." He delivered the following warning, "'I'm not letting you guys cut in front of me [any more].'"

More serious claims of unresponsiveness were levied by the men. They contended that when older inmates were victimized, they could not rely on the officers for assistance. Although they reported a low rate of victimization, none of the men who had been victimized informed the correctional officers of the situation. For example, after sustaining bruises in a fight with another inmate, Matthew chose not to report the incident to the officers. His failure to report the incident suggests a perception that the officers would be unwilling or unable to help. Daniel was the most vocal about the unwillingness of the correctional officers to intervene. He claimed that if he were to report mistreatment to the officers, he would receive a response of: "Deal with it, cry baby." Furthermore, Daniel and Robert maintained that the officers would write up an inmate for trying to address a situation that the officers were ignoring. According to Daniel, "[Some inmates] were trying to extort my cellie right now, as we speak. It's bad . . . and the guards don't care. They tell you [take the property back] but when [you] do, [you] get written up for it." Following the incident for which he was transferred to administrative segregation, Daniel was considering filing a failure-to-protect claim against correctional officers for allegedly not ending the fight: "It's strange, Maggie, that the guards disappear when you start to fight. . . . And the guard's nowhere around. . . . They're negligent. They're supposed to protect us in here. We're not supposed to have to fight nobody with a knife. That's what they get hazardous pay for."

Allegations of unresponsiveness extended into medical care. Robert described an incident in which he alleged that a correctional officer refused to assist him during a medical emergency, and as a result, he was forced to commit a serious disciplinary infraction to attract the attention of other officers:

> [I started to have] chest pains, so I took a nitroglycerin pill. And I didn't take no chances. I didn't wait for five minutes like I was supposed to and then take another one. [He asked a nearby inmate to inform the officer] that I'm having a heart attack and I need him to call medical. So [the officer] just goes and waves me off like "go lay down." So I said the only way that I can get help is to cause some kind of disturbance to draw attention to anybody else that's around. So I took a piece of newspaper and lit it and waved it in the air. He picked up the phone, I knew he was calling for back up, so I took the newspaper and put it out in a bucket of water. So four other officers came, and by the time they got there, I couldn't even

talk. So they're asking me, why did I set the fire. [I couldn't speak, so the other inmates told them I was] having a heart attack and the officer won't help us.

Robert won several thousand dollars in monetary damages in a lawsuit against the prison stemming from the incident.

The men shared other examples of perceived officer misconduct, ranging from making insensitive comments about mental health medication to harboring personal grudges against particular inmates to instigating harassment. Gabriel thought that one reason for the low reliance on mental health services was because of how mental health medications were delivered at the prison:

> I think that the way they do medication in here, sometimes, I think it's kind of like embarrassing. There's another stigma connected where, you know, people aren't willing to [go] because if you go to a doctor depressed, they put you on medication and so in the evening they holler medication, you know, officers are hollering or the officers who are kind of like not sensitive to the basic needs call medication "ice cream" or "cotton candy." And it's really a putdown. I don't think they realize that when they say that, and so when the call is made, people are looking to see who it is that's going. . . . It subjects them to a certain level of ridicule in the institution.

Several men claimed that instead of their being able to seek assistance from custodial staff, some officers went out of their way to make the correctional experience more arduous. Adam observed: "You have others that believe that their sole job is not to watch over us and keep us, and keep the public safe from us, but they also believe that they need to make our time a little bit harder because we're here to be punished. They feel that the courts probably didn't do enough for that, so they want to contribute to that."

Other men claimed that the grudges were particular to them. Speaking from personal experience, Walter stated: "A lot of them hold things against me because of my escape, because I embarrassed the prison system and everything." Daniel reported that correctional officers would interfere with the ability of the men to receive medical care. He claimed that correctional officers would destroy the sick call slips of inmates they disliked. In a separate incident, Daniel alleged that an officer had instigated a fight between him and a group of inmates. As a result, Daniel alleged that these inmates had threatened him and thrown feces under his cell door. According to Robert, in response to his successful case against the correctional officer for failing to call for medical assistance during his heart attack, he claimed that other correctional officers would manipulate situations so that he would "look like a rat," thus making him more vulnerable to victimization from other inmates. George claimed that he was transferred to a prison in California not "to get rehabilitated" but as a punishment for the lawsuits he had filed against the institution. He also claimed that he was never able to secure a job at the prison because "they worry about what I'll see and how I'll react."

Medical Staff

Besides the young correctional officers, the other group of staff members who incited the most negative statements were members of the prison medical staff. In the mid-2000s, the mid-Atlantic DOC hired a private medical contractor to provide medical services to its inmates.[3] One year later, the federal Department of Justice launched an investigation into the state's prison health care and found it to be in violation of the prisoners' civil rights. Of particular concern were the high inmate mortality rates, especially for HIV/ AIDS and suicide. A federal monitor was appointed to oversee reforms to prison health care. At the last interview, the men reported that several new medical contractors had assumed responsibility of the medical care. While the federal monitor reported that "significant progress" had been made, four men felt that the change in contractor had done little to improve the quality of the medical care. Nathan explained: "It's gotten worse. . . . You think it could never get any worse. These people are just as bad if not worse than the people before." George and Daniel claimed that one reason the quality of the care had not improved was because the new contractors retained a sizeable number of employees from the original medical contractor. Daniel summarized the situation as: "They kept the same staff and it really is basically the same. The name just changed."

Dissatisfaction with the prison medical care is a common complaint among older inmates (Aday 1994a, 88; Gallagher 1990, 260; Wilson and Vito 1986, 411). This group of older inmates was no different, as virtually all of the men interviewed were dissatisfied with the quality of the care they received. In response, some avoided being seen by the medical staff, or when they were seen, they reported feeling anxious or dread because, in Karl's word, "I don't think you get the proper treatment all the time." Alan claimed that the only time he felt anxious was when he went to the medical unit: "I'm afraid to go over there, to tell you the truth. . . . I get anxiety when I go over to the infirmary. I really get nervous going over there." As a result of their lack of faith in the quality of the medical care they were receiving, several men reported that they had stopped taking prescribed medication (e.g., Alan and Ryan) and treated medical conditions themselves: they had purchased over-the-counter medicine at the prison commissary, concocted home remedies, or taken another person's medication (e.g., Gabriel and Daniel). As seen in the statements below, three men would only use the health care services as a last resort:

I need to depend on me. I can't depend on them, because they don't have your best interests [in mind]. (Henry)

I haven't been up there in years. (Charles)

If I get sick, I take care of myself in my room. I get a cold, something like that, [or] I get in pain, I might buy something at the store. (Ryan)

The men were distrustful of the medical care because they felt decisions were motivated by what would generate the most profit rather than what was in the best interest of the patient:

These people in here, it's a set amount of money, that's the amount of money they get . . . because whatever's left over is their profit so the least amount of treatment you get, the worse the care is, the more money they make. (Nathan)

They don't want you to get old; they'd rather see you die so somebody else can take your place. They don't have no sympathy. They say they do, but it's a lie. (Noah)

The administration don't care about you. They don't really care about you like that. I mean if you get sick . . . it's all about that dollar bill. It's not that they're concerned and have a whole-hearted care about your health because the thing about it is they don't care if you live or die today. There's another inmate to take that spot, so you're a number. (Henry)

The men identified the perceived low quality of medical staff and delay as evidence of the desire to limit prison health care costs. According to the men, a disproportionate number of the medical staff were foreign-born. In addition to language barriers that impeded communication, the men felt that the private medical contractor was not hiring qualified employees because they could pay foreign employees less than Americans. George maintained:

They don't have the qualifications . . . that they would [require] in [a community] hospital or they've been gotten rid of. . . . And so what they do is come here and do as [little] as possible. . . . They have a lot of foreigners here because one of the things [with] state agencies [is] you do not have to be board certified.

Delay was also commonly mentioned. The group cited the delay in refilling prescriptions, receiving aids (e.g., hearing aids or dentures), or obtaining medical treatment as evidence of the cost-cutting strategies employed by the medical contractor. Most of the men were prescribed at least one medication, and they expressed frustration that they would not receive refills of their prescriptions in a timely manner:

They don't want to give you your medications. . . .You may go a few days without it . . . all your prescriptions run out at different times. They fix it that way. . . . They save money that way. (Matthew)

Putting me off for thirty days or two weeks of not getting my medication, they didn't have to pay for that medication. It's a penny-pinching process. I know what it is and they do it with everybody. (Victor)

Robert reported that he had suffered a third heart attack in 2010 because a doctor had taken him off his nitroglycerin medication: "I've been taking nitro for fifteen and a half years. [Last year,] one of my doctors decided to take my nitro away from me. She said that there was nothing in my file that I was sup-posed to have nitro. . . . [Two months later], I had a heart attack waiting to go to breakfast." Perhaps referencing the same doctor, Walter claimed that one of the doctors had the nickname of "Dr. Death," because "she discontinues all of their medicines to save money." In addition to medication, the men—especially James, the oldest of the group—found it difficult to acquire needed aids. In 2006 James claimed to need hearing aids in both of his ears, but at the time, he was only able to acquire one. He also was in need of better-fitting dentures and pulled his current pair out of his mouth to show me the sores on his gums. Five years later, he was having difficulty seeing and claimed he needed stronger lenses in his glasses but his prescription had not changed in twenty years.

Relatedly, another source of dissatisfaction was the length of time it took to be seen by medical staff. The men estimated that it took approximately two weeks from the time they submitted a sick call slip to the time they were seen by a doctor. Due to the delay between requesting medical attention and receiving it, the men were displeased that, by the time they received medical attention, acute illnesses, such as a cold, had passed, yet they were still obligated to pay the four dollar co-pay. While most men did not suffer serious harm as a result of the delay, Matthew claimed, "The medical department is ignoring us. And I'm blind in one eye because of it, makes me angry." Matthew was referring to an eye injury he sustained in a physical confrontation with an inmate and the delay in receiving medical treatment that he claimed resulted in permanent vision loss:

My eye, I had a lot of pain in it. And, well I thought it was a normal black eye, but it wasn't. It was more than a normal black eye. I had a torn retina, I didn't know it. . . . I put a sick call slip in. It was about a month . . . later. . . . My eye was bothering me, but I never thought about it enough because I could still see out of it. But I was having real bad headaches, so about a month later, I put a sick call slip in and by the time I saw the . . . doctor, I explained [the problem] to him, and he looked at it, and . . . said,

"Why don't we try a new pair of glasses?" [But], evidently, I had retina damage and he didn't pick up on it. And he said, "Well, I'll get you a new pair of glasses, I think it'll help." . . . This was in February . . . of 2000. . . . So, I went about six months, it went from February to October . . . of 2000, and I started to get a line across my eye. . . . I began losing my vision, and the next thing I knew, my vision was gone in that eye. And that was in October, so I put a sick call slip in, and I didn't see the . . . doctor until November, something like six weeks later. I saw the [same] doctor. He got scared, he says, "You have a torn retina. I'm going to put you in for . . . an eye exam and they're able to recognize eye diseases," something like that. He wasn't a specialist, so he put me in to see the [eye doctor], and that was in November. . . . Three months later, I'm still going around blind in one eye. And so anyway, I kept putting sick call slips in and filing grievances, and the next thing I know, I get back in to see him; it's been three months, he says, "You mean you haven't been out yet?" He got all excited, he recommended [it] again, see this has to be approved by prison medical. And prison medical wouldn't approve it, the doctor wouldn't approve it. They kept throwing [it] under the table or whatever. Anyway, the second time I got to see [the doctor], it was six months [later] and she said, "This has been going on too long. . . . You'll get some vision back, but you won't get it all back. You waited too long." So, by the time I had my surgery, I ended up getting something like twenty percent of vision in that eye. I'm legally blind in the eye. I can't even read. . . . I can see you but you won't focus. . . . It's like a fog.

Some of the men alleged that the bureaucracy in seeing a doctor, which fueled the delay, was intentional so as to deter inmates from relying on medical care, thus protecting the profits of the medical contractor. Gabriel provided an example of a time in which he gave up his attempt to receive medical attention:

I put a sick call slip in and it took three weeks just to get to the hospital after and I'm like, you know, [on my slip] I stated severe pain. It had gotten to the point where I couldn't sleep for like four straight days, because the pain was so severe and . . . I got scheduled and you have to see a nurse first before you see [the doctor], so you wait three weeks. You finally see the nurse and a nurse scheduled [you] for the doctor, I get up to see the doctor, I'm scheduled to see the doctor the next week and my appointment is canceled. So now I have to wait another week so, you know, in all the time I've never ever, ever had to see the doctor. You know I went through this for like six weeks and finally it was like, you know, forget it. I'm not, you know, my neck is not okay.

Francis, Adam, Anthony, and George offered a second reason for the delay. According to them, there was too high a ratio between the medical staff and the number of inmates, another cost-saving strategy. George characterized the medical situation as an "insurmountable" problem.

The delay in being seen by prison medical staff increased the length of time before an inmate could see a specialist or a surgeon, as seen in Matthew's experience described above. Several men, including Francis and Michael, reported waiting several years for surgery:

> I had been fighting with the administration for two years for an operation on my hernia. . . . They don't listen too well here. (Francis)

> I've needed an operation for the past five years, and it's an uphill battle to get the operation. . . . I got a varicose vein coming up my left leg going into my testicle. . . . It's mixed up with some other veins and it's got a seal over it and it's like somebody's just digging at you with a knife . . . but it's—everything's—delay by design . . . [because of] the money, money, money, they don't want to spend the money. (Michael)

Related, the men reported that there was little opportunity to be seen by specialists. Following cardiac bypass surgery, Walter alleged that he had not been seen by a cardiologist. Victor claimed that he had received no physical therapy following shoulder surgery. Other men were waiting to be seen by a dentist (e.g., Karl, Matthew, and Charles), a dermatologist (e.g., George), and an urologist (e.g., Francis).

One final example of the cost-savings strategy the men reported was that there was little preventive care. Walter and Michael claimed that the diabetic diet they were supposed to receive was the same food "they serve on the line." Additionally, the men alleged that each inmate was supposed to receive a physical and an eye exam each year; however, annual checkups did not occur. Matthew reported that he could not get screened for prostrate or colon cancer: "I've been waiting three weeks for them to screen me for colon cancer. That's three weeks they put me off, and they're going to keep putting it off and putting it off." He was also waiting for tests to be conducted for a potential artery blockage, but he was not optimistic that he would receive the tests until a potentially life-threatening event occurred: "They're waiting until I have [a] stroke before they do anything."

Another major complaint about the medical staff was that they were uncaring and unprofessional, as reflected in Henry's statement:

> They need a lot more TLC. . . . I can understand that with the number of people that you have here . . . and it's difficult for the nurses or the doctors or the staff to focus on certain individuals. I understand that . . .

but I think from being here and experiencing and seeing those nurses and doctors at work and what they do up there and for the most part, man, it's just a lot of lollygagging and doing nothing. You got people back there dying. I mean people back there, man, that you don't see . . . and the nurses are saying we'll get to them when we get to them. . . . I think they should start just with a little more TLC, being more loving, and being more concerned about your job.

The men also claimed that the medical staff was incompetent. They described specific incidents when, the men alleged, a nurse or a doctor had committed an error. Alan was doubtful that he had hepatitis C, a condition he was diagnosed with about five years earlier. Instead, he maintained that he was misdiagnosed and claimed that the medical staff had made errors previously: "It could be a mistake. They have misdiagnosed some other people with it and it wasn't so. . . . Then come to find out by accident one of the medications they was giving me, I was allergic to. And they never really told me that yet, I just found out by accident. That's one of the reasons I really stopped taking [it]." In another example of alleged misdiagnosis, Daniel had been treated for a boil caused by a staph infection that had developed on his skin. The nurse instructed him to care for it with a hot compress. Daniel later required hospitalization and surgery to treat the infection.

Following knee surgery, Walter claimed that a nurse should not have put a topical ointment in his knee. He stated: "That's for scratches. You don't put it inside of you, so I go back and wash it out. I [use] alcohol [to prevent infection]. I do a lot of it myself. . . . You got to treat your own self in here." In another encounter with the medical staff, Walter received a disciplinary write-up for verbally assaulting a nurse. A diabetic, he alleged that he became upset because the nurse was planning on reusing the needle she had used to administer his insulin shot. Noah and Nathan reported that they were encouraged by nurses to treat medical conditions by purchasing over-the-counter medication at the commissary that would be ineffective in treating the illness. Nathan asked, "What's a cold medicine going to do when I have the flu?" And when men did receive medication, they reported errors in its administration. Ryan, fifty-five years of age, stated: "Sometimes they give you the wrong medications. It's happened a couple of times." Consequently, Ryan refused to take the medication given him because he was concerned it would not be his actual prescription. As a result of the perceived errors made by the medical staff, Walter, Victor, and Alan each expressed the belief that "they didn't know what they were doing."

Many of the men had serious health conditions; as such, the lack of confidence in the ability of the medical staff to treat these conditions was especially problematic. Michael commented: "Especially as you get older. . . . I dread going in the hospital up there because that's more like a setup for a dispensary for cold medication and maybe help me with the flu." In the intervening years between the interviews, Joshua had a total of seven surgeries on his knees. Five were corrective surgeries as a result of post-surgery infections that developed. He claimed to have contracted the infections because of how "dirty" the prison was and described the deterioration of his physical health: "I had shit coming out of my leg that looked like yellow chicken fat, lumps of chicken fat, like, that just [kept] coming out of my leg and rolling down my leg. I lost fifty-one pounds in five weeks or six weeks, you know, I went from one hundred eighty-three down to one hundred thirty-one. And this here [pointing to his knee] was already sealed. The infection was on the inside [and] just ate away at the bone. That's why I don't walk right no more because they had to cut away so much of the bone." Joshua lost some of his coordination and now, in his words, "waddled like a duck." According to the surgeon, if his leg were to become infected again, amputation would be likely: "He told me last time, you know, you catch another infection, you're probably going to lose it. He didn't know if he was going to save it last year, but he did. He said, you were close, you're not going to walk as well as you used to, but he said you'll be able to walk."

Several men made serious accusations that inmates died of medical conditions that should not have been lethal. For example, Charles, who was one of the few men to describe his physical health in positive terms, commented that, while there were diseases that a person could survive if he was on the streets, "in here, you're going to die. It's just that simple." Nathan referred to the prison infirmary as "the house of death," because "the people that check into the infirmary, they die." A recent case mentioned by four men was the death of an inmate who had allegedly died because of inadequate treatment following an asthma attack. In another case, Victor claimed that an inmate was erroneously diagnosed with heartburn, went into cardiac arrest, and died three days later.

In response to the perceived inadequate medical care they received, some of the men had taken action to encourage outside intervention. Hoping to initiate an investigation, Robert wrote to the DOC, and Francis wrote to the local chapter of the National Association of the Advancement of Colored People (NAACP). Though his case was dismissed, George had filed a lawsuit claiming that the medical care was insufficient. Daniel received almost three hundred thousand dollars from his suit against the prison for the improper medical care he received for a staph infection. Walter was aware of pending litigation against the medical contractor, and Robert had "filed a lawsuit on the doctor that took my nitro[glycerin]." Though litigation was pending, he was still being treated by the doctor. In order to avoid any baseless claims that he had assaulted her, Robert reported taking the following steps: "Every time that she calls me over to see me about blood, or to draw blood, or medications or anything, I tell all the officers in there that I need an escort. Right. To cover my back because if I just stayed in the room just with her, she could take and rip her clothes and start hollering rape or something. . . . See, she could do stuff like that . . . I'm supposed to see her [tomorrow]. I got to have security in the room with me." Robert further explained that the need for a credible bystander to witness his interaction with the doctor was especially important because he was preparing a commutation application and did not want the doctor to sabotage his chances of release.

Mental Health Staff

In keeping with the pattern of not relying on staff for assistance, the men rarely mentioned the mental health staff as a source of support. The only interaction the men seemed to have with them was during group sessions or as part of a mental health evaluation, a requirement of the commutation application. Daniel was the only individual who specifically mentioned having a good rapport with a mental health staff member. Daniel and Walter reported taking sleeping pills; otherwise, none of the men reported taking medication to treat a mental health issue. None of the men were currently in counseling, although six men had undergone individual counseling earlier in their incarcerations. While some of the men had found the experience to be beneficial, Thomas disagreed: "Individual therapy was a waste of time . . . didn't do me any good."

As with other medical staff members, the men had largely negative opinions of the mental health staff. George and Thomas expressed resentment that mental health personnel allegedly used the experience they obtained through working in the prison as a "stepping stone" in their careers. In addition, the men reported that the mental health staff members were ineffective, in part because they lacked firsthand experience. Anthony commented, "It's different between reading something in a book and actually living it, you know, and they haven't actually lived it, so they don't really know." John, who had a history of drug use, agreed that drug treatment was not beneficial, because the program was "run by a twenty-something-year-old kid that doesn't know nothing about drugs."

Two final reasons for the reluctance in seeking the help of the mental health staff was a concern that it would jeopardize their chances of release and a concern about the side effects of medication. Anthony explained that staff equated mental health conditions with dangerousness, and consequently they were "not something you really want to discuss because they [the staff] take things the wrong way or brought it out of context." Lastly, several men commented that they were reluctant to take medications because they were concerned about the side effects, in particular lethargy. When newly incarcerated,

Matthew refused to take medication because he was worried that he would become one of the "walking zombies." Daniel claimed that the mental health staff prescribed mood-altering medications because it made the inmates easier to control: "I don't want to take no mind drugs like that. That's the first thing they want to do, Margaret, is to drug you up. Not so they can help you, just so you won't bother them."

Unexpected Acts of Kindness

Although prison staff were described mostly in pejorative terms, some men did offer examples in which a particular staff member was helpful or expressed concern or sensitivity. These staff members tended to be non-custodial employees who interacted with the men on an individual basis (e.g., counselor, teacher, chaplain, or cook). With these particular staff members, the men felt comfortable discussing personal problems. As new inmates, some of the men reported that they found certain staff members to be helpful in their transition to prison life. A few of the men continued to maintain close ties with a staff member. Matthew admitted that he struggled periodically with depression. I asked him, "When you are depressed, do you see the mental health staff?" He responded, "No, I'd go talk to the chaplain." Troy, who had learned to read while serving life without parole, had developed a close relationship with a teacher whom he described as his "moral compass." Troy's experience highlighted the kindness and generosity displayed by this teacher: "[I] had never opened a Christmas present since I've been in jail. . . . [My teacher] bought me five presents and made me promise not to open them up [until Christmas morning]. And that was the greatest thing. [My cellmate woke me up] because he wanted to open the presents."

Matthew was appreciative that a prison counselor intervened when he was to be moved to a special needs building for inmates who could not care for themselves. He claimed that the correctional officer who was charged with making housing assignments "didn't like older people, he just had it in for older people." The seventy-three-year-old explained: "I'm the oldest one in my building. . . . I don't think anyone wants to move. They tried to move me. [His counselor sided with him stating], 'You're able to take care of yourself, you're staying here.' Counselor has a lot of pull." Victor was grateful that one of his teachers paid for him to complete a college correspondence course. Perhaps, because of their perceived infrequency, the men expressed appreciation and gratitude for these acts of kindness. Some men remained in contact with the staff member after he or she retired, and some of the employees eventually became advocates for the inmate's release. The men appreciated when a prison employee would speak at a hearing on their behalf or write a letter of support to be included in their commutation application for they believed that the endorsement would carry more weight.

CONCLUSION

It is surprising that a group of men with seemingly so few coping resources could have the resiliency to withstand permanent incarceration. Of course, there is an inherent selection bias in this group of men. Other LWOP inmates who were not able to function in the prison environment, and as a result died young or were transferred to a mental hospital, would not have been interviewed; as such, their perspectives are missing from this account. For the present group of men, largely because of their own internal resources, they have done more than survive decades-long confinement. Many have built lives for themselves and pursued activities that they felt were personally meaningful.

Other researchers who have studied long-term inmates have arrived at the same conclusion. Wilfried Rasch (1981, 430) remarked that the results of his study, which showed little psychological deterioration in his sample of life-sentenced inmates in Germany, "suggest the existence of a seemingly infinite human capacity to cope with the stress of an inhumane condition—long-term imprisonment." A decade later, in describing the varied adjustment patterns and coping mechanisms of inmates, Hans Toch (1992, 8) noted, "Paradoxically, some offenders flourish in this context. Weaklings become substantial and influential; shiftless men strive and produce; pathetic souls sprout unsuspected resources."

The men appeared to have survived imprisonment primarily by depending on themselves instead of seeking support from other inmates, prison staff, or relatives on the outside. Other studies on long-term inmates have also found self-reliance to be the preferred coping strategy (Flanagan 1980a, 153; Richards 1978, 166). They relied on themselves to find ways to make their lives matter, for example, through work, educational courses, and helping others. As other researchers have noted (Flanagan 1981, 218; R. Johnson and Dobrzanska, 2005, 36–37), a desire to use time constructively (for example, for self-improvement) was commonly mentioned. The men developed new skills, earned degrees and certificates, and confronted personal issues. They attributed their resiliency to a positive outlook, which for some, was based on a hope of release.

CHAPTER 5

Growing Old in Prison

MOST OF THE MEN entered prison as young men, but at some point over the course of incarceration, they had grown old. They are a small part of an unprecedented number of older individuals incarcerated in the United States. Approximately 240,000 people over the age of fifty are incarcerated, that is, about 16 percent of the total population (Carson and Sabol 2012, 26). The increased use of life without parole has contributed to the rise. The men were aware of the "graying" of inmates (Flynn 1992, 77). Over the years, Gabriel, who had been incarcerated for twenty-six years, had observed a rise in the number of aging inmates: "I see a lot more canes and wheelchairs than I've ever seen. It used to be . . . you didn't see canes and wheelchairs. Now, you know, it's like I call it the wheelchair brigade because . . . there are, like, eight guys in my building being pushed with wheelchairs and, you know, five guys with canes. And so that's something that you see more frequently. [It] used to be just, you know, one building that had like one guy in the whole compound that used a wheelchair, now every building has some." As the older inmate population has grown, DOCs have faced a corresponding increase in the costs associated with the care of this group. Primarily because of increased medical care, the cost of caring for older inmates is approximately three times higher than for younger inmates (Adams 1995, 475), or about $70,000 per year for each older inmate (Mauer et al. 2004, 25). The men were aware of the high costs to treat their medical problems. During his interview, George, one of the oldest and longest-serving men in the group, cited the following statistic: "The projected cost of medical care alone for an inmate over fifty with chronic medical illness is $78,000 a year." Anthony, a sixty-two-year-old habitual offender, argued that, because of the health care costs of older inmates, "We're more of a burden to the State."

While it is not clear if older inmates use health care services more than non-incarcerated older people or younger inmates (Falter 1999, 160; Gallagher 1990, 260; Marquart et al. 2000, 90), it is known that older inmates, especially those with chronic medical illnesses, can be frequent visitors to the prison infirmary. In fact, chronic illness may be a better predictor of utilization than age or incarceration status. In his study of factors that increase utilization of prison medical services, Robert Falter (1999, 160) found that the most important predictors of the total prison medical encounters in a six-month period were hypertension, followed by heart disease, diabetes, chronic obstructive pulmonary disease, sentence length, and age.

Older inmates face physical health problems that are similar to those of older people in general, though older inmates appear to be in poorer health than their non-incarcerated peers (Fazel et al. 2001, 405). On average, older male inmates have three chronic health conditions; common medical problems include arthritis, diabetes, high blood pressure, heart disease, asthma, cirrhosis, hepatitis, and cancer (Leigey and Hodge 2012, 300). In the present group of aging LWOP inmates, the men described themselves as being in good physical health but poor mental health at prison admission. Over the course of incarceration their assessments had reversed, as they felt that their physical health had declined but they reported improved mental health.

PHYSICAL HEALTH

As two-thirds of the men were in their twenties and thirties when they began serving life without parole, it is not surprising that all of the men described their physical health at prison admission in positive terms. Although five men entered prison with a preexisting medical problem, including asthma, allergies, diabetes, hearing impairment, and obesity, they described any issue as minor and not posing a challenge to their daily life. However, because they were not receiving regular medical checkups, it could be the case that some of the men entered prison unaware of medical issues, as noted by other researchers (Dubler 1998, 150; Marquart et al. 2000, 86). For example, Thomas, one of the oldest men at the time of prison admission, stated that he "didn't believe in doctors" and rarely received medical care when he was on the outside.

Since prison admission, most of the men reported that their physical health had declined, and in the five years between the interviews it had continued to deteriorate. This perception of worsening physical health has been noted in other studies of older inmates (Aday 1994a, 86; Colsher et al. 1992, 881; Marquart et al. 2000, 87; Wilson and Vito 1986, 410). Hypertension was the most common medical condition reported by the men, and thirteen were diagnosed with the condition. Almost as common, eleven men reported chronic pain, most commonly back or knee pain. Eight men were diabetic and seven had high cholesterol. Less common medical issues that were reported by the men included asthma, arthritis, respiratory issues, hernia, kidney stones, dental problems, hepatitis, and tuberculosis. Overall, twenty men were prescribed medication to treat a chronic physical health issue, typically hypertension, diabetes, and cholesterol. Five men either required a cane or a wheelchair to help them move around the institution.

Several men reported more serious medical conditions. Nathan, who was fifty-seven years of age, had been diagnosed with bone cancer, and John, the second-longest-serving member of the group, had been diagnosed with prostate and skin cancer. Robert, who had spent half his life serving life without parole, had had three heart attacks. Seven men had had surgeries, for a hernia (Francis), prostate cancer (John), shoulder replacement (Victor), and knee replacement (Joshua). Walter and Robert had had multiple heart surgeries (seven and three, respectively). However, Thomas was in the worst health of the men. He had had a quadruple bypass operation and estimated the cost of the procedure to be "over a million dollars." According to Thomas, the doctors "gave me two weeks to live, six months ago . . . and here I am." At the time of his interview Michael was awaiting surgery to treat a varicose vein, and in 2011 Nathan was awaiting surgery to remove a mass from his spine.

The men believed that their physical health would continue to decline. Some were pessimistic about their future quality of life. Nathan and Joshua reported that their physical health was their biggest worry, primarily because they perceived the medical care at the prison to be inadequate. Looking into the future, Joshua, who was sixty-four years of age, remarked: "The next twenty [years] aren't going to be as good as the last thirty that's for sure." Transfer to the special needs unit (where George, James, and Walter were housed) was also a cause for concern. As an example, Troy, a habitual offender who had served thirty-four years, described an incident in which he became upset at other inmates who were discussing the special needs unit: "I was in the building where they have [a] tier for chronically care people, right, and guys were talking about them. My reality was yo, man, I don't appreciate that, because with my sentence I could be one of them people down on that tier." Describing it as "an old age dumping ground," Nathan claimed that he would rather be placed in a unit for disruptive inmates than be transferred to the special needs unit: "It's [a] dormitory, all the people, all the negativity, all the depression. . . . I would refuse [to go there] and make them lock me up. I'd rather be locked up back there by myself. . . . because I don't care how strong you are, how strong your body is, if you're put around something like that . . . eventually it's going to wear off [on you]." In 2006 Anthony was uncertain if he would be released from prison before he died from diabetes-related complications: "Yes, I do [believe that I will be released]. That is, if I don't die first, you know, from this illness because it's getting worse, you know, I've seen it progress over the years. If I can get that, lick that, I think that eventually I'll get out." Anthony's concerns about his health were warranted. He died in prison in 2009.

MENTAL HEALTH

In their study of long-term British prisoners, Stanley Cohen and Laurie Taylor (1972, 105) observed a profound fear of mental deterioration. They noted:"These men felt that all around them were examples of people who had turned into cabbages because they had not been sufficiently vigilant. Every day they encountered an old sex offender who spent hours merely cleaning and filling the teapot, a mindless activity which the old man appeared to be contented with." Though long-term inmates reported being fearful of mental deterioration, Cohen and Taylor's study did not demonstrate the actual occurrence of it (Bonta and Gendreau 1990, 348). In the present group of long-term inmates, seventy-three-year-old Matthew admitted he was concerned with maintaining his sanity but felt that was a commonly asked question: "Sometimes . . . I ask myself am I really sane? You know, am I sane? I think most people ask their selves that at one time or another."

The bulk of early research on the mental health of long-term inmates predicted a universal deterioration as a result of incarceration (Flanagan 1981, 203). However, as more rigorous research designs and statistical analyses were introduced (Flanagan 1995, 5), evidence began to mount that long-term imprisonment did not generally lead to mental deterioration. Doris MacKenzie and Lynne Goodstein (1985, 399) summarized the results of these studies: "Adverse effects of long-term confinement have not been demonstrated in the bulk of the empirical research conducted. Overall, the literature on impacts of long-term confinement in such areas as intellectual ability, personality, physical condition, and interpersonal relations does not demonstrate strong and consistent evidence of broad-scale deterioration." While most of the research is cross-sectional and relies on samples of long-term inmates outside of the United States, it is now generally accepted that long-term imprisonment does not uniformly lead to mental or physical decline (Bonta and Gendreau 1990, 357–360).[1]

This body of research indicates that long-term inmates may experience a multitude of mental stress in the early phases of incarceration as they transition into prison life (as the men in this book reported; see Chapter 2, Turbulent Transitions). However, mental health improves over time, in particular in regard to depression, anxiety, psychosomatic illness, boredom, guilt, stress-related problems, such as sleep disturbances and headaches, and self-esteem (Heather 1977, 383; MacKenzie and Goodstein 1985, 407; Rasch 1981, 426; Zamble 1992, 417, 419). A decline in the use of psychotropic medications over time was also noted (Zamble 1992, 420).

Unlike the positive assessments the men gave to their physical health prior to life without parole, only five men offered similar descriptions of their mental health. Instead, the men reported suffering from a variety of mental health issues, such as anger, bitterness, depression, and suicidal thoughts. Three men had received treatment for a mental health problem, and two men had spent time in a mental hospital as teenagers. Charles, a Vietnam War veteran, was diagnosed with combat fatigue syndrome after his return to the United States, and while serving permanent incarceration, his diagnosis was upgraded to post traumatic stress disorder. Incarcerated for the murder of his romantic partner, one man claimed to have suffered "a mental breakdown" and was initially declared incompetent to stand trial. He was confined to a mental hospital for about a decade until he was found competent to be tried.

The initial phase of adjustment to life without parole was difficult for some. Gabriel, Charles, and Alan reported that they had taken medication for a mental health problem during the first several years of incarceration but no longer did so. Consistent with the previous research noted above, sixteen men believed that their mental health had improved over the course of incarceration. In 2011 only Walter, who had recently been transferred to the special needs unit, was taking medication for difficulty sleeping, though Daniel hoped to be prescribed medication to treat the same problem in the near future. In particular, the men felt that they were less impulsive, angry, and bitter than they had been previously. They also felt they had acquired greater self-awareness and grown to become more empathetic, tolerant, and patient. Gabriel commented on the importance of empathy in his own self-development:

> I've seen human beings here at their best and at their worst. I think there's a level of empathy that I have today for certain situations and events in and out of prison. My conscience as far as this world [and] the world outside of here has, kind of like, grown. . . . I've opened myself up more to, you know, not just my own personal experience but to [the] life experiences of others. I think that's really helped me become a human being, closer to the human being that I'm supposed to be. . . . I never want to lose contact with the humanity even if I'm in one of the most inhumane of places.

He went on to express that his sensitivity extended to all forms of life; in fact, he was reluctant to walk on grass for fear that it would be harmful to the plants: "I became so conscience of what the man's effect on the earth [was that] I didn't even want to walk on grass because . . . [I saw] everything as a living organism." Troy had also grown to become more empathetic. He stated: "I think the thing that gets me now [when I watch TV and see] somebody victimized, you know, it infuriates me, and at the same time, it makes me remember you were that person."

The men felt that their mental health had continued to improve over the last five years. In 2011, when I asked him what changes had occurred in his life in the past five years, Matthew responded, "My mental health is better.

I'm more content." He did seem to be calmer and less agitated than in 2006. During the first interview, Matthew broke down and started crying at several points. In addition to behavioral cues, his statements also suggested that he was in distress. For example, when describing an injury to his eye, he remarked that it hurt "so much that I want to die." In addition, he claimed to be "in constant pain" because of a pinched nerve in his back. He was fearful that even the slightest infraction could result in the loss of his single cell as he stated: "You're in constant fear, not of being physically abused, [of] being afraid [of] being stuck somewhere where you don't have any privileges." Five years later, Matthew's demeanor and statements suggested that he was more content. He attributed his improved mental health to "the grace of God." The pain in his eye had abated and he had learned stretches that helped relieve his back pain. He made no mention that he was worried he could lose his single cell.

As compared to other older inmates with whom they interacted, the men felt their mental health was better, but they noted a decline in the mental health of some of their peers. The signs of deterioration mentioned included introversion, forgetfulness, weight loss, and abnormal behavior. For example, Daniel, who had been incarcerated for three decades, described an older friend who "used to salute you. That's all he'd do . . . he still thinks he was in the military." Gabriel described a less tangible indicator of mental illness: "[a loss of] that light . . . just that light in the . . . eye." The men attributed the mental deterioration of older inmates to a lack of mental stimulation and a loss of hope. According to George, "The more inactive you become . . . the more submissive you become to your environment." Additionally, Nathan and George claimed that the mental health of other older inmates had suffered because they had "given up."

Even though the men felt that their mental health had improved over time, many reported feelings of loneliness and regret. Over half the men reported that they felt lonely, and most reported feeling so frequently. Interestingly, Matthew suggested that he had felt lonely for such an extended period of time he no longer registered the emotion. He stated, "I've probably felt lonely for so long that, you know, you don't even recognize the feeling. I mean, it's funny that you ask, I never really, I never thought about myself as lonely. Yeah, I guess." Five men admitted that they went through bouts of depression or sadness. As with loneliness, Joshua felt that depression was unavoidable. He elaborated, "I was never too concerned about being depressed . . . because to me, you know, in jail, depression comes kind of normal."

Regret was another commonly mentioned emotion. Several men expressed regret for the course their lives had taken:

> I'm more angry at myself for allowing myself to get into that situation. . . .
> I had a lot of potential. (Anthony)

> [I think about] everything that I've lost, everything that I missed, you know, all of the opportunities that have went by. (Nathan)

The men regretted that they were unable to have a day-to-day presence in the lives of their children and grandchildren and felt guilty that they were unable to help their families when personal troubles arose. In addition to these, other specific events were identified. Troy regretted that he was arrested in front of his father. Nathan regretted that he had sacrificed his freedom in order to avoid being labeled as a snitch. He declined a plea-bargain deal that would have meant a lesser sentence in exchange for testifying against his accomplice. (He participated in a burglary in which a homeowner was killed though he did not commit the murder.) Instead, his case went to trial, and both he and his accomplice received a LWOP sentence. He explained:

> [I] probably would have been out of jail for fifteen years [by now] and me being the idiot that I was didn't do it because of the way that I grew up and the beliefs that I had, you know, you don't tell on people. . . . Do you know, believe it or not, that my codefendant . . . I can't blame him, just myself, because he told me right then and there to take the deal. [He told me,] "Do what you got to do to get out of prison." [I refused saying,] "We got in this together; we'll ride it out together." So I really can't blame him because he gave me the opportunity, I can only blame myself.

William was the only individual I interviewed who appeared (to a non-expert such as me) to have signs of pervasive psychological distress. Prior to the interview, I was warned by a correctional officer that William had a history of exposing himself to women. While he did not do so with me, his interview was the most difficult for me to conduct because he was either unwilling or unable to answer many of the questions I posed to him. He could not or would not tell me if he was in a segregated area of the prison for his safety or as punishment. I would ask him a question and his response would be completely unrelated to the topic. Much of our interview was spent with him discussing the women he had had intercourse with or the places he had traveled to when he was a young man. He made statements that were outlandish (e.g., Donald Trump was a close friend) or nonsensical (e.g., he was asked to be a correctional officer). Furthermore, he showed signs of paranoia. He claimed that some of the correctional officers had killed an inmate and that the officers were preventing him and Trump from communicating with each other. While William admitted that other inmates called him "crazy," he claimed: "I don't have any psychosis. . . . Sometimes I get a little irritable, you know, but I'm not really mentally ill." William did not respond to my requests to interview him in 2011; consequently, I am not sure of his current mental health state.

PERCEPTIONS OF AGING IN PRISON

Adam, who had been incarcerated for over thirty years and was approaching sixty years of age, observed, "Prison usually does one of two things for an inmate. It either preserves them or ages them." His observation accurately summarizes two competing perspectives on aging in prison. According to one viewpoint, prison insulates inmates from the aging process (Silfen et al. 1977, 65; van Wormer 1981, 90; Wilson and Vito 1986, 411). Older inmates may actually feel younger than their chronological ages because they are not exposed to unhealthy lifestyles or stresses that they would encounter if they were living in society. In support of this position, Monika Reed and Francis Glamser (1979, 358) noted: "Prisoners are not exposed to heavy industry, hard labor, or heavy drinking. They eat well, rest often, and have ready access to medical care. This is unlikely to be the case among lower and working class men on the outside."

In contrast, the opposing viewpoint is that older inmates have aged more quickly than non-incarcerated older people (Abramsky 2004, para. 46; Aday 1994b, 48; Dubler 1998, 151). For example, Sasha Abramsky (2004, para. 40) noted: "The rule of thumb among prison medical staff is that inmates (and people who cycle in and out of prison) tend to age ten to twenty years faster over the course of their lifetimes than their peers." The aging differential has been explained by a variety of pre-incarceration and incarceration factors including drug, alcohol, and tobacco use, unsafe sex or sexual promiscuity, lack of access to medical and dental care prior to incarceration, and living in a stressful prison environment (Abramsky 2004, para. 46; Anderson and Hilliard 2005, 59; Colsher et al. 1992, 882–883; Dubler 1998, 151; Smyer et al. 1997, 10). Even more nuanced, one study found that, while middle-aged inmates are more likely to report that incarceration has retarded the aging process, older inmates are more likely to report that confinement has accelerated the process of aging (Gillespie and Galliher 1972, 470–473).

The men endorsed the former position, as fourteen men felt that time had slowed and prison had preserved them. A majority of men in both 2006 and 2011 reported that they felt younger than their chronological ages. The exact age given by the men varied. Some felt as though they remained the age they were when they entered prison; others felt that they were a decade or so younger than their chronological ages. When asked to explain why they felt younger, six men had the perception that they were living in a time warp:

> You're in a place where you stand still. I think the natural perception because, you know, you're in the same place and you stand still, that everything stands still, but in actuality, it doesn't. (Gabriel)

> One of the things about being put in here is you're locked in a warp. . . . Being here, you're stuck . . . in a position where you don't think about age. (Troy)

John discussed the technological advances that had occurred since his imprisonment as evidence of living in the past. He explained: "Well, you come in, and whatever age you came in at [you remain], and you never grow old because that's the last thing you know. See, I mean we're speaking, when I came in, they had Eight-Track tapes. . . . They just started cassette tapes. . . . And I never used a cell phone, you know, technology has grown so much. . . . Things that you do on the computers and things like that, I've never experienced." Therefore, the notion of being "frozen in time" was a commonly held perception for these LWOP inmates.

Other men perceived that prison life protected them from the daily stressors that people on the outside experience and, as a result, decreased the probability of premature aging:

> You aren't able to drink, smoke, run the streets, party all night long or however you chose to, so you have a tendency, your body has a tendency of slowing down and aging more gracefully than when you were out there on the streets. (Noah)

> I know for a fact that if I was on the streets, oh man, I'd probably look like I was seventy-five [because of] not getting the proper rest, not getting the proper meals. (Robert)

> This place actually preserves you. . . . You don't get a lot of stress. . . . A man my age out on the street would have to work. I mean in here, the basic things I got to do is go to yard. (Troy)

Matthew maintained that the routine of prison life shielded inmates from aging: "It's a routine, you know, it's just, you're doing the same thing, day after day, week after week, getting up at the same time, going to the same places, seeing the same faces, you have no way of keeping track of time. And before you know it, ten years, twenty years is gone. . . . I'm serious it doesn't seem like more than two years."

While the men might have felt that they were aging at a slower pace, they were reminded that time had passed. They reported that, compared to when they were younger, they noticed declines in speed, agility, strength, and endurance. For instance, Samuel, a habitual offender who had served nineteen years, noted: "I've really slowed down so much. I get tired so easy from doing this, from doing that." The men were addressed with salutations, such as "old head," "poppy," "old-timer," and "pop-pop" that reflected maturation. Troy explained his initial surprise at being thought of as old but how he had grown to accept, and even appreciate, the designation: "When you hear guys call you that, it's a sign of respect. . . . At first it was shocking like who are you talking to? I'm not old. Then you come to realize, yes I am . . . so I just accepted it. It's endearing to me." Gabriel and Henry commented that the deaths of other inmates reminded them that they were also aging, while Walter, Joshua, and Victor observed that the retirement of correctional officers documented the passing of time. Physical signs of aging—for example, gray hair and wrinkles—also reinforced to four men that they were no longer young. Troy stated: "I [used to] wish my hair would turn white so when I went to the pardon board they'll think I'm old. One day I looked in the mirror and said damn, my beard turned white. When you see it, it's hard to believe . . . it happened so gradually."

Five men commented that they were aware they had grown old because they were experiencing health problems associated with advanced age (e.g., arthritis, poor eyesight, high blood pressure, and aches and pains). Interactions with family members also reinforced that years had passed. As an example, Troy's nephew told him: "You look like pop-pop." For others, it was the physical appearance of their relatives that confirmed the length of time they had been incarcerated. Matthew commented: "Time has gone by so fast. . . . It only seems like five years. I look at my family, my brothers and sisters, my grandchildren, and I can't believe it."

In contrast to the prevailing perception of feeling younger than their chronological ages, five men felt that physical health conditions had made them feel their ages or even older. Samuel and Adam reported that mentally they felt young, but because of medical problems, they felt old physically. This finding is consistent with previous research that found health status is a better predictor of self-perceived age than either chronological age or time served (Goetting 1983, 294).

STAYING YOUNG

The men identified several factors as important in maintaining mental and physical health. They attempted to treat their own medical issues so as not to rely on the prison medical care, which they perceived as being lacking. Some men credited their health to their positive outlook, motivated by a hope of release for many, to keep them young. For instance, Alan's hope of release motivated him to "start taking care of myself."

Remaining active was frequently cited as a means of staying young. For example, Victor, who was sixty-two years of age, commented: "If you stay active, you feel better. If you do things that keep your mind sharp, and I do things, I keep busy, I keep my mind busy. I read. I write. I have a little ministry in here that I do and I have eighty-two people that I write to." Even if they were no longer able to maintain the levels they once had, the men spoke of the importance of staying active. Anthony commented, "It's my belief that no you don't stop doing that. You just slow it down maybe a little bit but you don't stop." Exercise and diet were also mentioned as means of protecting their health.

Exercise

According to Adam, "We all know what we need to do to stay younger, keep up with your health [and] exercise." Over half the men reported that they exercised regularly. Some walked around the yard, while others performed calisthenics (e.g., sit-ups and push-ups) in their cells. A few of the men had maintained an exercise routine ever since they were first incarcerated. For example, John stated, "I know that I should do some type of exercise every day. I know that I should get my blood pumping. I know I should be doing something. I just can't lay around or I'm going to end up just dying like I see so many people doing. So, you know, I made it a habit years and years ago. I got to at least walk a half hour a day, if not more, you know, [and] do little exercises."

Despite their age and physical health, some were able to adhere to rigorous training regimens. For example, Alan, who was approaching seventy years of age, claimed he did "one hundred push-ups each day." In addition to bolstering physical health, the men found that exercise helped them cope with the stresses of imprisonment. While he admitted that he had started jogging as part of his plan to escape from prison, Joshua found that it helped him relieve stress: "To me it turned out to be something that I really started enjoying and something that made me feel good. You know, it took a lot of my tension away and I guess anxiety too."[2]

While six men exercised at the gym, the majority did not. They claimed there was not enough equipment, such as weights, for all of the inmates. As a result, James, the oldest in the group, and Daniel, one of the younger men, claimed that younger inmates refused to share with older inmates. Although he frequented the gym, Gabriel thought that the large number of inmates in a small space acted as a deterrent for older people: "I think that older people . . . are real conscious of space so . . . when you got a small area and you have like . . . eighty to ninety people packed into a small area . . . it can present . . . problems for people who are really space conscious." John and Michael claimed that they avoided the gym because they believed it to be a "hot spot" for violence.

Prison sports programs were the only other means of exercise available to the men. Only Gabriel and Henry participated as athletes, the rest were relegated to the auxiliary roles of referees, timekeepers, and coaches. Claiming to be the star pitcher of his softball team, Henry explained his motivation to participate: "I do it because it kind of keeps me kind of . . . not young but active." In 2011 both Gabriel and Henry reported that they were still involved in competitive sports programs; however, they remained the exceptions. When asked why they were not involved in sports leagues, some men commented that older inmates could not compete with younger inmates, as noted in Francis's statement: "Those guys run like racehorses up and down the court." The two other reasons given were preexisting injuries that prevented their participation or the potential for injury as some of the men were concerned they would get hurt in the course of a game or in a fight that could break out between the teams.

Diet

The men also reported that they tried to maintain their physical health by eating a healthy diet. Proper nutrition was especially important for those with diabetes, hypertension, and high cholesterol. However, the men alleged, it was often difficult to eat nutritional foods. The men with special dietary needs, including low sugar or low sodium diets, claimed that restricted diets were not available to them. Instead, they were forced to regulate their diets themselves. Michael commented, "The food is not nutritional. You get starch and sugar in all the food. I'm a diabetic so the food's hard for me. . . . I just eat what I can eat and stay away from what I'm not supposed to eat." The men attributed the unhealthy quality of prison food for increasing the number of inmates with a chronic disease or health condition such as diabetes, obesity, and hypertension. Instead of relying on the prison for all of his meals, Alan, in an effort to eat a more nutritious diet, had begun to eat more cereal and oatmeal that he purchased at the commissary. However, most of the food items sold at the commissary were junk foods and low in nutritional value.

THE END

In the final part of this chapter, the two possible forms of release—death or sentence modification—are discussed. Compared to other groups of inmates, a discussion of the fear of death and dying is perhaps most relevant for older LWOP inmates. Given the slim chances of sentence commutation, most LWOP inmates will die in prison. While medical parole, the release of a terminally ill inmate, is available in most states and in the federal system, it is not frequently granted. Human Rights Watch (2012, 2) estimated that over the last twenty years less than twenty-five federal inmates on average have been released via medical parole each year. Even if medical parole was granted with greater regularity, most LWOP inmates would not be eligible for inmates convicted of serious violent crimes are typically excluded (Anno et al. 2004, 41). Case in point, after Thomas's prognosis was determined to be terminal, doctors applied for medical parole on his behalf but the request was denied.

Dying in Prison

Data from the Bureau of Justice Statistics indicate that the leading cause of death in prison is illness, commonly cancer and heart disease (Noonan

2013, 1). Not surprisingly, the mortality rate among older inmates is much higher than it is among younger inmates. For example, the mortality rate for inmates over the ages of fifty-five is 1,771 per 100,000 inmates, as compared to 26 per 100, 000 for inmates between the ages of eighteen and twenty-four. Additionally, research suggests that older inmates die at a relatively young age. At Angola Prison in Louisiana, the mean age of a death resulting from natural causes is fifty-one years of age (Cain and Fontenot 2001, 120).

Some of the men acknowledged the strong likelihood of dying in prison, given the contemporary reality of a LWOP sentence. Henry, sixty-three years of age, assessed his chances of dying in prison as high: "I probably won't get out and I have natural life so there's no need for me to be lying to myself to be, oh man you're going home next year, do five more, because in reality I do have natural life and the statute says no parole. . . . There's a great possibility that I'm going to die here. You know, I think about it."

The men found that when other older inmates died, it forced them to acknowledge the real possibility that one day they will lie dying in the prison hospital:

I've seen people who have died or on their death beds up there. It makes me think, that could be me some day. (Karl)

Every now and then it kicks in, the reality kicks in. . . . This is a constant worry of yours. . . . It's not regular [the death of an older inmate] but it does happen and it does affect you. I think it affects older guys more than it does the younger guys because you think, man, that could be me. (Anthony)

Conversations with their relatives also caused the men to consider where or when their lives will end. Troy commented: "When my people talk about, it becomes a reality. You know, that my sentence says, that that's what will happen." In 2006 Daniel explained that he grew emotional when discussing the possibility of dying in prison with his family: "My daughter said, 'Dad, do you think you're going to die in here?' I just started crying. . . . It really touched me. My little granddaughter asked me. She said, 'Pop-pop, when are you coming home?' I said, 'Soon.' She said, 'You've been telling me that all my life.' She's only five years old. . . . That's what tears you up."

Suicide

About one-third of the men reported suicidal thoughts earlier in their sentences. For all but Walter, suicidal ideation passed. The fact that Walter did not expect to be released, was in poor health, and was estranged from his family may have made death seem attractive. The only scenario in which John mentioned that he would take his life would be if his health deteriorated to the point where he could no longer care for himself. He explained: "[If] I knew I was dying, I would get me something and kill myself, not kill myself painfully, but I'd ingest something . . . that would put me to sleep. I don't want to be [like] one of these people, wasting away. . . . It's not like committing suicide, it's pulling the plug." It is important to note, however, that several men commented that they were looking forward to death but were not planning to take matters into their own hands, as reflected in the following statements:

> [Death] would be [an escape]. Anything to get away from this would be welcome. (Walter)

> I must say I look forward to it. . . . It'd be nice to wake up in heaven. . . . I want to be free from my body, that's what I desire. . . . My spirit yearns to be free. (Matthew)

In 2006 Matthew reported that because of the physical pain he experienced, "I want to die. . . . I look forward to it you know. It would be so nice to go to sleep and wake up dead. . . . I'd love it. I [would] embrace it really." While he had hoped to die, he had not taken any additional measures to achieve this result. Matthew explained, "I wouldn't take my own life because that's a horrible sin. I wouldn't stoop that low."

Thomas and Anthony also thought of dying as an escape from prison. Anthony shared the following perspective: "Sometimes I believe that if I'm going to die in prison . . . come on and bring it. Cause this is not a nice life." Thomas equated dying to mean serving less time than what the State intended: "If I die, then this life sentence is over with and I'm cheating them. So, it doesn't matter." Despite this claim, however, Thomas's behavior after undergoing a quadruple bypass surgery showed a will to live: "The next day I got up out of the bed, put my tennis shoes on, got dressed, started walking that hallway . . . shocked the doctor . . . so you have to have the determination and not let them let you lay there and die because they'll let you lay there and die. They won't encourage you to get up and walk around, so you have to do it on your own. You have to have your own agenda. If you want to live, get up and walk, if you want to die, lay there and die. So, I got up and walked." Nine men were aware of other inmates similar to Thomas and Anthony, who believed that death was an escape. John remarked: "I heard a number of them say I'm cheating the State out of time. . . . Yeah it would be a blessing. I wouldn't have to wait all them years before I die if I die tomorrow." In *Aging Prisoners: Crisis in American Corrections* (2003, 129), Ronald Aday also found that inmates may look forward to death as an escape from their current lives: "Some inmates viewed death more like a friend that would take them away from their horrible life in prison."

Fear of Dying

Prison is hardly an ideal location to die. As argued by Nancy Dubler (1998, 152): "The good death—an acceptance of the inevitable and a reconciliation with family and friends, supported by spiritual counselors in a comfortable surrounding—is rarely available inside prison walls." About half the men reported that they were fearful of dying, as a result of the social stigma carried by dying in prison and the possibility of dying without loved ones nearby. These specific concerns are similar to those noted in other studies of older and long-term inmates (Aday 2005–2006, 209; Flanagan 1981, 212; Rideau and Sinclair 1984, 55; Wilson and Vito 1986, 411).

Noah and Troy reported that they would feel better about their lives if they were able to die on the outside:

> I don't want to die in prison. I would rather die a free man. That's point blank. I don't want to die here. . . . I would feel better about myself . . . just knowing that I was a free man and not an incarcerated person. I think I would feel a lot better about that within myself. (Noah)

> It is a fear. . . . I don't want to die in here. To me . . . it would be a waste of life. To stay here all of these years and never really reach the potential that I know I can. (Troy)

Even the men who were not fearful of dying acknowledged that a stigma existed. Gabriel explained why the failure to be released could cause some to feel as though their lives were a failure: "I think it represents the greatest failure, you know, I think . . . even if you have a mandatory life sentence . . . there is a belief, you know, that there's a glimmer of possibilities that . . . constitutes grasping at the one success that you had in your life. And I think that, you know, dying in prison is the ultimate failure to some people." John described how the local newspaper's treatment of an inmate's death intensified the feelings of stigmatization:

> The big thing about dying in prison is what they put in the paper when you die. . . . They put all bad stuff, you know, so and so in prison for so many years because he did this. You know, I mean, I don't think that should be put in there . . . every bad thing they did. I mean, there's a whole mess of us that do good. Why don't you say, "Hey, he did this and he did that towards the end of his life." . . . I don't want [to] have that as my last thing. Matter of fact, I don't want it so bad we told the newspaper not to put it in already because you can do that. . . . The only thing I want in the obituary is: "[His name] died."

Anthony was concerned that the stigma would extend to his family: "Dying in prison, that would be my worst legacy to leave to my children, my family, you know. I wouldn't want that, you know, [for] them to say, 'Well, my pop or my grandpa died in prison.' I wouldn't want . . . them to carry that burden." He died in prison in 2009.

Uncertainty over the specific location in which they would die in prison was of concern to Troy and Henry. Troy explained: "The only thing that concerns me now is . . . where is it going to happen? Will I be asleep in my cell or will [it] be out in the yard? Or will I be in some program?" Henry echoed a similar concern but also expressed the fear that he would be surrounded by people who would not care if he died. He stated: "Where am I going to die at? Could it happen at chow hall? Could it happen on the ball field? Could it happen in the yard? Who's going to be around when you die? . . . You start to wonder who's going to be there to help you? Nobody. Who really cares for you really? Nobody." Therefore, the uncertainty of the location of their deaths coupled with the perceived apathy of the witnesses of their deaths added to their anxiety. Similar to Henry, Noah, who was thirty years of age when he began serving life without parole and was now fifty-eight, was fearful that he would die in the absence of loved ones: "It's not being able to hold my daughter's hand, or my son's, or my granddaughter's, or grandson's hand." Two other fears were mentioned by the men. Matthew and Victor were concerned with becoming ill and, as a result of not receiving the proper medical attention, dying in pain. John and Daniel, both of whom claimed to be innocent of the crime for which they were incarcerated, were fearful that they would die in prison before they were exonerated.

While none of the men wanted to die in prison, about half the group reported that they were not fearful of dying, either in prison or in general. Seven men attributed the lack of fear to their religious beliefs. Francis, a sixty-eight-year-old habitual offender, elaborated: "No fear. I guess like most guys I would like not to expire in here but also [I] realize that's a possibility and Islam teaches . . . living is just moving toward [death]. So that's going to come, that's an eventuality, you know, I would like for it not to be here, but I know it could be here because of my sentence. But, no, there's no fear."

Nine men accepted the inevitability of death and as a result did not worry:

Everybody has to die. How is not up to us. . . . You have to come to an understanding. I did. [I] didn't like it, but I did. . . . You're not going to live forever. This world is not geared for that. (Alan)

What are you doing to do? You going to worry about that? No, I don't want to die in prison, but if you do, you do. (Charles)

I've accepted it, matter of fact. I realized years ago, you know, that there's no point worrying about anything, not only death, but there's no point in worrying about anything that you have no control over. (Robert)

I don't think about death hardly ever, dying either. You know what I mean, why? Why? You're going to die. You already know that, why worry about it? You know what I mean, I can't change it. It's going to come when it's ready. (Joshua)

While some were concerned with the stigma of dying in prison, Alan and Joshua disagreed and felt the location of death was of little significance. Alan remarked: "People die everywhere: in prison, out of prison, in trains, [and] in air. . . . What's the big deal about, you know, dying in prison?"

Interestingly, hope of release and a lack of hope were other reasons for the absence of fear. Nathan was confident that he would be released prior to his death: "I know that might sound awful cocky, [but] I don't plan on dying in this place." Likewise, Alan commented: "I'm almost sure that I'm not going to die in here." Alternatively, Thomas, Walter, Joshua, and Henry did not expect to be released from prison and had accepted that their deaths would occur in prison; as a result, they reported little fear. In his study of death anxiety among 102 older male inmates in Mississippi, Aday (2005–2006, 211) also found that, as inmates accepted the inevitability of dying in prison, their fear of death declined. In the present group, Walter explained: "I gave up thinking about it because I know I'm going to die in here. I know there's no getting out for me." And, as noted above, he was looking forward to dying. Walter died in prison in 2013 at the age of sixty-nine.

Burial Wishes

Related to dying in prison, another fear expressed by inmates is burial in the prison cemetery (Rideau and Sinclair 1984, 56) or in a potter's field for indigent individuals. Wilbert Rideau and Billy Sinclair (1984, 40–41), inmates at Angola Prison, explained the difference between burial in Point Lookout, a prison cemetery, as compared to one in the community: "While Point Lookout is a cemetery, it is different from the typical cemetery. No one goes to Point Lookout—except to clean the cemetery or to bury another prisoner. There are no visitors, either prisoner or free. Prisoners are not permitted to go and employees generally have no reason for going—and since those buried there are the dispossessed and unclaimed, there are no friends and relatives to come and lay flowers." Prisoners are buried in prison cemeteries or cremated either because their families cannot afford a burial in a community cemetery or because they are estranged from their families and their bodies were not claimed (Abramsky 2004, para. 3; Cain and Fontenot 2001, 122; Rideau and Sinclair 1984, 37, 57).

Only Robert and Daniel expressed concern that they could be buried in the state cemetery. Robert stated: "I really wouldn't want the State to bury me in . . . potter's field." Daniel expressed a similar sentiment: "I don't want to get buried there. [I made my children] swear that they're coming to get my body." However, they were the exception. A greater number of men claimed that they had no objections to being buried by the State. In fact, Thomas, Henry, Victor, and Adam reported that they preferred to be buried in the potter's field. As explained by two of these men, the reason was that they did not want to burden their families with the costs of burial:

> I don't want to be the guy to burden your family with the finances. If these people have kept me this long for these many years away from them, let them spend the finances to put me away. (Henry)

> [I] told them not to collect my body. Let the State go ahead and take care of my body. . . . I just can't see putting my family in financial responsibility of that. . . . The State has kept me so they can go ahead and pay for me. (Adam)

Thomas's desire appeared to be motivated by a final act of defiance as he stated: "The State raised me all of these years, let the State take care of the burial . . . spend their money." Thomas died in 2008. I am unsure of the location of his remains.

Two-thirds of the men had made arrangements for their burials. Several of the men reported that they would be buried in family plots; for the seven who were in the military, they would be buried in a veterans' cemetery. James planned to donate his body to science. Walter wanted his body to be cremated and his ashes spread in Florida, where he had spent most of his time after he escaped.[3] Matthew planned to be cremated and have his ashes spread in a wooded area where he used to hunt and fish as a young man. On the other hand, some had not made plans for their burials. For instance, Nathan commented: "I'm not even thinking about [it]." He expected to be released, and so he was unwilling to entertain the idea of dying in prison.

RELEASE

Almost all of the men expected to be released from prison, and their commitment to this belief persisted through the years of confinement. All of the men who reported in 2006 that they expected to be released from prison expressed a similar belief again in 2011. Adam, who in 2006 did not expect to be released, had changed his mind and in 2011 believed that he would be released. Other research has also found LWOP inmates to be hopeful of release (Abramsky 2004, para. 4; Villaume 2005, 274; Welch 1987, 7).

Hope of release remained even after the men acknowledged that the probability of release was extremely low. For some, their hope of release was based on sources that were tenuous at best. For example, Alan inferred that he would be released because an attorney alluded to release as a theoretical possibility.

He explained: "Why would she write that knowing I have life without parole? She must know something I don't know." When pressed, the men could only identify three LWOP inmates by name who had been released. These cases involved unusual circumstances that were not applicable to these men's situations. Four men were aware that Francis, a non-violent habitual offender, had been released in early 2011. Alan commented that Francis "sent some pictures back. He looks good. He looks good in street clothes." Troy's hope of release increased as a result of Francis's release. He elaborated: "It gave me all the hope in the world now. It was like okay finally because he had the same sentence I had. That's what gave me the hope that they're actually looking at these sentences and realizing that at some point you could be released." Similar to Troy, Daniel thought that his chances of release had improved, because Daniel had participated in more programs than one LWOP inmate who he claimed had been released.

Despite their knowing a few LWOP inmates who had been released, for Gabriel and Henry, hope was more measured. Henry, convicted of first-degree murder, reported that it was only habitual offenders, like Francis, who were being released. Gabriel acknowledged that the release of a handful of LWOP inmates did not necessarily increase his own chances: "I understand that everybody's case, you know, is different. And, you know, I don't get encouraged because it's happening or get discouraged because it isn't happening." Indeed, Francis's case was markedly different from most of the other men's. Francis was serving life without parole as a result of being designated a habitual offender after he was convicted of a series of burglaries. Unlike almost all of the other men, violence—or the threat of violence—was absent from all of Francis's crimes.

Only five men did not expect to be released from prison. Matthew, Thomas, and Joshua commented that, given the low likelihood of release for inmates serving lengthy parole-eligible sentences (e.g., sixty years) or life with the possibility of parole, those with a LWOP sentence had practically no chance. Matthew remarked: "I started to [apply for sentence commutation], but I didn't [finish it]. They're not letting guys go with parole. There are guys in here that got parole dates, they won't release them." Joshua, who admitted to killing a homeowner in a burglary that went awry, was aware that his accomplice, who was not in the home when the murder occurred, had his commutation applications denied. As a result, Joshua thought the prospects of his release were non-existent. He explained: "Look, you got to realize, I honestly don't foresee myself getting out of jail. You know, I just don't. I've adapted myself to probably this is it, until I'm rolled out of here on a gurney."

Some of these men chastised other LWOP inmates for failing to accept the reality of their situations. Walter criticized the hopeful for "living in a fantasy world." Joshua remarked: "Some guys around here think with sentences like mine that they have an opportunity of getting out, which is really wrong." However, despite their doubts, Henry, Walter, and Joshua were still challenging their cases in the courts or submitting commutation applications.[4] While he claimed to "not think it's possible," Matthew nonetheless possessed a small amount of hope that he could be released. He remarked: "[My release] would be a miracle. . . . I think there's always hope of it, you know. I've never one hundred percent given up." As examined below, the two means by which a LWOP inmate could be released were appeals and commutation.

Appeals

Through the years that they had been incarcerated, almost all the men had appealed their sentences. At our first interview, Troy estimated that he spent about three hours a day working on his case, but by 2011 Troy, like a lot of the men in the group, had exhausted all of his appeals. In 2011 only seven were still actively pursuing their cases, most of whom were those who professed their innocence. One challenge they faced was that, because of the length of time that had passed since their convictions, they were time barred from raising certain legal issues. Daniel felt it was unfair that he only had three years to raise legal issues, yet the State had an indefinite amount of time to file charges for there was no statute of limitations for murder: "They've got from now on to charge you with murder . . . so it's not equal. You're fighting for your life. . . . By the time I learned the laws and the statutes, they were changed and the time limit ran out so they said that I was time barred. . . . The only way I could get back in court [is] with the newly discovered evidence." Similar to Daniel, John and Charles were pursuing new dimensions of their cases and were hopeful that the courts would accept new evidence that exonerated them for the murder of their wives. Charles remained committed to working on his case despite the numerous denials of his previous appeals: "I don't know what's going to happen if I go to court, hell, I've been turned down so many times, I'm just . . . , like, it's the norm. But, I got to keep trying, I got to keep shooting at it, I got to keep going." Daniel echoed a similar sentiment when he remarked: "I'm trying to stay strong to prove my innocence and get out of here." For most, though, the courts were no longer an option, and the only chance at release for many of the men was commutation by the governor, an improbable occurrence.

Commutation

The men were well versed on the commutation process in the state. As they explained it, inmates were eligible to apply every three years. Three levels of approval were needed to secure sentence commutation. The first level of approval was from the DOC. If it recommended that the inmate be released, then the application was forwarded to the pardons board. After a hearing, in which interested parties could testify (e.g., the inmate, the victim or the victim's family, or the prosecutor), the board would determine whether to support or deny a request. If supported by the pardons board, the application was sent to the governor for final approval. Of the men who had applied, most claimed that they had been successful at the first stage of the process but did not receive a favorable recommendation from the pardons board. Only Nathan, George, and Francis have had their applications reach the governor. To date, Francis was the only one to be successful.

Less than half the men had applied for commutation in 2006. Five years later, about two-thirds of the men had made at least one attempt at commutation. In 2011 Gabriel, Noah, and Daniel reported that they were planning to apply for the first time. These men felt that they needed to serve a substantial period of time (e.g., twenty-five or thirty years) before the application would be given serious consideration, or in Gabriel's case, until he felt comfortable applying. In addition to the consideration of the length of time served, the men wanted to wait until they had accomplishments to report as evidence of their rehabilitation. For example, Noah had originally planned to wait until after he obtained his GED before applying. In 2011 Matthew was the only individual who had not submitted an application for commutation and had no plans of doing so. When I asked him why, he responded: "I don't see the need, they'd laugh at me."

The men identified several impediments to applying for commutation. Robert estimated that, because of copying and postage fees, it cost an inmate about one hundred dollars to submit a commutation application. Other men commented that they were not permitted to apply when they had a court case pending. For example, Daniel was waiting until his litigation against the prison had ended before he would apply. In 2006 several of the men who claimed to be innocent reported that they had not submitted an application because they were under the impression that they would have to admit guilt at the hearing. Daniel contended: "I'll go to my grave. I would rather die than say that I did it and I didn't do it." However, in 2011 the men informed me that they had been mistaken and were not required to admit guilt. As a result, Ryan, who maintained his innocence, had submitted an application for the first time. In addition, as most of the men did not have the funds to hire an attorney to represent them through the process, they were forced to wait until state-provided attorneys had the time to devote to their cases. Even when the attorney was available, some men questioned the quality of the legal counsel they received. For example, Henry doubted that the public defender had his best interests in mind; consequently, he decided to represent himself at the pardons board hearing. He explained: "A lot of people thought it was a bad move, could have been, but I'm saying to me, I can't afford a paid attorney. . . . If I'm going down there, what do they want to know? They want to know about me. Who's [a better] person to tell about me than I am?" Henry had a positive assessment of his performance: "I went down there and thought I'd done a fairly good job."

The men took into consideration changes in the State's political tides when determining a favorable time for them to apply. They were aware that the perception of being "tough on crime" was important to politicians and that granting commutations was a potential death knell "to your political career because they will use it against you" (Francis), especially if the released offender recidivated. For this reason, in 2006 several men maintained that it was an opportune time to apply for sentence commutation because the governor (Governor A) was not seeking reelection and was allegedly retiring from political life. As a result, some men felt as though Governor A would be more willing to grant commutation. However, Victor disagreed; he wanted to wait until after this governor had left office so that he could have a fresh start with the next one (Governor B). Ultimately, only Francis was successful in his bid during this time period. While Nathan's applications had twice been approved by the two lower levels, he was unable to secure the necessary approval from the governor.

In 2006 Nathan reported that he had received the approval of the DOC and pardons board and was "very confident" that he would be going home in the next couple of years. He predicted: "I'm going home. I'm going home." Ultimately, his request was denied by Governor A before leaving office. Five years later, Nathan reported that he had reapplied for sentence commutation and that once again he had been approved at the first two levels and had been awaiting a decision from Governor B for over a year. Despite the rejection several years earlier, Nathan was emphatic that he would be released: "I'm going to get out of here. There's not a doubt in my mind."[5] As the next gubernatorial election cycle was gearing up in 2011, Charles and Karl reported that they were waiting until after the election before they applied. Victor was disappointed as he had expected Governor B to approve more commutation applications than he did.

An Unalterable Past

The men were frustrated that a single event was used as the sole criterion to judge their worth. Instead of focusing on the positive changes they had made, they claimed that the pardons board and governor, when making commutation decisions, only considered the severity of the original crime. Henry provided a representative comment of statements made by pardons board members: "'The bottom line is that we knew you went to trial, you was found guilty by a jury of first-degree murder, and we feel that sentence needs to be carried out. But you can continue to do what you're doing [in prison] because you're doing a fine job.' [They] didn't say not to come back or come back but basically . . . left me hanging right there." As noted below, the uncertainty of how to proceed was a common source of frustration for the men.

The men felt it was unfair that the totality of their lives were judged based upon this one act, for they each felt that it was unrepresentative of who he was as a person, either then or now. Noah commented: "It's hard for me to accept that I took somebody's life because I feel as though that's not me." Several men stressed that they were good people. Victor claimed: "I had good morals but I just covered them up." Expressing a similar sentiment, Noah remarked: "I'm not a natural mean person, never been a mean-spirited person." John and Daniel, who maintained their innocence, felt that their previous misdeeds did not warrant the life sentence they had received. John described himself as "a good person [who] went bad on drugs." He blamed his drug use for leaving him vulnerable to the accusation that he had killed his wife. While Daniel admitted that he had committed more offenses than the ones that he had been punished for (he did not elaborate), he maintained that he was not involved in the murder and that his "good outweigh[s] the bad." In Nathan's case, as he was not in the residence when the homeowner was killed, he argued: "I'm not a bad person, you know? It's not like I came to prison because I was running around, killing, and assaulting people." Despite the fact that they had committed a homicide, some rejected the label of killer, murderer, or violent offender primarily because the homicide was not premeditated. For example, Alan claimed: "I'm not a violent person even though I had a violent crime." Michael alleged: "I'm not a murderer, I'm not." And Henry stated: "I'm not a killer although I'm in prison for killing. I'm not a killer. . . . This was an accident."

Instead of solely relying on the severity of the crime they had committed decades previously, the men argued that their personal transformations and low likelihood of recidivating merited consideration. The men felt that as a result of their awakenings they had become different people. Joshua, incarcerated since the age of thirty, reflected: "I know that I'm not the same person that I was in 1977." Nathan claimed: "I've rehabilitated myself in this prison system." Through maturation and participation in programming, the men contended that many LWOP inmates have changed. Noah explained: "We are not the same inconsiderate people that we used to be when we first got locked up. We have changed for the better. Let me rephrase that, a lot of us have changed for the better. . . . We have changed for the better. We aren't negative. We're more positive about different things in life. We stop and look before we leap. We think about what we are going to do before we do it. We appreciate ourselves, our lives, and the people that are around us." Robert claimed that he was proof that life-sentenced inmates could be rehabilitated: "I'm definitely a better person than when I came here. They say that some people can't change or you might have society feel that a person can't change, you might have judges, maybe juries, prosecutors that might think that you can't change, but the fact is I'm a living witness that a person can change."

Despite the positive changes they had made, the men were upset that the pardons board and the governor failed to acknowledge them. Henry explained: "A person can see a change in themselves in these couple of decades, and other people they [can] see the change, but the people that have this hold on you, they just look at the paper [crime reports]. And . . . they might say you have been found guilty for a murder charge [but] that happened thirty-four years ago." Daniel claimed: "Nobody notices [the] positive changes." John felt that the fact he was incarcerated for murder trumped all of the positive contributions he had made to the prison. Adam offered: "It becomes harder in realizing that no matter how much you change, society is not going to forgive you. . . . You're always constantly reminded and in here you do all of this rehabilitation just to be trying to do right, trying to make amends, trying to prove yourself." Samuel argued: "They need to consider what he's done over the past, you know, [number of] years that he's been here."

The men also asserted that their lack of dangerousness should be taken into consideration. While one-third of the men were of the opinion that some LWOP inmates should never be released because they pose too much danger to the public, they felt that the majority of older LWOP inmates no longer posed any threat. Walter claimed that his good behavior during his five-year escape demonstrated that older LWOP inmates pose little threat to the public: "I proved to them that I didn't get in any trouble. I was out for five years. I didn't go out [and] rob or murder. Kill anybody. I went out and worked the whole time. If I lasted five years, I know I could last the rest of my life."

Given the fact that most of the murders fit the "homicides under high pressure category" (see Chapter 2, A Typology of Their Offenses), and seemed to be impulsive decisions, John and Thomas argued that these LWOP inmates would not pose a danger to society if released. John commented: "All these people that got [life without parole], they didn't plan that [murder]. You know? They went in and [did] the crime with a gun under the influence. That's no excuse, but this is what it is and somebody got shot. You know. They shouldn't have a gun to begin with but they're not killers."

Thomas differentiated between LWOP inmates who committed their crimes under emotional stress and offenders who "kill people, and they don't think nothing about it." Both men went on to argue that most LWOP inmates should be released because of the extremely low probability that they would commit a similar crime in the future:

They're not going to go kill again. Statistics say that all over the world. You know what I mean, but people don't look at it that way. (John)

If they would let me out of here tomorrow, the chances of me killing somebody is a million to one. It would have to be extreme circumstances. (Thomas)

Adam agreed: "[Offenders who committed a] passionate crime, murder or whatever, they are the least likely to re-offend after being incarcerated for [a] certain period."

The men maintained that the contentious relationships they had with the victims of their offenses, many of whom were their former or current romantic partners, were atypical, and as a result, they were unlikely to use violence in the future. Thomas explained: "Crimes of violence are committed for a reason. . . . I've never killed anybody during the commission of a crime. . . . I killed her [my wife] because I thought I had to." Age and accompanying poor physical health were two other reasons why the men felt they posed no threat to society. Francis argued: "When you get to an age that . . . you're no longer a harm to society that [I think] some consideration would be due for your sentence." Walter asked: "What am I going to do? I'm in a wheelchair." Instead of being a danger to society, the men argued, they could make positive contributions, primarily through mentoring younger offenders and at-risk youth. For example, Daniel reported: "I believe I could help a lot of people . . . by teaching younger guys the trades like upholstery, roofing . . . and tell[ing] them about prison life, that this is not the way to go. I think I could be an asset in that way." Victor added, as additional benefits of the release of older LWOP inmates, the "ability to work, and pay taxes, and be a pillar in the community."

In addition to their frustration that evidence of rehabilitation and lack of dangerousness were not taken into consideration, the men shared two additional frustrations with the commutation process. George, Walter, and Nathan questioned the purpose of having a pardons board if its recommendations could be unilaterally rejected by the governor. Related to this, the men were frustrated because the governor provided no explanation for denial. In particular, George wanted greater clarification as to why the governor did not support the recommendation of the pardons board. He asked: "What information does [the governor] have that is different?" In fact, George and several other long-term inmates had filed litigation in federal court raising the issue that they received little direction as to what they could do to be released. He summarized the case: "We're not challenging the governor's right to overrule the board, but what we're saying is [when I reapply] how do I know what to address when it's never been given to us in writing?" According to George, other inmates were not supportive of this litigation as they were fearful that it would alienate Governor B and all future applications would be denied.

Despite the repeated rejection, most men planned on continuing to file commutation applications. In fact, they expected their initial application to be denied claiming that it was the pardons board practice to reject a first-time applicant. To borrow Robert's gambling metaphor, the only way in which the men were to win the lottery of release was to buy a ticket (in the form of a commutation application). Even the men who did not hope to be released from prison, with the exception of Matthew, continued to submit applications. For example, Walter reported that he applied for commutation as he hoped that a clerical error would be made and he would be mistakenly released. If they were to stop applying for commutation, the men felt, it would be forfeiting their lives. As Gabriel put it: "I know I will pursue it . . . and it's because . . . I'm not going to give up and just give my life . . . away like that." Anthony stated that he had had the wrong attitude at previous hearings and vowed that, at the next one, he would be more empowered: "I'm going to walk in there like they're sitting there especially for me."

Not all of the men were planning to keep applying every time they were eligible. At the follow-up interview Joshua, who was sixty-four at the time, expressed uncertainty as to whether he would apply for sentence commutation again should his next request be denied. He felt that he was at a critical juncture; if he was released in the next five years he would be able to care for himself, but any later than that, he expressed concern that he would become a burden to his family:

> So the earliest [I could go up] would be late next year, if not early 2013. And if you don't make that hearing, and they say no, you can only go up once every three years. So then I would have to wait to 2016 before I could reapply again. That's another five years down the road. I'll be sixty-nine, seventy. . . . I don't know. At that time [I] might think differently if I'm going to get out of here and be a burden on everybody. Might not want to go that route, I might just want to stay here and be a burden on the State.

The Downside of Hope of Release

As argued throughout this book, hope of release was one of the most powerful coping mechanisms that the men possessed. As noted by psychologist Paul Kwon (2002, 208–209), higher levels of hope are associated with greater life satisfaction, achievement, and positive interpersonal functioning. Yet, the hope of release for most LWOP inmates was unrealistic. Kwon (2002, 211) differentiated between genuine hope and false hope based on "whether the expectations are grounded in reality" and "whether the hope generates a constructive response." While most LWOP inmates fail to meet the first criterion because of the slim chance of release, it is undeniable that hope of release for these LWOP inmates had inspired their self-improvement, positive outlook, and good behavior. However, while hope of release was mostly spoken of in positive terms, its downsides were the uncertainty of not knowing if their release would ever come, not knowing how they could improve their chances of release, and feelings of frustration and disappointment when their commutation applications were rejected. The men found the indeterminacy of the LWOP sentence to be one of the most painful aspects of imprisonment. The recent suicide of Victor Hassine, a Pennsylvania LWOP inmate, is instructive. After serving nearly thirty years, Hassine hanged himself shortly after his most recent request for a commutation hearing was denied (Hassine 2011, xii).[6]

Henry described the mental toll associated with rejection: "When they deny you, it does something to you, especially when you put a hundred percent effort into trying to better yourself." The mental toll mounted with each denial, he added: "I still have hope but, you know, it takes something out of you every time going down there and getting denied." A few men claimed that their acceptance of the fact that they would never be released from prison had led to feelings of contentment and peace. Joshua remarked: "I'm still at ease with my sentence. I've accepted it. I know I'd accepted it when you were here last time, five years ago. I've kind of adjusted as best as I can to the situation." Matthew agreed. He stated: "I'm happy. I'm at peace with myself."

For most LWOP inmates, release is akin to a desert mirage. The glimmer of release at the edge of the horizon looks real enough that the inmate thinks it could be within his grasp. The encouragement of prison staff and family and the rare instances of the commutation of a LWOP inmate provide just enough motivation to spur the LWOP inmate on as he presses through the desert of life imprisonment. However, for most, after walking in the desert for many years, they were ultimately no closer to release than they were at the start. This begs an important question: Given the low likelihood of it actually occurring, should a LWOP inmate's hope of release be encouraged, tolerated, or squashed?

The men felt that prison administration benefited from the sizeable number of life-sentenced inmates who had hope of release and consequently the prison staff actively cultivated it. Troy explained the prison staff's motivation: "The institution don't like you to think [about dying]. If you got a man that he's thinking he's going to die [in prison], what hope does he have? So what's the chance of him having respect for other people? So they don't really want you sitting, you know, around focusing on that. [They say things like] 'Oh, you shouldn't think like that, you can go up to the [pardons board].'" Walter expressed a similar view and, using the metaphor of fishing, claimed that the pardons board and governor exploited hope of release as a worm to lure them into good behavior. He explained the thought process of a life-sentenced inmate: "They got that hope, you know, they got that fishing rod from the governor's office. . . . They keep throwing that worm out, throwing that fishing hook. And you keep saying, okay, okay, I'll be good. . . . You're going to get tired of it. I am." In fact, Walter had grown frustrated, as he perceived himself to be a deserving candidate for release and yet was denied. In the mid-1990s, after multiple denials from the pardons board, he escaped. He explained: "I went to the pardon board for the sixth time and then they told me to serve the rest of my life with no further consideration. I was a model prisoner . . . and I said, 'That's it.' . . . I had twenty years [in] . . . I was hurt at the time when I was told to serve the rest of my life. . . . I said, 'The hell with it all. I'm going.'" Daniel agreed that there would be an increase in disciplinary problems if LWOP inmates lost their hope of release. Speaking about how his own behavior would change, he claimed: "If I thought that [there was no hope], I would be raising holy hell."

Troy provided the following example to illustrate the prison's response to inmate pessimism about release. He stated, "[Some years ago], I put in for a living will. They sent me to see mental health." According to Troy, the prison made it too difficult for him to pursue a living will so he abandoned the project, though he claimed to understand the prison's position: "I'm in a building where about seventy-five of the guys are doing time where they may not get out of here. Well, can you imagine if those seventy, seventy-five people started losing hope?" While this incident occurred some time ago, according to Troy, the prison continued to be reluctant to acknowledge the chances of an inmate dying in prison. He remarked: "The administration won't even allow [us] to put [an inmate's death] in the inmate paper. So, it's like, you know, the elephant that's in the room that nobody talks about. That's their attitude around here." No memorial or funeral services were offered at the prison when inmates died. Troy felt that the lack of remembrance had the effect of erasing the inmate from the collective history of the prison. He remarked: "[Older inmates] pass away, and they don't even discuss it. It's like tomorrow, it's like you wasn't even here."

CONCLUSION

Consistent with previous research, the men described their mental health in positive terms and felt that their mental health had improved over the course of incarceration. On the other hand, the men reported their physical health had worsened. The men suffered from many of the chronic health conditions common to the older population in general (e.g., hypertension and high cholesterol). However, despite the decline in their physical health, most of the men believed that prison had shielded them from the aging processes as they claimed to feel younger than their chronological ages. Though they believed that prison had preserved them, they knew that time had passed. They were aware, for example, of changes in their or their relatives' physical appearance.

Fear of dying, either in prison or in general, was not widely reported. Religious beliefs and the inevitability of dying were the two most common reasons for the lack of fear. While suicidal ideation was reported by only one individual, a small portion of the group thought of death as an escape. These men tended to be those with little or no hope of release. However, they were in the minority, as most men remained steadfast in their hope that they would be released from prison one day, despite the lack of success in their appeals and extant commutation applications. While most claimed that they would continue to apply for commutation, the men were frustrated with the process, chiefly because they felt that the positive improvements they had made while incarcerated and their low level of dangerousness did not receive as much consideration in the release decision as the severity of the crime they had committed. The men maintained that they had undergone profound changes over the period of incarceration and wanted to be judged for who they were now—not for the single episode of lethal violence they had committed decades earlier.

CHAPTER 6

Forgotten No More

THERE ARE NOW MORE people permanently incarcerated in the United States than ever before. Unless dramatic changes take place, the number of LWOP inmates will only continue to increase. Within the population, there is a sizeable number who continue to age in place. Despite the severity of life without parole and the number of LWOP inmates, there has been little research focused on the experience of aging LWOP inmates. The purpose of this book was to give voice to the long-serving permanently incarcerated. While the number of men interviewed was small, and as a result the applicability of these findings to the entire aging LWOP population in the United States is unknown, this project contributes to an emerging record of the experiences of the permanently incarcerated. If the men's narratives could be reduced to a single observation, it would be that this group of men displayed remarkable resiliency in their abilities to adapt to the deprivations of life without parole. Most inmates had adjusted to the limited contact they had with their loved ones. They chose to find meaning and purpose in their lives and to help others. Largely in the absence of structured recreational activities, they developed routines to fill their days. They employed preventive measures to maintain their physical and mental health. They were hopeful of release. Overall, this research speaks to the profound capacity for individuals not only to exist but to live in a sparse environment for an extended period of time.

POLICY RECOMMENDATIONS

Below are policy recommendations related to the current utilization of life without parole and the treatment of the permanently incarcerated. The first three are related to the release of LWOP inmates. I argue that true life without parole should be replaced with a modified sentence of life with the possibility of parole (LWP) in which inmates would be eligible for release after serving a specified number of years. A modified version of life with the possibility of parole would do as well or better than true life without parole in meeting the purposes of punishment. The remaining policy recommendations focus on the treatment of older LWOP inmates during incarceration. Nathan, who had been incarcerated for thirty-four years for his involvement in a burglary that resulted in the death of a homeowner, argued: "Even if they're going to spend the rest of their life here, they need a chance of, you know, a halfway decent quality of life." The policy recommendations proposed in this section are designed to ensure that the needs of older LWOP inmates are considered and that they are treated with dignity for the duration of their lives. If humanitarian reasons are not enough, the avoidance of litigation is one incentive for DOCs to implement institutional policy for older long-term inmates. Specific areas in which litigation could be pursued include age-based discrimination in prison programming, noncompliance with the Americans with Disabilities Act, inadequate medical treatment, or failure to protect older LWOP inmates from victimization (Goetting 1985, 19; Kerbs 2000, 222; Kerbs and Jolley 2009, 132). It would seem that the cost of implementing programs for older inmates would be cheaper than the potential costs of litigation.

Policy Recommendation One:
Implement Modified Life With the Possibility of Parole Sentences

The most far-reaching policy implication is a reexamination of current LWOP statutes at both the state and federal levels. Jurisdictions should abolish true LWOP sentences, in which parole ineligibility exists for the duration of the sentence, to modified LWP terms, in which an inmate would become eligible for parole after serving a set number of years. Ten states use or have used this type of sentence with the mandated period of parole ineligibility ranging from twenty-five to forty years (DPIC 2013c; Wright 1990, 546).

A modified LWP sentence would meet many of the criteria used to justify the necessity of a true LWOP sentence. Because of the specified parole ineligibility for a lengthy period of time, modified life with the possibility of parole ensures a harsh punishment and prevents the release of an inmate prior to serving an appropriate amount of time. According to Julian H. Wright, Jr. (1990, 563–564), Kentucky's modified LWP term of twenty-five years parole ineligibility was implemented to incapacitate violent offenders during their most crime prone years but then to provide mechanisms for release when they no longer posed a threat to public safety. As the proposed modification only offers review by the parole board and not a guarantee of release, it would also prevent the release of LWOP inmates who remain dangerous. In supporting the abolition of true LWOP sentences, the men featured in this book agreed that they deserved lengthy prison sentences because they took another's life. As an example, Matthew, who had been incarcerated for twenty-seven years for the murder of his wife, stated: "I know that I deserved it, to be punished for what I did. It was wrong." However, the men also felt that release should be a realistic possibility for those among them who had changed. Joshua, who entered the prison at thirty and was now sixty-four years of age, argued that modified life with the possibility of parole was a better sentence than true life without parole for it considers the seriousness of the crime committed but also the potential for offenders to change: "I ain't saying you got to give them a little sentence. I ain't saying that. I'm saying give them twenty-five years to life. After twenty-five years, you come up for parole. No guarantee of getting out. If you don't change, you don't get out."

While ensuring a harsh punishment, modified life with the possibility of parole would overcome many of the criticisms of a true LWOP sentence (see Chapter 1, Life without Parole: Support and Opposition). It is more humane than either capital punishment or permanent incarceration for it provides deserving LWOP inmates with the opportunity to return to society. The uncertainty of release is one of the greatest pains of permanent imprisonment. Joshua reflected on the ambiguity of a LWOP sentence and argued that the death penalty and life with the possibility of parole should be the two most severe penalties in the mid-Atlantic state because "either the crime is horrendous enough that the jury decides to put you to death or [it should] give you a sentence that you can turn around from." Law professor Robert Blecker offers a similar perspective (Liptak 2005, para. 15): "Life without parole is a very strange sentence when you think about it. . . . The punishment seems either too much or too little. If a sadistic or extraordinarily cold, callous killer deserves to die, then why not kill him? But if we are going to keep the killer alive when we could otherwise execute him, why strip him of all hope?"

While acknowledging the gravity of the crime committed, modified life with the possibility of parole also recognizes the personal transformations that LWOP inmates have undergone while incarcerated. The men were asking for a realistic chance at release. Noah, who had been incarcerated for almost thirty years, pleaded: "Give me somewhat of a chance. Give me just that much of a chance [indicates a small amount]." As release decisions would be made on a case-by-case basis, life with the possibility of parole allows for greater individual attention to the men's records, which is of importance to them:

> You should treat everybody's case different, you know, don't classify us all as the same thing. (John)

> It's a lot of bad people in here but it's a lot of good people in here too. . . . Don't judge everybody by just one or two people. (Daniel)

Finally, as life without parole was touted as being more cost-effective than capital punishment, modified life with the possibility of parole would be even cheaper than life without parole. Researchers at The Sentencing Project calculated that the total cost of incarcerating a life-sentenced inmate from ages thirty to sixty was approximately $600,000 per inmate. As the inmate continues to age and requires greater medical treatment, the ten-year period from age sixty to age seventy was estimated to cost an additional $400,000 (Mauer et al. 2004, 25). Using these figures, state and federal governments would save almost half a million dollars per LWOP inmate if he or she was released after thirty years instead of remaining incarcerated for the duration of his or her life.

Furthermore, the current implementation of life without parole is incompatible with aspects of all of the punishment philosophies, including retribution. The widespread heterogeneity that currently exists in LWOP-eligible offenses and offenders is inconsistent with retribution. This punishment philosophy mandates that the punishment should be equal to the harm caused by the crime. At present, life without parole is not reserved to punish "the worst of the worst"; only about two-thirds of LWOP inmates in the United States were convicted of murder. The rest were convicted of other serious, but non-lethal, violent offenses (27.8 percent), property offenses (4.0 percent), and drug offenses (2.0 percent) (Nellis 2013, 7). In addition, those subject to permanent incarceration also include habitual offenders who have not committed murder (e.g., Anthony, Troy, and Samuel) or even a violent offense (e.g., Francis). And under the felony-murder rule, as a result of the offenders' involvement in a precipitating offense, such as burglary or robbery, offenders are liable for homicide even when they play no role in the actual killing (e.g., Nathan). In his comprehensive analysis of how the current utilization of life without parole violates retribution's key tenet of proportionality, Paul Robinson (2012, 146) argued that while the final offense committed by a habitual offender or the underlying offense in a felony-murder "might well be serious, it is not as serious as a planned intentional killing, and to treat the two cases the same is to trivialize the greater blameworthiness of the more serious offense."

Even if it is limited to murder, life without parole is an overutilized and disproportionate sentence. The men asserted that some offenders should spend the rest of their lives incarcerated. Henry, who had been incarcerated for over three decades, offered examples of murderers who were deserving of permanent incarceration, for example, serial killers or "someone who assassinated the president." However, most men did not think that the crimes they committed were severe enough to warrant permanent incarceration. Of the men who had been convicted of murder, most believed that a lower degree of murder more accurately reflected their level of intent than first-degree. Given that the offenses were not well planned and were committed in a highly emotional state, the men felt that second-degree murder and a punishment of fifteen years to life with the possibility of parole more accurately reflected their culpability.

Retribution also seeks to ensure that all offenders who commit the same crime and have the same culpability should receive the same sentence (Cullen and Jonson 2012, 39–40). However, the men felt that life without parole was not uniformly imposed. Henry remarked that "there's no consistency here in [mid-Atlantic state]." In reference to defendants convicted of murder who receive a lesser sentence, he asked: "What makes them different than me?" Moreover, a retributivist would be alarmed by the fact that much empirical evidence exists to suggest that race is taken into consideration when making punishment decisions, including the imposition of the death penalty (Kanshal 2005; Walker et al. 2012). While no studies could be identified that specifically examine how race affects the imposition of life without parole, a preliminary examination shows that national figures are disconcerting. Blacks comprise about 12 percent of the nation's population, yet they represent 58 percent of the national LWOP population, and in seven states (i.e., Alabama, Georgia, Illinois, Louisiana, Michigan, Mississippi, and South Carolina), the proportion is greater than two-thirds (Nellis 2013, 10).

As released life-sentenced inmates pose little threat to the public, the only reason the men remain in prison is because of the horrible crimes that they committed. Anthony, a habitual offender who died in prison, claimed: "It's just a revenge atmosphere. . . . We took a life, so they took our life." The crimes that some of the men committed were heinous and they should receive harsh punishments for those crimes. Incarceration for thirty or forty years should satisfy the retributive mandate of proportionality. As pointed out by the men, they have missed out on much in their lives. Nathan argued that incarceration "does what it's made to do . . . you can't be happy in a place like this." They have been punished severely, and as Francis, the rare exception of a LWOP inmate being released from prison, contended: "There's some point in time where people should have received their pound of flesh."

While it is necessary for LWOP inmates to receive a punishment that is commensurate with the severity of the crime, a retributive philosophy punishes people for the crimes they have committed and is not interested in preventing crime in the future (Cullen and Jonson 2012, 48–49). Punishment should have a utilitarian purpose; it should have a wider-reaching effect beyond a particular case. It should be imposed because it has some benefit to society. Joshua explained that while a retributivist approach to punishment ensures that the offender will be punished, society remains unchanged:

> There's fair retribution that society requires, right, and it doesn't matter up to that point, whatever that point is set by society, if you don't reach that point, then, you know, you're not getting out of jail, that's all there is to it. And I guess, you know, I guess it's fair, but I think giving guys sentences with life without parole really doesn't serve a purpose other than it lets him know that he's never getting out, let's society know that he's never getting out, but society's the same. It's not changed none. People are [still] killing each other over nothing.

As the overutilization cannot be justified on retributive grounds, the widespread use of true life without parole is not supported by the utilitarian philosophies of rehabilitation, deterrence, or incapacitation. While life without parole "forswears altogether the rehabilitative ideal" (*Graham v. Florida* 2010, 2030), rehabilitation can happen among LWOP inmates nonetheless. Based on their behavior in prison, the men featured in this book—and other life-sentenced inmates—show evidence of rehabilitation (Irwin 2009). They seldom received disciplinary write-ups, had earned degrees, participated in programs, and helped those around them. Robert, who had spent half his life incarcerated, believed that he was proof that LWOP inmates were capable of change: "They say that some people can't change or you might have society feel that a person can't change. You might have judges, maybe juries, prosecutors that might think that you can't change . . . but the fact is I'm [a] living witness that a person can change." Focusing solely on the crime committed fails to recognize the positive changes and self-growth that many LWOP inmates have made. Victor, who had served more than twenty-five years for the murder of an acquaintance, questioned why a LWOP sentence could not be amended when the men had changed: "I understand my sentence, don't get me wrong, but things change, people change, lives change, [and] events. Why not the law?"

The pervasive use of true life without parole cannot be justified on the grounds of deterrence. Even advocates of the sanction concede that achieving a general deterrent effect through life without parole is limited. For example, Danya Blair (1994, 202), a proponent of permanent incarceration, conceded: "There is little evidence that the punishments imposed on convicted offenders have any impact on the behavior of potential offenders." Deterrence presumes that offenders behave in a rational manner (Cullen and Jonson, 2012, 67), yet substance use and stress can impair a person's ability to reason. One-third of the men (and over one-half of LWOP inmates in a national sample, see Appendix B The National Picture of Older LWOP Inmates) were under the influence of alcohol, drugs, or both at the time of their offense, and more than one-fourth of the cases were classified as homicides precipitated by emotional stress (Irwin 2009, 44). As further illustration of the limitations of deterrence, the men underestimated the likelihood of getting caught and of receiving a LWOP sentence. All in all, there is no reason to believe that true life without parole would exert a greater deterrent effect than modified life with the possibility of parole.

Another reason to punish is to protect society by incapacitating dangerous offenders (Cullen and Jonson 2012, 110). George and Joshua both commented on the public's affinity for incapacitation. George, one of the oldest and longest-serving men, observed: "The only thing they seem to be interested in here is containment." In a similar vein, Joshua remarked: "I think all that they [the public] would want to know is that they're safe and sound. They're there safe and sound and we're here." However, the vast majority of released LWOP and life-sentenced inmates are law-abiding, which indicates that continued incapacitation of LWOP inmates en masse is unnecessary.

The recidivism of released murderers has been examined in five states: Texas, Massachusetts, California, Pennsylvania, and Ohio. Of the 109 murderers released in Texas, including some who were *Furman*-commuted death-sentenced inmates (n=21) and others who were sentenced to life (n=88), only two committed new violent offenses after they were released, and only one committed another murder (Marquart and Sorensen 1988, 688). Overall, upon release, less than 2 percent committed another violent offense, and less than 1 percent committed another murder. Commuted murderers in Massachusetts and California had similarly low levels of recidivism. In Massachusetts, between 1972 and 2008, none of the approximate forty commuted and released LWOP inmates committed a new offense; only two were returned to prison for violating parole conditions (Black 1990, 68; Haas and Fillion 2010, 17). In California, of the 850 individuals who received life sentences following convictions for murder and who were paroled, less than 1 percent have returned to jail or prison for a new offense (Weisberg et al. 2011, 17). And none had committed a crime in which the prescribed sentence was life imprisonment. In its analysis of the recidivism of long-term inmates in Pennsylvania and neighboring Ohio, the Pennsylvania General Assembly concluded (2005, 4): "Little recidivism data is available regarding inmates who were incarcerated for at least twenty-five years and released at the age of fifty or older. Ohio provided data showing that, of twenty-one offenders in that category who were released in 2000, none had committed a new crime during the following three years. The Pennsylvania Board of Probation and Parole provided data showing that, since the inception of parole in the Commonwealth, ninety-nine commuted lifers have been released on parole at the age of fifty years or older, one of whom was recommitted to prison for a new crime."[1]

National data highlight the interaction of age and offense on recidivism. Older inmates, those above the age of forty-five, were less likely than all other age groups to be rearrested, reconvicted, or re-incarcerated in a three-year period following release (Langan and Levin 2002, 7). In addition, inmates who were incarcerated for homicide were less likely to recidivate than inmates who were incarcerated for other violent offenses, property offenses, drug offenses, and public-order offenses (Langan and Levin 2002, 8). Analyzing both these factors together is illuminating. Of male inmates who were incarcerated for homicide, served more than four years, and were thirty years of age or younger at the age of release, about 13 percent were reconvicted and received a new prison sentence in the three-year period of study (as compared to 25.0 percent when all offenses were included). Keeping gender and time served the same, about 7 percent of inmates who were between the ages of thirty-one and forty and were incarcerated for homicide were returned to prison (versus 24.2 percent for all offenses). Less than 1 percent of inmates who were incarcerated for homicide and who were at least forty-one years of age or older when they were released were returned to prison (as compared to 8.0 percent when all offenses are included) (Bureau of Justice Statistics 2013).

The behavior of Walter and Francis while they were in free society provides additional evidence into how older LWOP inmates behave upon release. Walter escaped and lived on the outside for five years prior to his recapture. During that time period, he was not arrested for any serious offenses. Francis had his sentence commuted and returned to society. Since his release in early 2011, he also has had a record of good behavior. Michael, sixty-three years of age in 2006, vowed that he, too, would abide by all parole conditions and follow even the most minor of laws if released: "I wouldn't spit on a sidewalk. If they said be in the house at nine o'clock, that's where [I'd] be."

In sum, the bulk of empirical and anecdotal evidence suggests that, while isolated exceptions exist, the vast majority of older LWOP inmates would not present any harm to society if released. While it may be necessary to incarcerate violent offenders during their crime-prone years, continued incapacitation does not seem warranted. The fact that the reason for punishment can change over time, and that punishment may no longer be necessary after a certain point, was precisely the reason why the European Court of Human Rights determined that the review of LWOP cases was necessary:

> It is axiomatic that a prisoner cannot be detained unless there are legitimate penological grounds for that detention. . . . These grounds will include punishment, deterrence, public protection and rehabilitation. Many of these grounds will be present at the time when a life sentence is imposed. However, the balance between these justifications for detention is not necessarily static and may shift in the course of the sentence. What may be the primary justification for detention at the start of the sentence may not be so after a lengthy period into the service of the sentence. It is only by carrying out a review of the justification for continued detention at an appropriate point in the sentence that these factors or shifts can be properly evaluated. (*Vinter and Others v. The United Kingdom* 2013, 39–40)

Therefore, based on the principle of alternative-means-proportionality that suggests that "if a less severe punishment will achieve essentially the same benefits, the more severe penalty is excessive" (Frase 2010, 55), a modified LWP sentence is a better option than true life without parole. It would be as least as successful—if not more so—in meeting the purpose of punishment through the utilitarian perspectives of rehabilitation, deterrence, and incapacitation. At the same time, a modified LWP sentence would meet the retributive need of proportionality between the offense and the punishment, and it would prevent the permanent incarceration of individuals who unfairly received a LWOP sentence.

A Reality Check

The replacement of true life without parole with modified life with parole is no simple feat. As the men acknowledged, a constellation of elements would need to align for meaningful sentencing reform to occur. Legislatures and executive officers may fear political reprisal for appearing "soft on crime" if they supported modified life with the possibility of parole. Even if laws were changed, a realistic chance at release could elude LWOP inmates. In the current national climate, many LWP inmates remain incarcerated. For example, a study of parole-granting practices for California LWP inmates found that the chances of the Board of Parole Hearings granting parole have fluctuated widely over the last thirty years from virtually zero to 20 percent, with a current likelihood of about 18 percent. However, in murder cases, the governor has the power to reverse the decision of the board. For those inmates convicted of murder (as two-thirds of those serving life without parole nationally were), the likelihood of being granted parole by the board and the likelihood that the governor would approve the decision is much lower, about 6 percent (Weisberg et al. 2011, 4). Thus, a drawback to the proposed modified LWP legislation would be that it could have a displacement effect only and not lead to the increased release of LWOP inmates. In other words, the number of LWP inmates would balloon, yet the hope of release would remain hollow.

Finally, modified life with the possibility of parole requires faith in offenders that they are capable of change and that criminal justice officials can accurately discern which LWOP inmates are safe to release and which should remain incarcerated (Barkow 2012, 200). While assessments such as the Level of Service Inventory–Revised (LSI-R) have been found to increase the accuracy of predicting recidivism (Girard and Wormith 2004, 172), whenever predictions are made to determine future behavior there is the potential for error (Cullen and Jonson 2012, 114). Two such types of error predictions are false negatives (i.e., erroneously predicting that a

LWOP inmate is no longer a risk to society but then he or she recidivates upon release) and false positives (i.e., erroneously predicting that a LWOP inmate continues to pose a danger to society and subsequently he or she remains incarcerated). The recidivism data examined above indicate that most released life-sentenced inmates were false positives (as the men of this book claim to be). However, despite the small numbers, there were also false negatives, and released life-sentenced inmates committed additional offenses, some of which were violent. Given the choice between the two, Rachel E. Barkow (2012, 202) argues that the public would prefer erring on the side of caution and committing greater false positive errors in order to prevent false negative errors. Because of the political fallout, pardon boards and governors also have a vested interest in ensuring that release errors are minimized; consequently, they may opt to sacrifice the many false positives to prevent the recidivism of the few false negatives.

A recalibration of the punishment continuum is also necessary before modified life with the possibility of parole could be widely accepted as the nation's harshest prison sentence. Alongside its embrace of the principles of justice and fairness, the United States maintains a punitive punishment ideology (see Simon 2012a, 282). To Americans, a modified LWP sentence of twenty-five years of parole ineligibility may not seem harsh enough to punish serious offenders. Some evidence indicates that public support is greater for a modified LWP sentence such as twenty-five years of parole ineligibility accompanied with a provision of restitution rather than a true LWOP sentence (Bowers et al. 1994, 90; Lake Research Partners 2010 as cited in DPIC 2013e, 4). Other evidence suggests that the public is not supportive of the release of violent offenders (Angus Reid Public Opinion 2012, 1). However, a modified LWP sentence is the most serious sentence available in thirty-two European countries (*Vinter and Others v. The United Kingdom* 2013, 25). Unlike the United States, these nations do not have the death penalty, and the possibility for review and release must be present in LWOP sentences, per the recent decision of the European Court of Human Rights in *Vinter and Others v. The United Kingdom* (2013).

Given recent developments, perhaps there is reason to be optimistic. While there was a 22 percent increase in the number of LWOP inmates nationally from 2008 to 2012, the federal system and two states (Arkansas and Connecticut) experienced declines in their LWOP populations. Over the same period, Rhode Island and New Mexico had no growth in their populations. Four states (Iowa, Maine, Montana, and North Carolina) experienced increases of less than 5 percent (Nellis 2013, 6; Nellis and King 2009, 7–8). In addition to the lack of growth or slow growth in the LWOP population, sentencing reforms related to life-sentenced inmates have been implemented in the legislative, executive, and judicial arenas. In 2012, although they rejected the abolition of the death penalty, California voters amended the state's three strikes legislation to require that the third strike, which carries a mandatory sentence of twenty-five years to life, must be a serious or violent offense (Lagos and Huet 2012, para. 1). Approximately twenty-eight hundred California inmates are eligible to petition the courts for resentencing (Lagos and Huet 2012, para. 4). During her time in office from 2002 to 2010, Michigan governor Jennifer Granholm granted commutation to approximately fifty life-sentenced inmates, including thirty-five incarcerated for murder, many of whom were in advanced age and in poor health (Gill 2010, 23). Other states—for example, Pennsylvania and Wisconsin—have eased the restrictions placed on commutation, though the number of LWOP inmates who receive executive clemency remains low (Nellis 2013, 19).

Finally, the US Supreme Court has considered the constitutionality of life without parole for juvenile offenders. Its decision in *Graham,* which established homicide as the only offense for which a juvenile can receive a LWOP sentence, marked the first time that the Court had determined that a non-capital sentence was unconstitutional since *Solem v. Helm* (1983) (Barkow 2010, 49). *Miller v. Alabama* (2012) and *Jackson v. Hobbs* (2012) imposed an additional restriction on the use of life without parole to punish juvenile offenders prohibiting the mandatory imposition of the sentence. While some scholars are doubtful that the Court would impose similar limitations for adult LWOP inmates anytime soon (Barkow 2010, 51; O'Hear 2010, 1–2; Simon 2012a, 305), others are optimistic that the arguments made to restrict juvenile life without parole (e.g., capacity for change) would also be applicable to adults (Nellis 2013, 18).

Policy Recommendation Two:
Mandatory Lifetime Parole for Released Life-Sentenced Inmates

While those life-sentenced who have been released have demonstrated that they pose little risk to public safety, the release of LWOP inmates may garner more support if they were to be placed on parole for the duration of their lives. This would allow the criminal justice system to have greater oversight over this population, and if parole conditions were violated this would be a mechanism by which LWOP inmates could be returned to prison. Permanent parole is standard practice in England for released life-sentenced inmates (Ministry of Justice 2012, sect. 11), and in the United States others have also recommended lifetime parole (Haas and Fillion 2010, 3). Michael supported permanent parole for released LWOP inmates and recommended a gradual reduction in restrictions if the parolee was abiding by the agreement. He explained:

[A LWOP inmate] might be a person you would keep on a parole status indefinitely and conditions of it may change, you know. You may report maybe once a week, you know, every week . . . and then when things are going good, you have a certain amount of time [in] and then cut [reporting] down to once a month or twice a month and then over a period of time, you know, maybe up to six months or something. I believe that . . . the conditions [would be] laid down [and] that you would follow that up to the letter. You would not deviate from them; if you did, you would be putting yourself back in. In other words, the option to pull you right back in [would exist] because you violated conditions.

While permanent parole would impose a greater burden on the parole system, which is already severely overtaxed, imprisonment is ten times as expensive as parole (Petersilia 2001, 364), and the ratio would be even higher for aging offenders given the increased costs of incarceration. Furthermore, as extant evidence suggests that released life-sentenced inmates are not a difficult population to manage, the permanent parole of this group should not create an extraneous workload for parole agencies.

Policy Recommendation Three:
Inclusion of LWOP Inmates in Early Release Programs

Because of the low probability of recidivism, LWOP inmates should be considered for early release programs, such as Project for Older Prisoners (POPS) and medical parole. Perhaps the best known early release program, POPS was established by George Washington University Law professor Jonathan Turley and provides early release for inmates who are fifty-five years of age or older, who have served the average sentence for their crime, and who are unlikely to recidivate. To ensure that released inmates will not re-offend, POPS employs a rigorous screening process for potential applicants and, once they are released, assists older inmates with securing employment, housing, and access to government benefits (Turley 2007, sect. 3–4). Since 1989 POPS has facilitated the release of almost four hundred older inmates; none of whom has recidivated (Strupp 2010, 2).

Another early release mechanism is medical parole. Most states and the federal government allow for the medical parole of terminally ill inmates whose conditions are not expected to improve and whose prognosis is less than six months to live (Aday 2003, 210). These released inmates would spend the remainder of their lives either at home or in non-correctional medical facilities (e.g., hospitals or hospices) (Dubler 1998, 154). Medical parole is subject to revocation, for example, if an inmate's health improves to the point where he or she can be treated in prison or if the inmate endangers public safety (Anderson and Hilliard 2005, 61).

Despite their numerous benefits, including the humane treatment of offenders and the cost savings to the DOC (Anderson and Hilliard 2005, 61), the overall impact of early release programs on the nation's prison population is limited. Only five states have POPS chapters (Strupp 2010, 2), and medical parole is infrequently granted (Anno et al. 2004, 80–81; Human Rights Watch 2012, 2). Older LWOP inmates are not commonly eligible for either program because of their crime of conviction (Anno et al. 2004, 41; Turley 2007, sect. 4). However, similar to the argument advanced above in regard to the adoption of modified life with the possibility of parole, the threat to public safety should guide the criminal justice response to aging and dying inmates. The crime committed should not be the sole criterion used when assessing whether an inmate poses a risk to society in the present. Instead, an inmate's recent history should factor into release decisions.

Policy Recommendation Four: Reentry Services to Prevent Recidivism

It would be unwise to begin the release of older inmates who have been incarcerated for several decades without support services in place to assist them in their reintegration. The perfect zero percent recidivism of POPS participants reflects not only the meticulous screening of candidates selected for release but also the necessity of assisting former inmates as they transition back into society. The men agreed that reentry services are essential in order to ensure a smooth reintegration for released older LWOP inmates. To be sure, they would face considerable obstacles as they transitioned back into society. In their interviews with eighty older male inmates in England, Crawley and Sparks (2006, 73–74) found that worries commonly associated with reintegration included release logistics, access to medical care, assistance with daily activities, and reunification with family.

Six men acknowledged the difficulties they would encounter should they ever be released; two particular concerns were first the bleak job prospects and subsequent inability to support themselves and then the lack of familiarity with new technology. Returning ex-offenders of all ages report difficulty in finding employment that offers a living wage because of the lack of job skills, a stable work history, and a criminal record (Bahr et al. 2010, 682; Seiter and Kadela 2003, 367). However, employment prospects may be especially dim for older inmates, as argued by Stan Stojkovic (2007, 112): "For most elderly prisoners, prison was not a time in which skill development occurred. Many have limited or no skills that could translate into successful employment subsequent to release from prison. Most have never worked a steady job in their entire lives. They are a population that has been the least tractable and when finally released from prison, they have, again, limited skills to make themselves marketable upon release."

Because of poor health, older ex-prisoners may be unable to perform labor intensive work, which because of their lack of education (Williams et al. 2010, 1040), could be all that is available to them. Furthermore, as length of time served is negatively associated with employment after release (Western et al. 2001, 418), returning older LWOP inmates face additional challenges, as acknowledged by the men. When thinking about release, Troy, a habitual offender who had been incarcerated for thirty-four years, reported: "I start to think about how hard is for a fifty-year-old man to get a job with a criminal record." While some men would be able to rely on government benefits (e.g., Social Security and veterans' benefits), most would not have pensions or retirement savings to depend on if they were unable to find employment. The following statement from Matthew, who did not expect to be released from prison, reflected this concern: "[I'm] just fearful thinking about getting out and starting all over again with my health and all of that. I mean how would I support myself?" Joshua spoke of the challenges that would exist if he were released: "I'm so restricted [because of my physical health]. I mean I think about things like no Social Security because you haven't worked nowhere. Ain't going to be able to retire from no place, you know. I would be able to get Social Security, but right now it would only be about $140 a month. That don't cut it. I guess that's okay if you're halfway healthy and can get a decent some kind of a job, you'd be alright."

Much has changed in the decades that the men have been incarcerated. If they were released from prison, they would encounter a world that looked very different from the one they had left. None of the men had ever used a cell phone, and most had never used a computer. During our interviews, several men marveled at the increasingly smaller size of recorders and that they no longer needed tapes. Charles, Daniel, and Troy reported that the technological advancements were intimidating. Troy remarked: "I think the only thing I'm concerned about is getting out of here and dealing with technology . . . but I'm excited too." Daniel, who entered prison at the age of twenty-six and had served thirty-one years, echoed this concern as he stated: "It's hard to know what to expect. So many things have changed . . . all the technology." Charles, who had been incarcerated for over thirty years for a crime he claimed he committed in self-defense, felt that older inmates who had been incarcerated for a substantial period of time would need support to help them function in contemporary society: "[They] can't drive, can't use computers. They're stuck in time, man, they can't move. They are uncomfortable being in 2006, so if they went in [to prison in the] 1960s and it's now 2006, they can't live with that. If you let them out now, you'll have to go teach them how to function."

Considering the many challenges to successful reentry, Joshua, Henry, and Thomas advocated for halfway houses specifically designed for older inmates.

They believed that released older inmates would have smoother adjustments if they gradually earned their freedom. The men endorsed the use of halfway houses as an interim step between incarceration and full release. Henry explained why gradual release would be a better approach than straight release: "To make a change from being locked up for thirty-four years to being released on the streets, I'm not giving myself a chance at all. . . . I have no shot, but if you put me in some sort of center or program and let me phase out, [I would do better]." Thomas, who was incarcerated for two decades for the murder of his wife, shared his idea for a halfway house that would take into consideration the varying employment skills and health statuses of older offenders: "They could rent a little apartment . . . and the ones that are able to work, they could go out and work every day . . . and pay the bills, and the ones that are really unable to go out and perform duties on the job, could stay there and clean the house and do the cooking."

For a few men, they felt that it was preferable for them to remain in prison. Alan, who was approaching seventy years of age, admitted that he was "not quite ready" to have to support himself and pay for his living expenses, which he listed as "gas, food, and rent." Matthew would rather remain in prison than be transferred to a nursing home. He explained: "If they keep me here until I'm disabled, I'm unable to take care of myself. I won't even want to leave. Why should I? I'd rather be in here than be in a nursing home." As employment opportunities would be dim, it would be difficult for the men to be able to secure independent housing; as such, they would be forced to live with family members. However, because of the length of separation, the nature of the crime committed, the relatives' advanced age or poor health, family members may be unwilling or unable to take in an elderly ex-prisoner. Joshua and Matthew were reluctant to be released because they were fearful of being a burden on their families. Joshua explained that there were few desirable housing options available to him if he were to be released: "You [could] go with family, [but] I'd really rather not do that if I don't have to. . . . If I thought if I'd just get out of here and be a burden on them, I probably wouldn't go. I really wouldn't. Might go under that bridge and join the hobos . . . and live happily ever after under there."

As a result of the challenges that older LWOP inmates would inevitably encounter, reentry services—for example, housing and life skills—would be essential. In addition, a reconsideration of parole conditions may be necessary. Maintaining employment is a common condition of parole; however, for the reasons outlined above, it would be particularly difficult for older ex-inmates to meet this condition. As a result, parole agencies could consider volunteering as a substitute for work. For example, upon release, Francis was unable to find a job; in lieu of a requirement to work, Francis is required to complete a certain number of community service hours each week.

PRISON AS PUNISHMENT NOT FOR PUNISHMENT

Policy Recommendation One: Age and Sentence Specific Programming

As indicated by the men, the separation from family is one of the greatest pains of permanent imprisonment.[2] Recent policy changes at Institution One pertaining to honor visits had further diminished the already low number of visits received by older LWOP inmates. Instead of implementing policies that decrease the communication between older LWOP inmates and their loved ones, efforts should be made to maintain or increase the strength of these relationships. Timothy J. Flanagan (1982a, 93) recommended several measures to strengthen the family ties of long-term inmates, which would also be effective for the permanently incarcerated: family counseling, the placement of long-term inmates in a facility within close geographical distance to their families, and extended visits that allow inmates and their visitors to interact in a private area for several days. Family counseling would be beneficial as it would be a forum in which inmates and their family members could discuss the offense committed by the inmate, his absence from the family, the likelihood of release, and his burial wishes. The assignment of older LWOP inmates to facilities that are closer to their families could also minimize the challenges associated with visits (e.g., missed work and travel costs). An extended visit program would be a major incentive for older LWOP inmates to continue to be well behaved—the men reported that they were deterred from engaging in institutional misconduct out of fear that they would lose special visitation privileges. In addition to these recommendations, Daniel offered two more means by which older LWOP inmates could maintain their attachments. As older LWOP inmates and their aging relatives continue to experience physical health issues and because of the challenges associated with traveling, Daniel recommended video chats (e.g., skyping) as a low-cost means of communication. His other recommendation was intended to foster greater connections between older inmates and their grandchildren as their relationships have been impaired by permanent separation. Daniel advocated for the implementation of a program in which inmates could record themselves reading books and send the recordings to their grandchildren.[3]

The physical health of older inmates must also be addressed. As can be seen with the men featured in this book, their physical health was in decline, and diseases and medical conditions were common. Policies should be implemented to improve or maintain the physical health of older LWOP inmates, such as age-specific recreation programming and health and wellness education. The men were in need of greater physical activity but were unable or unwilling to participate in sports or exercise programs with younger inmates. The lack of recreational activities geared toward older inmates in this mid-Atlantic state is consistent with national trends. For example, of forty-nine correctional systems surveyed, only approximately 31 percent of systems at the city, state, federal, and international levels reported that they had formal recreational programs specifically designed for the older inmate population (Anno et al. 2004, 65). The men expressed a desire to have senior competitive sports teams and separate gym times in order to increase their levels of physical activity. Recreational programs that would not require a great deal of physical exertion—including mini golf, bocci, shuffleboard, gardening, and horseshoes—would also provide opportunities for exercise (Bintz 1974, 89; Vito and Wilson 1985, 24; Welch 1987, 8; Wilson and Vito 1986, 415).

Preventive care education could also promote the physical and mental health of older LWOP inmates. Potential topics could include nutrition, exercise, weight management, smoking cessation, stress management, strengthening family ties, and death and dying (Florida Corrections Commission 1999, 24; Gallagher 1990, 263; Morton 1992, 18; Morton and Anderson 1982, 15). These programs could provide a forum for older inmates to interact with each other and share personal issues. For the prevention of health issues, vitamins and specialized diets such as low-sugar and low-sodium diets should be made available to improve the inmates' nutritional health (Kratcoski and Pownall 1989, 33; McCarthy 1983, 74; Morton and Anderson 1982, 15). Several men with restricted dietary needs reported that specialized diets were not offered to them, and consequently, they regulated their diets themselves. Given the lack of food options available to inmates, this approach may have limited success.

Closer monitoring of the health status of older inmates could help to increase the early identification and early treatment of health conditions. Other researchers have noted the benefits of providing regular physical and mental health assessments so that treatment of illnesses could begin sooner (McCarthy 1983, 74; Morton and Anderson 1982, 15; Smyer et al. 1997, 15). The men at Institution Two reported that doctors actively monitored the health status of older inmates. Joshua explained: "If you're fifty or older, they got like a chronic care list. . . . The doctor sees you like every ninety days. He does that for, you know, a good period of time, until he says well, you're in relative good health. Then he might [see you] every six months." However, none of the men at Institution One, where most older LWOP inmates were housed, reported a similar practice. Daniel, who was incarcerated at Institution One, recommended that older inmates be eligible for regular physicals that would be exempt from the four-dollar copay. These preventive health measures could lower the costs associated with treating the health needs of older inmates. It is more cost effective to prevent illnesses or to initiate early treatment procedures than it is to treat diseases when they have developed into advanced stages. As an example, Joann Morton (1992, 18) argued: "Early treatment of elevated blood pressure is far more efficient than maintaining the victim of a massive stroke."

Issues related to death and dying are extremely important to older LWOP inmates. If LWOP inmates are to die in prison, policies that provide some level of dignity to the process must be in place. Good food was a luxury for the men. Allowing special foods and beverages could provide a small comfort to dying inmates (Dubler 1998, 153). While not widely reported in the present group of older LWOP inmates, one fear of dying in prison mentioned was the fear of dying alone. Visitation policies should be relaxed so inmates can have loved ones close to them in their final moments. Special effort should be made to permit the opportunity for dying inmates to reconcile with estranged family members, which would decrease the chances of an inmate being buried by the state. If inmates are to be buried in state cemeteries, then arrangements should be made to permit outside contacts, other inmates, and prison staff members to remember the dead (Dubler 1998, 153). Burial procedures at Angola Prison provide an example of the dignity that prison funerals can have. Angola inmates play an active role in the funeral arrangements and burial procedures as inmates make the coffins and the hearse, maintain the cemetery, and are permitted to attend funeral services (Cain and Fontenot 2001, 122).

Policy Recommendation Two:
Allow Older LWOP Inmates a Voice in Housing Assignment Decisions

One of the key decisions that correctional administrators face is determining whether older inmates should be housed in the general population or segregated in special units or facilities. The debate over segregation is well documented in the corrections literature; however, despite this, special housing areas for senior inmates have not been widely implemented (Anno et al. 2004, 66–67). A compelling case can be made for segregation. Separate facilities would provide older inmates with housing units that are specifically geared to them, both in the design of the physical environment and in prison programming (Kerbs and Jolley 2009, 122–123). These facilities would include the resources, such as medical care, that this population requires (Kerbs and Jolley 2009, 122), and at the same time, it would make it easier to monitor the health of older inmates (Neeley et al. 1997, 121). Additionally, others have argued that segregating older inmates would reduce the stress of incarceration (Yates and Gillespie 2000, 172), increase the self-respect of older inmates, reduce loneliness, and protect older inmates from victimization and harassment by younger inmates. Furthermore, because the majority of older inmates are not considered to be security risks, their removal from higher security institutions would afford space for more dangerous inmates, which has the potential to reduce costs of confinement for the state (Adams 1995, 484; Aday 2003, 208, 209; Florida Corrections Commission 1999, 21; Flynn 1992, 87; E. Johnson 1988, 163; Kerbs and Jolley 2009, 126; Morton 1992, 11–12; Morton and Anderson 1982, 15; van Wormer 1981, 94; Yates and Gillespie 2000, 172).

Conversely, arguments for mainstreaming the older inmate population are also persuasive. Mainstreamed older inmates would have the same access to programs and work assignments as younger inmates (Adams 1995, 484; Falter 1999, 166–167; Johnson 1988, 163; Morton 1992, 11). Additionally, older inmates are regarded as having a calming effect on younger inmates and can act as positive role models (Adams 1995, 484; Aday 1994b, 52; Florida Corrections Commission 1999, 20; Flynn 1992, 86; Johnson 1988, 163; Yates and Gillespie 2000, 172).[4] It is important to remember that older inmates are not a homogenous population, and subsequently, some older inmates would prefer to have interaction with younger inmates (Adams 1995, 484; Florida Corrections Commission 1999, 20; Johnson 1988, 163; Wilson and Vito 1986, 416). In addition, if the age-segregated facility is further in geographical distance from the inmate's family, this could also negatively impact his social networks by reducing visits (Alston 1986, 255; Marquart et al. 2000, 81; Morton and Anderson 1982, 15; Neeley et al. 1997, 121). One last danger associated with separate facilities is that it might lead to stereotyping of older inmates, which could subsequently lead to discrimination in programming options (Goetting 1985, 19).

While some studies have found that older inmates preferred segregation (Aday 1994a, 89; Marquart et al. 2000, 89) and had increased feelings of security compared to older inmates housed in other facilities and units (Marquart et al. 2000, 90), the men in this book were split in their support of segregation. Eight men were supportive, eight were not, and four offered mixed support. Opinions on this issue remained consistent. In comparing responses from 2006 to 2011, only two men changed their positions. At the first interview, Daniel and Noah were not in favor of segregation; however, at the second interview, they expressed support.

Among those who were opposed to segregation, Noah went so far as to claim that being confined in a separate facility would be a form of punishment. The two primary reasons offered for why they would prefer the mainstreaming of older inmates was the interaction with younger inmates and a concern that segregation would cause them to age more quickly. Seven men reported that they enjoyed interacting with younger inmates. Adam explained: "I'd like the interaction with some of the younger ones. It's refreshing. It helps keep current with different changes in the community, you know, you can only glean so much from the TV or the radio or magazine . . . or family and friends." Interaction with younger inmates is one of the few ties that older LWOP inmates have with the outside world, and their segregation would further remove them from society. Another reason the men wanted to stay in a mixed-age facility was so that they could mentor younger inmates. Matthew contended, "It's good to have the older guys mixed in with the population. . . .

I think older guys are good role models in general." In addition, Troy, Nathan, and Adam reported that they would not want to be in a separate facility because it would cause them to age more rapidly, as reflected in the following statements:

> Why would I want to be around a bunch of old guys that's sickly? No. I'd rather be around the younger ones, that would keep me more going. (Troy)

> If you're around something long enough, you know, it will start rubbing off on you. . . . I don't want to be housed with a bunch of older people. Like I said, I don't consider myself old. I mean, I'm fifty-two years old, but I don't think I act like anybody fifty-two years old, you know. I don't think like that, I don't limit myself to things, you know, I don't let my age limit me in anything. (Nathan)

Along the same lines, Gabriel claimed that the environment would be "negative" and "pessimistic." Nathan felt that his mental health would be adversely affected and claimed that he would become depressed if he were to be transferred to a separate unit.

A possible factor driving the lack of support for segregation overall was the negative frame of reference, specifically the conditions in the special needs unit at Institution One. The prison had a special needs dormitory for inmates who had physical health care needs that made them unable to care for themselves. As it was a dormitory, the men were displeased that they had would lose the privacy of their single cells. Three men (George, James, and Walter) were housed there. While George reported that he liked to change his housing assignment periodically in the interest of variety, and Walter requested to be transferred to the unit as he had thought that he would have greater access to the yard, both George and Walter identified the chief drawback of living in the unit as the lack of privacy. Walter had hoped that he could be transferred back to his single cell: "I'm trying to get out of there now. I want to try and get a single cell. I like being by myself. I don't like being around forty-nine other inmates. You know, that's a lot of people to be around. And you really, you don't have no privacy what so ever. I should have stayed in the back. I had a single cell." Other men at Institution One had negative perceptions of the special needs unit. With the help of a counselor, Matthew was able to block his transfer to the unit and remain in his single cell. Despite the fact that inmates of all ages could be incarcerated there, Nathan described the unit as "an old age dumping ground." He claimed that if he were to be transferred there, he would commit a disciplinary infraction so that he would be placed in the security housing unit and retain a single cell.

Alternatively, about one-third of the men preferred to be housed in a separate facility because of the special needs and different preferences of older inmates. These men anticipated that in a separate unit they would receive greater medical attention and the environment would be quiet and peaceful. The men also reported that they would appreciate the increased interaction with other aging inmates, as reflected in Joshua's statement: "Well, I could see where it would have advantages. Because, number one, you probably would have more people in your age group to communicate with where a lot of these younger guys are just into things that the older guys just aren't into anymore. So, yeah, I wouldn't mind it." As older inmates were not a disciplinary problem, the men anticipated that the unit would have a lower security level, which could mean more privileges. John, who had served thirty-five years for a crime he claimed he did not commit, explained:

> They should have people fifty and above stay in that building and give them something extra. . . . See, because we do have special things that we need that we can't get . . . we have, you know, the young dudes, you know, acting up making a whole lot of noise; young guys stealing stuff, bringing heat, you know, where the guards come in and tear up the cells. You know it's them, why don't you do them, why do you got to do us? . . . We've done so much time. We're tired of all of the bullshit that's going on. . . . We just want to go to work. We just want to go to school. We . . . want to keep busy and leave us alone. You know, we ain't about causing no more trouble.

Researchers have cautioned against using an age cutoff as the sole criterion for designation to a segregated facility and have argued that both mainstreaming and segregation should be available to meet the needs of this diverse population (Morton 1992, 12; Wilson and Vito 1986, 416). In addition, because "older inmates who have some sense of control over their daily lives adjust better" (Neeley et al. 1997, 123), they should have some input in housing assignment decisions (Wilson and Vito 1986, 416). Some men agreed that a segregated housing unit should be available for those who want to live there, but they argued against the automatic transfer of inmates when they reach a certain age. Gabriel's statement summarizes this position:

> No, I want to be where the work is and my thing is to . . . continue to impact . . . young people and try to have an impact on their lives so that they don't come here. But I definitely see . . . the merit in the idea and I definitely will support it. . . . I wouldn't want to make it mandatory that . . . at a certain age, that . . . you have to go there . . . [but] if there was an option for guys . . . who felt the need to do that. I definitely would support it.

As can be seen in his statement, while Gabriel would not want to be seg-regated from younger inmates, he did think the option should be available for those who are so inclined. Consistent with other research, it appears that having both housing options available to older inmates and allowing older inmates a role in the decision-making process would increase the well-being of the older inmates and tailor decisions based on their individual preferences.

Policy Recommendation Three: Fostering Greater Institutional Thoughtfulness

The last policy recommendation is to cultivate greater consideration of the needs of aging LWOP inmates. One way to do this would be to provide accommodations to older inmates with physical health issues. The men faced physical impediments in prison such as top bunks, stairs, and the distance between buildings. Prison administrators who maintain facilities with an older inmate population should consider providing this population with accommo-dations that ease these physical obstacles, such as requiring older inmates to be on the bottom bunk, assigning them a cell on the first floor, and providing them with extra time to eat, shower, and move around the institution. Another way to accomplish greater thoughtfulness would be to give staff training in regard to the needs of older inmates and the physiological and psychological changes that accompany age (Aday, 1994a, 89; Gallagher 1990, 263; Marquart et al. 2000, 93; McCarthy 1983, 74; Morton 1992, 13; Smyer et al. 1997, 15; Wilson and Vito 1986, 415).

EPILOGUE

I hope to interview the men for a third time in 2016, ten years after the original interviews. In looking ahead, I can only expect that the size of the group will continue to decrease. I do not believe that the attrition will occur as a result of sentence commutation and release. While Francis was released following a sentence commutation, he was an anomaly, a habitual burglar who had never been convicted of a violent offense. Almost all of the other men have at least one violent offense on the record, and eighteen of the surviving men have been convicted of first-degree murder. Given the politicization of release decisions, I doubt that any of the other men will be released. Nathan arguably has the best chance, given the facts of his case and his record of good behavior in prison; however, his two most recent commutation applications have been rejected by two governors. I anticipate that future commutation applications will end in the same way. Instead of by release, I expect that the group will continue to decline as a result of the deaths of the men. In 2016 all of the men will be at least sixty years of age. Five will be in their seventies, and one will be in his mid-eighties. Death has already claimed a few mem-bers of the group. Between the first and second interviews, Thomas, Anthony, and Samuel died. Since 2011 Walter died. I expect that several more men will succumb to illness or disease in the next several years.

At the next interview, I anticipate that the physical health of the men will have continued to deteriorate. I expect that when I see them again they will be facing even more serious health challenges and requiring greater medical treatment. It is likely that more of them will have been transferred from their single cells to the special needs dormitory at Institution One. I would also anticipate that their ties to the outside world will have become even more tenuous. As their loved ones continue to encounter their own physical health issues and to die, their communication with their relatives will be further reduced and, should the men outlive their relatives, cease all together. If this were to occur, then they will have become truly forgotten.

In 2016 all of the men will have been incarcerated for at least a quarter century, with over half of them having served in excess of thirty years, and one having served more than forty years. What remains to be seen at the next interview is whether their mental health continues to remain intact, whether they continue to be satisfied with their communication with their relatives, and above all, whether they continue to remain hopeful of release. At our first interview, Noah, who had been incarcerated for nearly three decades, argued: "I'm not doing this for another twenty-five years, I can't do this no more." The question is how much longer can he, and the others, go on?

Pseudonym	Age at Incarceration	Primary Offense	Relationship to Victim	Age in 2006	Time Served in 2006	Age in 2011	Time Served in 2011
Adam	25	murder	acquaintance	55	28	59	32
Alan	49	murder	family member	64	15	69	19
Anthony	45	robbery	stranger	62	17	N/A	died in 2009
Charles	29	murder	romantic partner	59	27	64	32
Daniel	26	murder	stranger	52	26	57	31
Francis	50	burglary	stranger	68	18	73	released in 2011
Gabriel	28	murder	romantic partner	50	21	55	26
George	37	murder	acquaintance	66	29	72	34
Henry	31	murder	acquaintance	58	26	63	31
James	58	murder	stranger	75	17	80	22
John	29	murder	romantic partner	59	31	65	35
Joshua	30	murder	stranger	59	29	64	33
Karl	24	murder	romantic partner	50	26	55	31
Matthew	45	murder	romantic partner	67	22	73	27
Michael	32	murder	romantic partner	63	30	N/A	N/A
Nathan	23	murder	stranger	52	28	57	34
Noah	30	murder	stranger	53	22	58	27
Robert	33	murder	stranger	62	28	67	33

(continued)

Pseudonyms and Demographics of Respondents
(continued)

Pseudonym	Age at Incarceration	Primary Offense	Relationship to Victim	Age in 2006	Time Served in 2006	Age in 2011	Time Served in 2011
Ryan	30	murder	stranger	50	19	55	24
Samuel	32	burglary	stranger	52	19	N/A	died in 2011
Thomas	46	murder	romantic partner	68	21	N/A	died in 2008
Troy	22	robbery	stranger	50	28	55	34
Victor	33	murder	acquaintance	57	24	62	26
Walter	32	murder	romantic partner	63	31	68	36 (died in 2013)
William	42	murder	acquaintance	61	19	N/A	N/A

Appendix B: Researching the Forgotten

AS THE PURPOSE OF this research was to examine the experience of growing old in prison for a group of LWOP inmates, in 2006 I established three conditions to determine who should be interviewed. First, the person needed to be serving a LWOP sentence. While other researchers also include those serving virtual life (Villaume 2005, 267) or death-in-prison sentences (Henry 2012) in their analyses, only those who were formally sentenced to life without parole were approached for participation. Second, the person needed to be fifty years of age or older. Although there is no universally agreed upon designation of the term "older" in the aging inmate literature, this is the most commonly used cutoff. Clearly, this age is significantly lower than the Social Security Administration's designation of retirement age as sixty-five. The rationale offered is that inmates have had a more physically and mentally taxing life than non-incarcerated individuals, both prior to and during incarceration. For example, chronic drug, alcohol, and tobacco use, poor eating habits, limited access to medical care before incarceration, and the stress of confinement are believed to accelerate the process of aging for older inmates (Anno et al. 2004, 8–9; Kratcoski and Pownall 1989, 30). The final criterion was that the individual must have served at least fifteen years of the LWOP sentence. This requirement was implemented to capture the experiences of those who had been incarcerated for a substantial period of time and had aged while confined.

In order to identify eligible participants, I obtained an inmate locator that contained the names of all inmates under the jurisdiction of the mid-Atlantic state. First, I scanned the locator and identified all inmates who were at least fifty years of age. Second, based on the prison admission date listed in the locator, I eliminated all inmates who had been incarcerated for less than fifteen years. Once all inmates who were at least fifty years of age and who had been incarcerated for at least fifteen years were identified, I used the LexisNexis database to locate the appellate records for eligible participants in order to confirm the sentence and length of incarceration. When there was no appellate record available online or when an inmate's sentence was not clearly indicated, I went to the county courthouse and reviewed sentencing hearing records.

At the beginning of this research project, I intended to speak with both male and female LWOP inmates. However, there were only three female inmates in the mid-Atlantic state who met the research criteria. Because of the small number and also because I believed that the correctional experiences of older female LWOP inmates would be substantively different from those of older male LWOP inmates, I decided to limit my analysis to male LWOP inmates. The above outlined method of identification yielded twenty-seven male inmates who met the three eligibility requirements.

Breaking In

The next step was to contact the state's DOC and ask for permission to enter its prisons to conduct the interviews. At first my phone, fax, and mail inquiries to the commissioner of corrections went unanswered. As time passed, I became increasingly concerned that I would not receive his consent to carry out the project and was unsure of how to proceed. I wanted to demonstrate my commitment to the research project, yet I did not want to alienate the commissioner or his office staff. Thus, I decided to place a phone call to the commissioner once a week, at various times and on alternating days, in an attempt to speak with him. I began calling his office in mid-May 2006. It was not until two months later that he took my call. I believe that there were two main reasons for the delay. First, as will not be a surprise to many, the DOC is a bureaucracy and my research proposal needed to be screened at various levels before it advanced through the hierarchy to the commissioner of corrections. Second, and of particular relevance to the population of this study, several years earlier, a staff member had been taken hostage by an inmate serving a lengthy sentence. The situation ended with the fatal shooting of the inmate. The incident received intense media attention and extensive investigation by state agencies. Consequently, I believe that the DOC was reluctant to permit a university researcher to enter the prison and interact with long-term inmates.

After receiving the permission of the commissioner, I sent each of the twenty-seven prospective inmates a letter identifying myself, explaining the purpose of the research, outlining the scope of their participation, and assuring them of confidentiality in their responses. In early September 2006, I entered Institution One to begin the interviews. Opened in the 1970s, Institution One is a mixed-security-level prison with an average daily population of twenty-five hundred inmates. Twenty-two interviews took place at this facility. All but two of the interviews occurred in a small room in an area typically used for attorney-client meetings. The room had a table with two chairs and a small window near the ceiling. At the officer's request, I sat in the chair closest to the door and the respondent sat on the other side of the table across from me. In order to protect the confidentiality of the men's statements, the door to the room was closed during the interview. Periodically, the officer assigned to this location would walk by the room. The other two interviews (with William and Robert) occurred in the shared visiting area of the security housing unit and protective custody unit. While this room was intended to accommodate multiple visitors, I was alone in the room when conducting the interviews. These two interviews were the only instances in which I was separated by a panel of glass from the interviewee. In some cases, due to the medical conditions of the respondents, such as hearing loss, I sat in close proximity to the respondent.

I interviewed one person each day, most weekdays through the month of September. My routine for the month was as follows: I would leave my home each morning by nine A.M. and drive the relatively short distance (less than fifty miles) to Institution One. Upon arrival at the prison, I would pass through security where me and my belongings, including a tape recorder, a folder containing consent forms and interview guides, and a small plastic bag filled with extra tapes and batteries, were screened with a metal detector. Next, I would make my way through the prison to the interview location. The first several days I was escorted to the interview location by a correctional officer; however, I soon moved through the prison on my own. Most of the interviews began at ten A.M., though there were delays due to inclement weather and morning counts. The interviews ranged in length from two to three hours. Two correctional officers at Institution One were especially helpful in answering questions, providing me with a tour of the facility, and allowing me the necessary space to conduct the interviews in private but also being accessible when I needed assistance.

The other three interviews occurred at Institution Two. Opened in the 1930s, Institution Two is also a mixed-security-level prison with an average daily population of approximately one thousand inmates. Because the prison was further away than Institution One (approximately a hundred miles from my home), interviews at Institution Two were conducted over a two-day period, in which I conducted one and a half interviews each day. I spent the night in a local motel to reduce travel time. These interviews took place in an empty recreation room near the honors housing unit where the men resided. A counselor at Institution Two provided valuable assistance to me as she gave me a tour of the prison, introduced me to prison staff, and escorted me around the facility. She had known the three men for a substantial period of time and was able to provide insight into the effects of long-term incarceration.

There was a litany of reasons why the men at Institutions One and Two might have declined my interview request. They could have been fearful of potential retaliation by correctional officers or administration if they were critical of the institution or the DOC. Perhaps their fears were justified; George, Daniel, and Robert reported that they had been punished for criticizing the DOC in the past. In addition, the subject matter of the interview was highly personal and could have discouraged participation. I was asking questions about sensitive topics such as death and dying, aging, and relationships with family. For the men who had committed murder, I was asking them to discuss probably the worst experience of their lives, when they took the life of another. In addition, the men could have been fearful that they would lose status in the inmate community and open themselves up to potential victimization if their statements were made public or it was perceived that they were "snitching on" other inmates.

In order to increase their willingness to speak with me and as a means to minimize any negative consequences of their participation, I made several assurances of confidentiality to the men. First, I would not use their real names when reporting the results. Consequently, pseudonyms are used in place of their actual names (see Appendix A). Second, I would not reveal any identifying information that would make it possible for statements to be connected to any particular person. As such, the name of the state in which the interviews were conducted is referred to only as "the mid-Atlantic state," and the two institutions in which the interviews were conducted are identified only as "Institution One" and "Institution Two." Throughout the book, material that would reveal the identity of a particular person may be referred to in general terms and not assigned to a pseudonym. Overall, I feel that these concessions were a small price to pay to have the opportunity to speak with the men and for them to feel comfortable enough to be honest and forthcoming with me.

Despite the many reasons for refusal, of the twenty-seven men I asked to interview, only two declined. One wrote me a letter in which he expressed interest in the project but explained that the interview would conflict with his work schedule; the other stated that he did not wish to speak to me and did not offer any further explanation. These cases of refusal were the exception; most men readily agreed to be interviewed, though there were several who expressed reluctance. For example, I met with Anthony on more than one occasion prior to receiving his consent to be interviewed. One source of concern for the prospective participants was uncertainty pertaining to who would have access to the recordings of the interview. My assurances that I would be the only one who listened to the tapes appeared to assuage their fears, although one interviewee asked that the recording be destroyed following the completion of the research project. In addition, my recruiting efforts were aided because of the "good press" I was receiving from the early interviewees. Respondents whom I interviewed later in the project stated that the early interviewees had reported that the interview was enjoyable and that no adverse effects had occurred. For participation in this research, I deposited five dollars into each man's commissary account.

THE ORIGINAL INTERVIEW

A qualitative methodology was used because I was interested in the respondents' life histories. The interview schedule contained 125 questions on a variety of topics including social networks, institutional misconduct, victimization, physical and mental health, perceptions of death and dying, and policy recommendations. The interview followed a semi-structured format, meaning that all of the questions contained in the interview schedule were put to the respondents in the same basic order; however, depending on the response, follow-up and clarification questions were individualized (Rubin and Rubin 1995, 5). Borrowing the ethnographic term (Geertz 2001, 57), my goal was to elicit "thick descriptions" of each individual's correctional experiences in order to have a well-informed understanding of long-term imprisonment and aging in prison.

As I devoted much energy into gaining access to the prisons, I felt less prepared to conduct them when I finally received permission. This contributed to the anxiety I experienced prior to the start of the interviews. While I had conducted interviews in prison previously, I had never done so with men who had been convicted of first-degree murder or who had been incarcerated for as long as these men had. I was not sure how they would receive me. Ultimately, my fears in this area were unfounded. I do not pretend to know the respondents well, but in my time with them, I found the men to be both courteous and articulate.

The Follow-Up Interview

Much changed for me in the intervening period from 2006 to 2011. In 2007 I received my PhD from the University of Delaware. Later that year, I relocated to California to accept a position as a faculty member. Although I was geographically removed, I frequently thought of the men and shared their experiences with my students and colleagues. In 2009 I contacted the mid-Atlantic DOC for an update on the men. In particular, I was interested in learning if any had been successful in their commutation applications and had been released. It was through this correspondence that I learned that Thomas and Anthony had died, of natural causes, in the prison medical unit. During this time period, George was the only respondent with whom I communicated. At his request I sent him a copy of my dissertation. Several weeks later, he sent me his review of it: "You done excellent job, contained valuable information, which feel we can utilize in the future." Since I wanted to "give voice" to this population's experiences, I was pleased to receive positive feedback from him regarding the merits of the project.

After three years living in California, I moved back to the East Coast in 2010 to accept a position at The College of New Jersey. I had not initially planned on conducting follow-up interviews with the men. However, when I returned to the East Coast and realized that it had been almost five years since the original interviews, I recognized that it would be an opportune time to reenter the prisons and speak with them again.

While the process of gaining access to the prisons remained a time-consuming process, I was better prepared for it the second time. In the five-year interim period, most of the DOC personnel had changed. There was a new commissioner of corrections and new wardens at Institution One and Institution Two with whom I needed to make contact. In the spring of 2011, I received permission from the commissioner of corrections to conduct the five-year follow-up interviews. I was able to conduct them at Institution Two during the summer. As I did in 2006, I completed the interviews (in the same order as in 2006) over a two-day period in July. As a result of a delay in receiving permission from the warden at Institution One, those interviews were completed in fall 2011.

Upon receiving permission from each warden to conduct the interviews, I again contacted the twenty-three surviving respondents of the 2006 sample. Because I was interested in examining how their lives and their perceptions of confinement had changed over time, I only contacted the respondents whom I had interviewed before and opted not to widen the sample to include additional inmates who would now meet the original eligibility requirements of participation (i.e., aged fifty or older and incarcerated for at least fifteen years). Considering that some time had passed since my last contact with the men and they might have found the original interview to be a negative experience, I was pleased with the quick response that I received from most respondents and their willingness to be interviewed a second time. As seen in their statements below, several expressed the fact that they found the original interview to be a positive experience:

> I was very surprised to hear from you again. It was nice to see that you received your Ph.D. Congratulations! Yes, I would be more than happy to be interviewed again. (Karl)

> I look forward to working with you again. Until I read your letter, I didn't realize how much time has passed since your last study. (Gabriel)

> Yes, I would gladly take part in your interview, the last one gave me a chance to unwind, so yes I'm fine with this. (Noah)

> I'm very much welcome you come to prison for interview. Just like before. After interviewed, I feel much better. (James)

> It's nice that you are doing a follow-up, that's a good thing. (Daniel)

Only Michael and William did not agree to be interviewed a second time. As my repeated attempts to contact them went unanswered, I am unsure for the reason they declined. Samuel had agreed to be interviewed but his health deteriorated rapidly. Several days before our scheduled interview, I received a phone call from his sister alerting me to his failing health. Samuel had asked her to call me to let me know of his condition and to apologize for cancelling the interview. He died soon after.

While conducting the follow-up interviews, I experienced an overwhelming sense of déjà vu as I interviewed the men at Institution One in the same area as I had five years earlier and adopted similar habits in my routine. What was different the second time around was my self-assurance. I was more confident in my interviewing skills and felt comfortable moving around the institution without an escort. Only minor changes were made to the original interview schedule. A couple of additional questions were included in areas not fully explored in 2006, such as "Do you think you ever had a reputation as being a problem inmate?" and "Did you ever have a drug or alcohol problem?" Otherwise, the only change made to the interview guide was to narrow the reference period of questions to focus on any changes in the last five years: "In the last five years, has your physical health changed?" For participation in the follow-up interview, each respondent's commissary account was credited ten dollars.

BRIDGING THE SOCIAL DISTANCE

Where I was in my life compared with where respondents were in theirs could not have been further apart; the social distance (Dohrenwend et al. 1968, 410–411) between us was vast. Gender, age, education, socioeconomic status, health, and quality of life placed us on opposite sides of life. At various points, the social distance between us surfaced in the interviews. For example, when describing how the burial plans in the Islamic tradition differed from those followed by the DOC in the Christian tradition, Francis, correctly assuming that I was of a Christian faith, commented: "I don't want to be buried as a Christian, no disrespect."

I had good reason to be concerned that the differences between us would hinder the quality of the interviews. Of particular importance, I was worried that the mixed gender combination of interviewer and respondent would affect our ability to establish rapport. After all, I was familiar with their cases so I was aware that a sizeable number of them had killed their female romantic partners. In 2006 gender was central to the following exchange between Matthew and me when I asked him to describe the offense for which he is serving life without parole: "I can talk about it. It doesn't bother me because I've come to that point where . . . I talk about it like everything else. But you're a lady, with you it's different because you're not a member of this population. I can't even look at you."

I believe that I was successful in bridging the social distance between us largely because I consciously adopted the role of an interested party who did not know much about their experiences or prison life in general. Since I did not pretend to be an expert, the men were able to assume the role of the instructor and teach me about prison life. This helped in the establishment of a connection with each man, as it was a comfortable expectation that, as the elder, he would assume the role of a teacher and I would adopt the role of an interested student. I soon found that my early fears of rudeness were baseless. Most men were polite. During both the original and follow-up interviews, William was the only respondent who commented on my physical appearance, and his statement, made during his only interview, was non-offensive. I was surprised that the area of my life that aroused the most curiosity was my religious affiliation. The following question from Matthew was a typical one: "Are you saved, are you a Christian?" Several men commented that I reminded them of their daughters as I was more or less of a similar age.

Instead of serving as barriers, I believe that our gender and age differences helped to foster an environment in which the respondents were able to express a wide range of emotions. Becoming emotional, such as crying or getting choked up, was a common occurrence. In addition, the men talked about their feelings of loneliness, vulnerability, sadness, and regret. I am not sure if they were able to do so because they felt less threatened because of my age, gender, personality, or some combination thereof, but research supports my experience. Studies indicate that male respondents are more willing to discuss their feelings with female interviewers than males (see Manderson et al. 2006, 1329).

I quickly realized that there was little threat to my physical well-being. Most of these men—because of their good behavior—had earned preferred housing assignments, prestigious work assignments, and special visitation privileges. They guarded them fiercely. It is not surprising that they responded positively when treated with courtesy. For example, I shook their hands, before and after the interview, addressed each as "Mister," and promptly deposited the small gratuity into their commissary accounts.[1] I also apologized to them when they were kept waiting, regardless of whether it was my fault or not, as in the encounter between John and me described below:

JOHN: Yeah, they [the officers] weren't telling us [that only one person was interviewed each day.]

ML: Well, I apologize. I wouldn't want you to waste your morning sitting and waiting.

JOHN: No, I know it's not your fault.

I found these small acts of courtesy helped in establishing a connection with the men.

Confronting Ethical Dilemmas

In the course of conducting the interviews, I encountered several ethical dilemmas. In 2006 during our interview, Daniel expressed his anger at a co-defendant who had implicated him as the actual killer in their crime. (Daniel maintained that he was innocent.) He admitted that, when he would see his co-defendant, he sometimes had violent thoughts toward him. I asked him if he had ever acted on them or was planning to act on them, and he answered "no" to both questions. Still, when I left the prison that afternoon, I was concerned that perhaps the interview had exacerbated his feelings of anger and that Daniel might physically attack the inmate. One exception to the guarantee of confidentiality that I made to respondents was that if they expressed harm toward another inmate or staff member, I would be forced to notify the warden. I wrestled with whether I should report Daniel's comments. After seeking advice from several colleagues, I chose not to. As far as I am aware, there were no confrontations between them. In 2011 I asked Daniel if he remained angry with his co-defendant and he responded: "A little bit. How would you feel if you did all these years [for a crime that you did not commit]? He don't have no conscience." This was the only situation in which the suggestion of a threat to another person's safety was made.

In 2011 a dilemma I faced was whether I should move beyond my role as a researcher to an advocate. As Joshua and Victor were preparing their commutation applications, both asked me to write a letter of support. At our interviews I agreed to their requests, with the stipulation that my letter would be limited to an expression of appreciation for participation in my research project and would not address whether they should be released or make any type of predictions as to how they would behave if released. As I was preparing to write the letters, I had a nagging feeling that the letter of support could be misinterpreted by the DOC. I contacted a senior DOC official and explained the situation and reiterated that the letter would be akin to a certificate of participation, commonly given to inmates after the completion of a program. He advised against writing the letters. I struggled with questions that I am sure other researchers have faced. What did I owe my respondents? Can the roles of researcher and advocate be performed at the same time? It was a difficult decision to make, but I wrote Joshua and Victor expressing my apologies that I would not be able to write a letter of support and that a perception by the DOC that my objectivity had been compromised would impede my ability to continue my research efforts. I did not hear back from either of them.

Another request that I declined was to accept money on behalf of a respondent. After our interview, Robert sent me a letter asking me if I would hold some of his money in my personal banking account until he was released. As he was estranged from his family and had few friends on the outside, he wrote, I was the only person he trusted. This request immediately struck me as inappropriate. I quickly responded to Robert's letter, thanking him for his trust but declining on the grounds that it would change our relationship from a professional one to a personal one. This was the sole instance in which a respondent asked me for a personal favor.

THE ANALYSIS

After completing the original and follow-up interviews, I began transcription. While it is time- and labor-intensive, a resulting benefit was that I quickly became familiar with the interviews and could quickly begin to identify themes across the respondents' histories. Because of the lack of research concerning this population, I found grounded theory to be an appropriate framework when analyzing the interview data (Glaser and Strauss 1967). The primary purpose of this research was to examine how this group of inmates felt about incarceration and the changes that had occurred over the course of confinement. The similarity in the experiences of older LWOP inmates to other groups of inmates previously studied was not known. As such, I was not testing any preconceived theories with this research. Instead, the data drove the creation of codes, which then became the building blocks for categorical themes. Consistent with grounded theory, the data were used to inductively generate the formulation of these broader themes (Glaser and Strauss 1967). In determining if a theme existed, I adopted the approach used by Saundra D. Westervelt and Kimberly J. Cook (2012, 25) in their study of death-sentenced exonerees. These researchers established the rule that a theme existed when at least 20 percent of respondents offered a similar experience or perception. Thus, in my project, a theme was identified when at least five respondents in 2006 and four respondents in 2011 provided similar statements or expressed similar sentiments.

The 2006 and 2011 interview data were analyzed using a line-by-line coding scheme whereby individual codes were created around a central category, such as violent victimizations or fear of death and dying. Following the creation of broad primary themes, associated material was identified and coded (e.g., effect of violent victimization, fearful of dying in prison because of inadequate medical care, etc.). The line-by-line coding served to limit the potential projection of my own biases on the data (Charmaz 2001, 341–342). While I analyzed and organized the content into codes, I let the men speak for themselves. I have tried my best to present a scholarly account of the life experiences of this group of incarcerated individuals. I have made only minimal corrections to their statements and only did so when clarification was necessary; otherwise, the language remains unchanged. In order to assess the reliability of coding, the 2006 interview data were analyzed a second time using the Atlas software program. No significant difference was found in the interpretation of data based on the coding method. As a result, I felt comfortable using line-by-line coding as the only coding scheme with the 2011 data. Overall, a total of seventy-five pages of codes were generated.

THE NATIONAL PICTURE
OF OLDER LWOP INMATES

How does this group compare to the national population of older LWOP inmates? In order to answer this question, Bureau of Justice Statistics data were analyzed to construct a national profile of older LWOP inmates.[2] Overall, as can be seen in the table on the next page, the mid-Atlantic sample differed from the national sample in key areas. While both groups were similar in terms of current age, the disproportionate number of minorities (though the disparity is more pronounced in the mid-Atlantic sample), and marital status at incarceration, the groups differed on primary offense, prior incarceration, length of time served, substance use prior to the offense, and existence of children.

Based on prior incarceration and primary offense, it appears that the mid-Atlantic sample had a more serious criminal history than the national sample. About 40 percent of the national sample had been incarcerated previously as compared to 68 percent of the mid-Atlantic sample. Additionally, a larger percentage of the mid-Atlantic sample was serving a LWOP sentence for homicide than the national sample (84 percent versus 66 percent). Put another way, the percentage of inmates serving time for a non-homicide offense was two times greater in the national sample (34 percent) as compared to the mid-Atlantic sample (16 percent). In the mid-Atlantic group, the three offenses triggering a LWOP sentence were homicide, robbery, and burglary; more variance existed at the national level. In addition to inmates serving life without parole for these three offenses, inmates in the national sample were incarcerated for other violent offenses (e.g., rape/sexual assault and kidnapping), drug offenses (e.g., trafficking and possession), and public-order offenses (unspecified). Though both groups included inmates who had been incarcerated for over three decades, the mid-Atlantic sample had been incarcerated for about ten years longer than the national sample.[3] As compared to the national sample, less mid-Atlantic inmates were under the influence when the offense occurred. While over half the national sample (55 percent) claimed to be under the influence of drugs and/or alcohol at the time of the offense, only about one-third of the mid-Atlantic sample (33 percent) reported the same. Lastly, while almost all of the mid-Atlantic inmates had children (84 percent), only slightly more than half (55 percent) of the national sample reported being fathers.

Demographics of the Mid-Atlantic and
National Samples of Older LWOP Inmates

	Mid-Atlantic Sample n=25	National Sample n=47
Race/Ethnicity		
White Non-Hispanic	36%	62%
Black Non-Hispanic	56	36
Hispanic	4	0
Other Non-Hispanic	4	2
Age		
Range	50–75	50–77
Mean	59	57
Social Attachments at Prison Admission		
Married	28%	23%
Children	84%	55%
Primary Offense		
Murder	84%	66%
Rape/Sexual Assault	0	9
Kidnapping	0	2
Robbery	8	11
Drugs (Trafficking & Possession)	0	9
Public-Order	0	4
Burglary	8	0
Under the Influence	33%	55%
Prior Incarceration	68%	40%
Age at Incarceration		
Range	22–58	21–67
Mean	34	46
Length of Time Served (in 2006)		
Range	15–31	0–30
Mean	24	12

LIMITATIONS TO THE RESEARCH METHODOLOGY

There are several limitations of this study that must be noted. First, because of the small sample size, the generalizability of the findings is limited. There were only twenty-seven inmates identified in the mid-Atlantic state who met the eligibility requirements for participation, and only twenty-five agreed to participate. Although this research had an extremely high participation rate of 93 percent, and I reached a saturation point with the final interviews in that little new information was emerging, the similarity of this sample's correctional experiences to other state or national samples of older LWOP inmates is unknown. I do not believe that the findings from this project constitute the singular account of what it is like to spend a lifetime incarcerated with little chance of release, but it does represent this group's experience.

Second, this research did not verify interview responses with formal institutional records, such as disciplinary reports or medical records. In a project based on individual perception, the pursuit of personal truth is more important than empirical truth. I wanted to hear the central narratives that the men had constructed for themselves and how they made sense of their lives. As such, I largely accepted the information that the men were telling me as part of their narratives. When a discrepancy or point of confusion arose in the interview, I asked for clarification and verification of previous statements before continuing with the interview so that it made sense to me. Overall, I believe respondents were honest with me. Most men had their own cells and were eligible to receive special visitation privileges; taken together, these indicate that the men were well behaved, or at least their misconduct was not detected by correctional staff. I also was struck by the similarities between the 2006 and 2011 interviews. In the second interview, some men gave almost the same response as they had in the original interview. I interpreted this favorably for it reinforced that the information was important to their personal narratives. Furthermore, respondents expressed a desire to be helpful and honest when responding to questions as indicated in the following statements:

Did I do any good [at the interview]? (John)

I hope I've been some help. (Michael)

I want to be truthful with you in this interview. (Matthew)

The men seemed pleased to have the opportunity to talk about their lives. During the first interview, Matthew interjected: "I'm enjoying this. I really am. I'm enjoying this. It allows me to voice myself." I hope that because the majority of the respondents were pleased to have the opportunity to share their experiences, and they were guaranteed confidentially, they reported their experiences in an honest and accurate manner.

Some questions posed to respondents asked them to recall feelings or experiences they had at least fifteen years ago, such as "What was your initial reaction when you were sentenced to life without parole?" Therefore, a related limitation in this research is that the specific details and memories associated with the thoughts, behaviors, or feelings experienced by these older LWOP inmates during their adjustments to prison could have diminished over time. This was apparent when the men could only provide a general time frame, such as a decade, for when they experienced certain events, engaged in certain behaviors, or felt particular emotions. When this lack of specificity arose in the course of interviewing, I probed the men in an attempt to pinpoint a more precise time. While the retrospective nature of the present research is a limitation, it is also a benefit. One of the primary objectives of this research was to acquire a better understanding of how the men came to terms with serving a LWOP sentence and their adjustment to incarceration. They have had a great deal of time to reflect on the courses of their lives; therefore, they can offer a thoughtful and less emotionally driven account than perhaps they would have been able to do when they were newly incarcerated.

NOTES

CHAPTER 1   THE RISE IN THE PERMANENTLY INCARCERATED

1. While Alaska does not have a formal sentence of life without parole, it does prescribe the mandatory sentence of 99 years in certain first-degree murder cases (§AS 12.55.125).

2. The term "global support" refers to the percentage of respondents who answered in the affirmative to the question: "Are you in favor of the death penalty for a person convicted of murder?" (Newport 2010, para. 2).

3. Supporters of Proposition Thirty-Four included Gil Garcetti, former district attorney of Los Angeles County; Jeanne Woodford, former warden of San Quentin State Prison (the site of California's death chamber); Don Heller, who helped author California's present death penalty statute; and organizations, including Amnesty International USA, Human Rights Watch, Death Penalty Focus, the California State National Association for the Advancement of Colored People (NAACP), the California Democratic Party, the California League of Women Voters, and the National Coalition to Abolish the Death Penalty (ACLU of Northern California 2013c, 2013g).

4. For these reasons, in 1989, Mario Cuomo, then governor of New York, advocated for life without parole in an editorial published in the *New York Times* on June 17, 1989: "There is an effective alternative to burning the life out of human beings in the name of public safety. That alternative is just as permanent, at least as great a deterrent and—for those who are so inclined—far less expensive than the exhaustive legal appeals required in capital cases. That alternative is life imprisonment without the possibility of parole. No 'minimums' or 'maximums.' No time off for good behavior. No chance of release by a parole board, ever. Not even the possibility of clemency. It is, in practical effect, a sentence of death in incarceration."

5. The Court acknowledged the irrevocability of life without parole as similar to that of the death penalty: "It is true that a death sentence is 'unique in its severity and irrevocability'; yet life without parole sentences share some characteristics with death sentences that are shared by no other sentences. The State does not execute the offender sentenced to life without parole, but the sentence alters the offender's life by a forfeiture that is irrevocable. It deprives the convict of the most basic liberties without giving hope of restoration, except perhaps by executive clemency—the remote possibility of which does not mitigate the harshness of the sentence" (842).

6. This type of sentence is also referred to as "fixed" life without parole.

7. Opponents included former governors Pete Wilson and George Deukmejian, twenty-seven district attorneys, the California State Sheriffs' Association, California Police Chiefs Association, California Correctional Peace Officers' Association, and Marc Klaas, father of murder victim Polly Klaas (Californians for Justice and Public Safety 2013b).

8. The inmate who committed murder first killed his girlfriend and then committed suicide (Marquart and Sorensen 1988, 687).
9. Article 3 states: "'No one shall be subjected to torture or to inhuman or degrading treatment or punishment'" (33).
10. However, as Newcomen (2005, 3) points out, it is possible that extremely long sentences can exist in countries without the formal sentence of life imprisonment.
11. When evaluating the constitutionality of Graham's sentence, the Court for the first time relied on the proportionality test it had previously reserved for capital cases (for an extensive discussion see Barkow 2010).
12. In *Michigan v. Bullock* (1992), the Michigan Supreme Court reduced the mandatory LWOP sentence for possession of 650 or more grams of cocaine to a sentence of life with the possibility of parole after serving a ten-year minimum period.

CHAPTER 2   THE FORGOTTEN

1. As mentioned in Appendix B, self-report data are subject to exaggeration or minimization of misconduct. However, as most of the respondents were housed in single cells and eligible for honor visits, it appears that their misconduct had lessened over time or was not detected by staff.
2. While none of the men at Institution Two had his own cell, all three were housed in a special unit reserved for well-behaved inmates.

CHAPTER 3   THE PAINS OF PERMANENT IMPRISONMENT

1. Married inmates in the mid-Atlantic state did not receive any special visitations with spouses, such as conjugal visits.
2. At Institution One, the term "no-contact visits" refers to visits in which inmates and their visitors are separated by a partition of plexiglass.

CHAPTER 4   COPING WITH PERMANENT INCARCERATION

1. Eight men were Protestant, four were Catholic, and three were Muslim. Another eight identified themselves as religious or spiritual but not belonging to a particular faith. Not all of the men relied on their spiritual or religious beliefs to cope with incarceration, as Thomas and Joshua were atheists.
2. As the admitted killer in a burglary gone awry, Joshua had little hope of release; as such, it seemed as though he was living vicariously through his friends' post-release experiences, which might explain the romanticized account he provided.
3. The privatization of prisons and prison services is one of the major controversies in corrections today. Allegations that private prison operators provide inadequate medical care, in order to protect their profits, are common.

CHAPTER 5   GROWING OLD IN PRISON

1. Others, however, have found deleterious effects of long-term incarceration. For example, in their longitudinal study of Austrian men incarcerated for murder, Lapornik et al. (1996, 125) found that concentration and memory declined after only three and half years of incarceration. As the average age of the sample was about thirty-two years, it does not appear that the decline in concentration and memory can be attributed to advanced age.
2. However, by 2006 Joshua was no longer able to run because of knee problems. In 2011 after a series of surgeries, several of which were to treat infections that he sustained, Joshua's surgeon cautioned him that amputation of the leg may be necessary if his knee were to become infected again.

3. Walter died in 2013. I am not sure if his burial wishes were carried out.
4. Thomas was waiting until he had served thirty years before he applied for commutation; he died after serving twenty-three years.
5. As of September 2014, Nathan remains incarcerated.
6. While it is unwise to make a causal connection between these two events, Hassine's death in the days immediately following his denial does provide insight into his state of mind.

CHAPTER 6   FORGOTTEN NO MORE

1. Although the offense in the case was non-violent, the potentially dangerous repercussions must be acknowledged. The individual, who was incarcerated for a sex offense, was re-incarcerated after falsifying his criminal record on an employment application at a school (Pennsylvania General Assembly 2005, 4).
2. The section title is derived from Alexander Paterson's well-known statement: "'[Individuals] come to prison *as* a punishment and not *for* punishment'" (1951, 13.)
3. Breaking Barriers with Books is a model that could be used (College of Education and Human Services 2013).
4. However, as Elmer Johnson (1988, 163) cautioned: "In speaking of older prisoners in this regard, prison officials are referring mostly to those with ages from thirty-five to fifty years. The inmates older than sixty-five years are generally seen as too passive and dependent to influence younger peers significantly."

APPENDIX B   RESEARCHING THE FORGOTTEN

1. However, Daniel corrected that behavior when he informed me that the proper greeting in prison was a "fist bump" because others could be hiding a weapon—a razor blade or other sharp object—in the palm of their hands.
2. Forty-seven older LWOP inmates were included in the analysis. The sample was obtained by merging two versions of the Survey of Inmates in State and Federal Facilities (1997, 2004).
3. There were only eighteen respondents in the national sample who had been incarcerated for at least fifteen years. As such, all of the older LWOP inmates in the national sample were included regardless of the length of time incarcerated. This would explain the increased average length of time and younger age at incarceration for the mid-Atlantic sample.

References

Abramsky, Sasha. 2004. "Lifers." *Legal Affairs*. Accessed December 4, 2013. http://www .legalaffairs.org/issues/March-April-2004/feature_abramsky_marpar04.msp.

Adams, William E., Jr. 1995. "The Incarceration of Older Criminals: Balancing Safety, Cost, and Humanitarian Concerns." *Nova Law Review* 19:465–486.

Aday, Ronald H. 1994a. "Aging in Prison: A Case Study of New Elderly Offenders." *International Journal of Offender Therapy and Comparative Criminology* 38:79–91.

———. 1994b. "Golden Years behind Bars: Special Programs and Facilities for Elderly Inmates." *Federal Probation* 58:47–54.

———. 2003. *Aging Prisoners: Crisis in American Corrections*. Westport, CT: Praeger.

———. 2005–2006. "Aging Prisoners' Concerns toward Dying in Prison." *OMEGA* 52:199–216.

Agnew, Robert. 2006. *Pressured into Crime: An Overview of General Strain Theory*. Los Angeles, CA: Roxbury Publishing Company.

Alarcón, Arthur L., and Paula M. Mitchell. 2011. "Executing the Will of the Voters? A Roadmap to Mend or End the California Legislature's Multi-billion Dollar Death Penalty Debacle." *Loyola of Los Angeles Law Review* 44:S41–S224.

Alston, Letitia T. 1986. *Crime and Older Americans*. Springfield, IL: Charles C Thomas.

American Civil Liberties Union (ACLU). 2014a. "Capital Punishment." Accessed January 17, 2014. https://www.aclu.org/capital-punishment.

———. 2014b. "End Juvenile Life without Parole." Accessed January 17, 2014. https:// www.aclu.org/human-rights_racial-justice/end-juvenile-life-without-parole.

American Civil Liberties Union of Northern California.

———. 2013a. "Broken beyond Repairs." Accessed December 18, 2013. http://www .safecalifornia.org/facts/system.

———. 2013b. "Costs and Savings." Accessed December 18, 2013. http://www .safecalifornia.org/facts/savings.

———. 2013c. "Endorsements from Organizations and Unions." Accessed December 18, 2013. http://www.safecalifornia.org/about/other-organizations.

———. 2013d. "Families of Murder Victims." Accessed December 18, 2013. http:// www.safecalifornia.org/facts/victim-old.

———. 2013e. "Innocence." Accessed December 18, 2013. http://www.safecalifornia .org/facts/innocence.

———. 2013f. "Supporters." Accessed December 18, 2013. http://www.safecalifornia .org/about/coalition.

———. 2013g. "Unsolved Rapes and Murders." Accessed December 18, 2013. http:// www.safecalifornia.org/facts/unsolved.

Americans with Disabilities Act of 1990. 42 U.S.C. §§ 1210112213 (2000).

Amnesty International and Human Rights Watch. 2005. *The Rest of Their Lives: Life without Parole for Child Offenders in the United States.* New York: Human Rights Watch.

———. 2014. "Abolish the Death Penalty." Accessed January 17, 2014. https://www.amnesty.org/en/death-penalty.

Anderson, Elizabeth, and Theresa Hilliard. 2005. "Managing Offenders with Special Health Needs: Highest and Best Use Strategies." *Corrections Today* 67:58–61.

Angus Reid Public Opinion. 2012. *Americans Would Not Grant Pardons to Murderers and Armed Robbers.* Vancouver, BC: Angus Reid Public Opinion.

Anno, Jaye, Camelia Graham, James E. Lawrence, and Ronald Shansky. 2004. *Correctional Health Care: Addressing the Needs of Elderly, Chronically Ill, and Terminally Ill Inmates.* Washington, DC: National Institute of Corrections.

Applegate, Brandon K., Francis T. Cullen, Michael G. Turner, and Jody L. Sundt. 1996. "Assessing Public Support for Three-Strikes-and You're-Out Laws: Global versus Specific Attitudes." *Crime and Delinquency* 42:517–534.

Appleton, Catherine, and Bent Grøver. 2007. "The Pros and Cons of Life without Parole." *British Journal of Criminology* 47:597–615.

AS Code of Criminal Procedure. §12.55.125 (2013).

Bahr, Stephen J., Lish Harris, James K. Fisher, and Anita H. Armstrong. 2010. "Successful Reentry: What Differentiates Successful and Unsuccessful Parolees?" *International Journal of Offender Therapy and Comparative Criminology* 54:667–692.

Baranauckas, Carla. 2010. "Is This Man Tim Pawlenty's 'Willie Horton'?" *Politics Daily*, December 8. Accessed December 19, 2013. http://www.politicsdaily.com/2010/12/08/is-this-man-tim-pawlentys-willie-horton/.

Barkow, Rachel E. 2010. "Categorizing *Graham.*" *Federal Sentencing Reporter* 23:49–53.

———. 2012. "Life without Parole and the Hope for Real Sentencing Reform." In *Life without Parole: America's New Death Penalty?* edited by Charles J. Ogletree, Jr., and Austin Sarat, 190–226. New York: New York University Press.

Beccaria, Cesare. (1764) 1995. "On Crimes and Punishments." In *On Crimes and Punishments and Other Writings*, edited by Richard Bellamy, 1–113. Translated by Richard Davies. Cambridge, UK: University Press.

Beck, Allen J., and Darrell K. Gilliard. 1995. *Prisoners in 1994.* NCJ 151654. Washington, DC: Bureau of Justice Statistics.

Bentham, Jeremy. (1811) 1830. *The Rationale of Punishment.* London: Robert Heward, Wellington Street, the Strand.

Bintz, Michael T. 1974. "Recreation for the Older Population in Correctional Institutions." *Therapeutic Recreation Journal* 8:87–89.

Black, Chris. 1990. "Horton Case Keeping the Jail Cells Shut." *Boston Globe*, July 8.

Blair, Danya W. 1994. "A Matter of Life and Death: Why Life without Parole Should Be a Sentencing Option in Texas." *American Journal of Criminal Law* 22:191–214.

Blecker, Robert. 2010. "Less Than We Might: Meditations of Life in Prison Without Parole." *Federal Sentencing Reporter* 23:10–20.

Bonta, James, and Paul Gendreau. 1990. "Reexamining the Cruel and Unusual Punishment of Prison Life." *Law and Human Behavior* 14:347–372.

Bowers, William J., Margaret Vandiver, and Patricia H. Dugan. 1994. "A New Look at Public Opinion on Capital Punishment: What Citizens and Legislators Prefer." *American Journal of Criminal Law* 22:77–150.

Bowker, Lee H. 1982. "Victimizers and Victims in American Correctional Institutions." In *The Pains of Imprisonment*, edited by Robert Johnson and Hans Toch, 63–76. Beverly Hills: Sage Publications.

Bureau of Justice Statistics. 1997. *Survey of Inmates in State and Federal Correctional Facilities, 1997.* Machine-readable data file. U.S. Bureau of the Census (Producer). Ann Arbor: Inter-University Consortium for Political and Social Research (Distributor).

———. 2004. *Survey of Inmates in State and Federal Correctional Facilities, 2004.* Machine-readable data file. U.S. Bureau of the Census (Producer). Ann Arbor: Inter-University Consortium for Political and Social Research (Distributor).

———. 2013. "Prisoner Recidivism Analysis." Accessed December 23, 2013. http://www.bjs.gov/index.cfm?ty=datoolandsurl=/recidivism/index.cfm.

Burns, Rebecca. 2013. "Is Life without Parole Any Better Than the Death Penalty?" *In These Times*, March 22. Accessed December 18, 2013. http://inthesetimes.com/article/14773/death_penalty_abolition_life_without_parole/.

Butkus, William. 2012. "Voting 'YES' on Prop 34 Means Eliminating the Risk of Executing the Innocent Forever!" Accessed December 18, 2013. http://www.amnestyusa.org/emails/W1209EODP1.html.

Cain, Burl, and Cathy Fontenot. 2001. "Angola's Long-Term Inmates." *Corrections Today* 63:119–123.

California Secretary of State. 2012a. "General Election Official Voter Information Guide." Accessed December 18, 2013. http://voterguide.sos.ca.gov/propositions/34/.

———. 2012b. *Statement of Vote: November 6, 2012, General Election.* Sacramento, CA: California Secretary of State.

Californians for Justice and Public Safety. 2013a. "Killers Who Kill Again." Accessed December 19, 2013. http://www.waitingforjustice.net/killers-who-kill-again/.

———. 2013b. "Mend It, Don't End It." Accessed December 19, 2013. http://www.waitingforjustice.net/mend-it-dont-end-it/.

———. 2013c. "We Oppose Prop 34." Accessed December 19, 2013. http://www.waitingforjustice.net/endorsements/.

———. 2013d. "Who Earns a Death Sentence." Accessed December 19, 2013. http://www.waitingforjustice.net/who-earns-a-death-sentence-2/.

Capers, Bennett. 2012. "Defending Life." In *Life without Parole: America's New Death Penalty?* edited by Charles J. Ogletree, Jr., and Austin Sarat, 167–189. New York: New York University Press.

Carson, E. Ann, and William J. Sabol. 2012. *Prisoners in 2011.* NCJ 239808. Washington, DC: Bureau of Justice Statistics.

Charmaz, Kathy. 2001. "Grounded Theory." In *Contemporary Field Research: Perspectives and Formulations,* 2nd ed., edited by Robert M. Emerson, 335–352. Prospect Heights, IL: Waveland Press.

Cheatwood, Derral. 1988. "The Life-without-Parole Sanction: Its Current Status and a Research Agenda." *Crime and Delinquency* 34:43–59.

Cohen, Stanley, and Laurie Taylor. 1972. *Psychological Survival: The Experience of Long-Term Imprisonment.* New York: Pantheon Books.

College of Education and Human Services. 2013. "Breaking Barriers with Books." Oshkosh, WI: University of Wisconsin Oshkosh. Accessed December 31, 2013. http://www.uwosh.edu/coehs/collaborations/breaking-barriers-with-books.

Colsher, Patricia L., Robert B. Wallace, Paul L. Loeffelholz, and Marilyn Sales. 1992. "Health Status of Older Male Prisoners: A Comprehensive Survey." *American Journal of Public Health* 82:881–884.

Coughlin, Thomas A., III. 1990. "Problems and Challenges Posed by Long-Term Offenders in the New York State Prison System." *Prison Journal* 70:115–118.

Council of Europe. 1977. *Treatment of Long-Term Prisoners.* Strasbourg, France: Council of Europe.

Crawley, Elaine. 2005. "Institutional Thoughtlessness in Prisons and Its Impacts on the Day-to-Day Prison Lives of Elderly Men." *Journal of Contemporary Criminal Justice* 21:350–363.

Crawley, Elaine, and Richard Sparks. 2006. "Is There Life after Imprisonment? How Elderly Men Talk about Imprisonment and Release." *Criminology and Criminal Justice* 6:63–82.

Cullen, Francis T., and Cheryl Lero Jonson. 2012. *Correctional Theory: Contexts and Consequences.* Los Angeles: Sage.

Cunningham, Mark D., Thomas J. Reidy, and Jon R. Sorensen. 2005. "Is Death Row Obsolete? A Decade of Mainstreaming Death-Sentenced Inmates in Missouri." *Behavioral Sciences and the Law* 23:307–320.

Cunningham, Mark D., and Jon R. Sorensen. 2006. "Nothing to Lose? A Comparative Examination of Prison Misconduct Rates among Life-without-Parole and Other Long-Term High-Security Inmates." *Criminal Justice and Behavior* 33:683–705.

Cunningham, Mark D., Jon R. Sorensen, and Thomas J. Reidy. 2005. "An Actuarial Model for Assessment of Prison Violence Risk among Maximum Security Inmates." *Assessment* 12:40–49.

Cuomo, Mario M. 1989. "New York State Shouldn't Kill People." *New York Times*, June 17. Accessed December 31, 2013. http://www.nytimes.com/1989/06/17/opinion/new-york-state-shouldn-t-kill-people.html.

Death Penalty Information Center (DPIC). 2013a. "Costs of the Death Penalty." Accessed December 18, 2013. http://www.deathpenaltyinfo.org/costs-death-penalty.

———. 2013b. "Life without Parole." Accessed December 19, 2013. http://www.deathpenaltyinfo.org/life-without-parole.

———. 2013c. "Life without Parole Laws in States that Recently Repealed the Death Penalty." Accessed December 19, 2013. http://www.deathpenaltyinfo.org/lwop-post-repeal.

———. 2013d. "Survey of Life without Parole Instructions in Death Penalty States." Accessed December 19, 2013. http://www.deathpenaltyinfo.org/documents/LWOPSurvey.pdf.

———. 2013e. *Facts about the Death Penalty.* Washington, DC: Death Penalty Information Center. Accessed December 18, 2013. http://www.deathpenaltyinfo.org/documents/FactSheet.pdf.

DeRosia, Victoria, R. 1998. *Living inside Prison Walls: Adjustment Behavior.* Westport, CT: Praeger.

Dohrenwend, Barbara Snell, John Colombotos, and Bruce P. Dohrenwend. 1968. "Social Distance and Interviewer Effects." *Public Opinion Quarterly* 32:410–422.

Dubler, Nancy. N. 1998. "The Collision of Confinement and Care: End-of-Life Care in Prisons and Jails." *Journal of Law, Medicine, and Ethics* 26:149–156.

Egelko, Bob. 2012. "Death Row Inmates Oppose Prop. 34." *San Francisco Gate*, September 24. Accessed December 19, 2013. Retrieved from http://www.sfgate.com/news/article/Death-Row-inmates-oppose-Prop-34-3891122.php.

European Court of Human Rights. 2012. *European Convention on Human Rights, as amended by Protocols Nos. 11 and 14, supplemented by Protocols Nos. 1, 4, 6, 7, 12 and 13.* Strasbourg, France: Council of Europe.

Fabian, Jordan. 2009. "Pawlenty: I Would Not Have Granted Clemency to Police Shooter." *The Hill*, December 1. Accessed December 19, 2013. http://thehill.com/blogs/blog-briefing-room/news/69921-pawlenty-i-would-not-have-granted-clemency-to-clemmons.

Falter, Robert G. 1999. "Selected Predictors of Health Services Needs of Inmates over Age 50." *Journal of Correctional Health Care* 6:149–175.

Farber, Maurice L. 1944. "Suffering and Time Perspective of the Prisoner." *University of Iowa Studies in Child Welfare* 20:153–227.

Fattah, Ezzat A., and Vincent F. Sacco. 1989. *Crime and Victimization of the Elderly*. New York: Springer-Verlag.

Fazel, Seena, Tony Hope, Ian O'Donnell, Mary Piper, and Robin Jacoby. 2001. "Health of Elderly Male Prisoners: Worse Than the General Population, Worse Than Younger Prisoners." *Age and Ageing* 30:403–407.

Flanagan, Timothy J. 1980a. "The Pains of Long-Term Imprisonment: A Comparison of British and American Perspectives." *British Journal of Criminology* 20:148–156.

———. 1980b. "Time Served and Institutional Misconduct: Patterns of Involvement in Disciplinary Infractions among Long-Term and Short-Term Inmates." *Journal of Criminal Justice* 8:357–367.

———. 1981. "Dealing with Long-Term Confinement: Adaptive Strategies and Perspectives among Long-Term Prisoners." *Criminal Justice and Behavior* 8:201–222.

———. 1982a. "Correctional Policy and the Long-Term Prisoner." *Crime and Delinquency* 28:82–95.

———. 1982b. "Lifers and Long-Termers: Doing Big Time." In *The Pains of Imprisonment*, edited by Robert Johnson and Hans Toch, 115–128. Prospect Heights, IL: Waveland Press.

———. 1995. "Long-Term Incarceration: Issues of Science, Policy, and Correctional Practice." In *Long-Term Imprisonment: Policy, Science, and Correctional Practice*, edited by Timothy J. Flanagan, 3–9. Thousand Oaks, CA: Sage Publications.

Florida Corrections Commission. 1999. *An Examination of Elder Inmates Services: An Aging Crisis*. Tallahassee, FL: Florida Corrections Commission.

Flynn, Edith E. 1992. "The Graying of America's Prison Population." *Prison Journal* 72:77–98.

Frase, Richard S. 2010. "*Graham's* Good News—And Not." *Federal Sentencing Reporter* 23:54–57.

Gallagher, Elaine M. 1990. "Emotional, Social, and Physical Health Characteristics of Older Men in Prison." *International Journal of Aging and Human Development* 31:251–265.

Geertz, Clifford. 2001. "Thick Description: Toward an Interpretative Theory of Culture." In *Contemporary Field Research: Perspectives and Formulations*, 2nd ed., edited by Robert M. Emerson, 55–75. Prospect Heights, IL: Waveland Press.

Gill, Molly M. 2010. "Clemency for Lifers: The Only Road Out Is the Road Not Taken." *Federal Sentencing Reporter* 23:21–26.

Gillespie, Michael W., and John F. Galliher. 1972. "Age, Anomie, and the Inmate's Definition of Aging in Prison: An Exploratory Study." In *Research Planning and Action for the Elderly: The Power and Potential of Social Science*, edited by Donald P. Kent, Robert Kastenbaum, and Sylvia Sherwood, 465–483. New York: Behavioral Publications.

Girard, Lina, and J. Stephen Wormith. 2004. "The Predictive Validity of the Level of Service Inventory-Ontario Revision of General and Violent Recidivism among Various Offender Groups." *Criminal Justice and Behavior* 31:150–181.

Glaser, Barney G., and Anselm L. Strauss. 1967. *The Discovery of Grounded Theory: Strategies for Qualitative Research*. Chicago: Aldine Publishing.

Goetting, Ann. 1983. "The Elderly in Prison: Issues and Perspectives." *Journal of Research in Crime and Delinquency* 20:291–309.

————. 1985. "Racism, Sexism, and Ageism in the Prison Community." *Federal Probation* 49:10–22.

Goffman, Erving. 1961. *Asylums: Essays on the Social Situation of Mental Patients and Other Inmates*. Garden City, NY: Anchor Books.

Gottfredson, Michael R., and Travis Hirschi. 1990. *A General Theory of Crime*. Stanford, CA: Stanford University Press.

Haas, Gordon, and Lloyd Fillion. 2010. *Life without Parole: A Reconsideration*. Jamaica Plain, MA: Criminal Justice Policy Coalition.

Haines, Herbert H. 1996. *Against Capital Punishment: The Anti–Death Penalty Movement in America, 1972–1994*. New York: Oxford University Press.

Hassine, Victor. 2009. *Life without Parole: Living in Prison Today*. 4th ed. Edited by Robert Johnson and Ania Dobrzanska. New York: Oxford University Press.

————. 2011. *Life without Parole: Living and Dying in Prison Today*. 5th ed. Edited by Robert Johnson and Sonia Tabriz. New York: Oxford University Press.

Heather, Nick. 1977. "Personal Illness in 'Lifers' and the Effects of Long-Term Indeterminate Sentences." *British Journal of Criminology* 17:378–386.

Henry, Jessica S. 2012. "Death-in-Prison Sentences: Overutilized and Underscrutinized." In *Life without Parole: America's New Death Penalty?* edited by Charles J. Ogletree, Jr., and Austin Sarat, 66–95. New York: New York University Press.

Hughes, Lily. 2014. "Why Did Death Penalty Repeal Fail in California?" *California's Campaign to End the Death Penalty's Blog*. Accessed December 19, 2013. http://www.nodeathpenalty.org/why-did-death-penalty-repeal-fail-california.

Human Rights Watch. 2012. *The Answer Is No: Too Little Compassionate Release in US Federal Prisons*. New York: Human Rights Watch.

Irwin, John. 1970. *The Felon*. Englewood Cliffs, NJ: Prentice-Hall.

————. 2005. *The Warehouse Prison: Disposal of the New Dangerous Class*. Los Angeles, CA: Roxbury Publishing.

————. 2009. *Lifers: Seeking Redemption in Prison*. New York: Routledge.

Jackson, Penny, Donald I. Templer, Wilbert Reimer, and David LeBaron. 1997. "Correlates of Visitation in a Men's Prison." *International Journal of Offender Therapy and Comparative Criminology* 41:79–85.

Johnson, Elmer H. 1988. "Care for Elderly Inmates: Conflicting Concerns and Purposes in Prison." In *Older Offenders: Perspectives in Criminology and Criminal Justice*, edited by Belinda McCarthy and Robert Langworthy, 157–163. New York: Praeger.

Johnson, Robert. 2002. *Hard Time: Understanding and Reforming the Prison*. 3rd ed. Belmont, CA: Wadsworth/Thomson Learning.

Johnson, Robert, and Ania Dobrzanska. 2005. "Mature Coping among Life-Sentenced Inmates: An Exploratory Study of Adjustment Dynamics." *Corrections Compendium* 30:8–9, 36–38.

Johnson, Robert, and Sandra McGunigall-Smith. 2008. "Life without Parole, America's Other Death Penalty: Notes on Life under Sentence of Death by Incarceration." *Prison Journal* 88:328–346.

Jonsson, Patrik. 2012. "Did Haley Barbour's Pardon Spree Go Too Far?" *Christian Science Monitor*, January 11. Accessed December 19, 2013. http://www.csmonitor.com/USA/2012/0111/Did-Haley-Barbour-s-pardon-spree-go-too-far.

Kanshal, Tushar. 2005. *Racial Disparity in Sentencing: A Review of the Literature*. Edited by Marc Mauer. Washington, DC: The Sentencing Project.

Karnowski, Steve. 2010. "Jeremy Giefer, Tim Pawlenty Pardon, Could Haunt Republican after New Molestation Charges." *Huffington Post*, November 30. http://www

.huffingtonpost.com/2010/11/30/jeremy-giefer-tim-pawlenty-pardon_n_790148
.html.

Kerbs, John J. 2000. "The Older Prisoner: Social, Psychological, and Medical Considerations." In *Elders, Crime, and the Criminal Justice System*, edited by Max B. Rothman, Burton D. Dunlop, and Pamela Entzel, 207–228. New York: Springer Publishing.

Kerbs, John J., and Jennifer M. Jolley. 2007. "Inmate-on-Inmate Victimization among Older Male Prisoners." *Crime and Delinquency* 53:187–218.

———. 2009. "A Commentary on Age Segregation for Older Prisoners: Philosophical and Pragmatic Considerations for Correctional Systems." *Criminal Justice Review* 34:119–139.

Koenig, Harold G. 1995. "Religion and Older Men in Prison." *International Journal of Geriatric Psychiatry* 10:219–230.

Kratcoski, Peter C., and George A. Pownall. 1989. "Federal Bureau of Prisons Programming for Older Inmates." *Federal Probation* 53:28–35.

Kwon, Paul. 2002. "Hope, Defense Mechanisms, and Adjustment: Implications for False Hope and Defensive Hopelessness." *Journal of Personality* 70:207–231.

Lagos, Marisa, and Ellen Huet. 2012. "Prop. 36: 'Three Strikes' Changes Approved." *San Francisco Gate*, November 7. Accessed January 1, 2014. http://www.sfgate.com/politics/article/Prop-36-Three-strikes-changes-approved-4014677.php.

Langan, Patrick A., and David J. Levin. 2002. *Recidivism of Prisoners Released in 1994*. NCJ 193427. Washington, DC: Bureau of Justice Statistics.

Lapornik, R., M. Lehofer, M. Moser, G. Pump, S. Egner, C. Posch, G. Hildebrandt, and H. G. Zapotoczky. 1996. "Long-Term Imprisonment Leads to Cognitive Impairment." *Forensic Science International* 82:121–127.

Le Coz, Emily. 2013. "What 'Life' Is Like a Year after Mississippi Pardons." *USA Today*, January 14. Accessed January 25, 2014. http://www.usatoday.com/story/news/nation/2013/01/14/one-year-after-mississippi-pardons/1832675/.

Leigey, Margaret E., and Jessica P. Hodge. 2012. "Gray Matters: Gender Differences in the Physical and Mental Health of Older Inmates." *Women and Criminal Justice* 22:289–308.

Liptak, Adam. 2005. "Serving Life, with No Chance of Redemption." *New York Times*, October 5. Accessed December 19, 2013. http://www.nytimes.com/2005/10/05/national/05lifer.html?pagewanted=all.

MacKenzie, Doris L. 1987. "Age and Adjustment to Prison: Interactions with Attitudes and Anxiety." *Criminal Justice and Behavior* 14:427–447.

MacKenzie, Doris L., and Lynne Goodstein. 1985. "Long-Term Incarceration Impacts and Characteristics of Long-Term Offenders." *Criminal Justice and Behavior* 12:395–414.

Maguire, Kathleen, Ann L. Pastore, and Timothy J. Flanagan, eds. 1993. *Sourcebook of Criminal Justice Statistics, 1992*. NCJ 143496. Albany, NY: Hindelang Criminal Justice Research Center.

Manderson, Lenore, Elizabeth Bennett, and Sari Andajani-Sutjahjo. 2006. "The Social Dynamics of the Interview: Age, Class, and Gender." *Qualitative Health Research* 16:1317–1334.

Marquart, James W., and Jonathan R. Sorensen. 1988. "Institutional and Postrelease Behavior of *Furman*-Commuted Inmates in Texas." *Criminology* 26:677–693.

Marquart, James W., Dorothy E. Merianos, and Geri Doucet. 2000. "The Health-Related Concerns of Older Prisoners: Implications for Policy." *Ageing and Society* 20:79–96.

"A Matter of Life and Death: The Effect of Life-Without-Parole Statutes on Capital Punishment." 2006. *Harvard Law Review* 119:1838–1854.

Mauer, Marc, Ryan S. King, and Malcolm C. Young. 2004. *The Meaning of "Life": Long Prison Sentences in Context.* Washington, DC: The Sentencing Project.

McCarthy, Maureen. 1983. "The Health Status of Elderly Inmates." *Corrections Today* 45:64–65, 74.

McCorkle, Richard C. 2004. "Personal Precautions to Violence in Prison." In *The Inmate Prison Experience*, edited by Mary K. Stohr and Craig Hemmens, 203–213. Upper Saddle River, NJ: Pearson Education.

McGinnis, Kenneth L. 1990. "Programming for Long-Term Inmates." *Prison Journal* 80:119–120.

McLaughlin, Michael. 2012. "In 2012, Executions Hold Steady, but Death Penalty Imposed Less." *Huffington Post*, December 18. Accessed December 18, 2013. http://www.huffingtonpost.com/2012/12/18/2012-death-penalty-executions -information-center_n_2323135.html.

McShane, Marilyn D., and Frank P. Williams III. 1990. "Old and Ornery: The Disciplinary Experiences of Elderly Prisoners." *International Journal of Offender Therapy and Comparative Criminology* 34:197–212.

Ministry of Justice. 2012. "Life-Sentenced Prisoners." London: Ministry of Justice. Accessed January 1, 2014. http://www.justice.gov.uk/offenders/types-of-offender/life.

———. 2013. *Offender Management Statistics Quarterly Bulletin: October to December 2012, England and Wales.* London: Ministry of Justice.

Minor-Harper, Stephanie, and Lawrence A. Greenfeld. 1985. *Prison Admissions and Releases, 1982.* NCJ 97995. Washington, DC: Bureau of Justice Statistics.

"Mississippi Ends Decades-Old Mansion Trustee Program." 2012. *ABC News Radio*, January 20. Accessed December 19, 2013. http://abcnewsradioonline.com/national -news/mississippi-ends-decades-old-mansion-trustee-program.html.

Mohr, Holbrook. 2012. "Haley Barbour Pardons: Mississippi Supreme Court Rules Pardons Are Valid." *Huffington Post*, March 8. Accessed December 19, 2013. Retrieved from http://www.huffingtonpost.com/2012/03/08/haley-barbour-pardons -mississippi-supreme-court_n_1332769.html.

Montopoli, Brian. 2009. "Mike Huckabee on Maurice Clemmons: I'm No Bleeding Heart." *CBS News*, December 3. Accessed December 19, 2013. http://www.cbsnews .com/news/mike-huckabee-on-maurice-clemmons-im-no-bleeding-heart/.

Morton, Joann B. 1992. *An Administrative Overview of the Older Inmate.* Washington, DC: National Institute of Corrections.

Morton, Joann B, and Judy C. Anderson. 1982. "Elderly Offenders: The Forgotten Minority." *Corrections Today* 44:14–16, 20.

Mumola, Christopher J. 2005. *Suicide and Homicide in State Prisons and Local Jails.* NCJ 210036. Washington, DC: Bureau of Justice Statistics.

Neeley, Connie L., Laura Addison, and Delores Craig-Moreland. 1997. "Addressing the Needs of Elderly Offenders." *Corrections Today* 59:120–123.

Nellis, Ashley. 2013. *Life Goes On: The Historic Rise in Life Sentences in America.* Washington, DC: The Sentencing Project.

Nellis, Ashley, and Ryan S. King. 2009. *No Exit: The Expanding Use of Life Sentences in America.* Washington, DC: The Sentencing Project.

Newcomen, Nigel. 2005. *Managing the Penal Consequences of Replacing the Death Penalty in Europe.* London: Centre for Capital Punishment Studies.

Newport, Frank. 2010. *In U.S., 64% Support Death Penalty in Cases of Murder.* Princeton, NJ: Gallup.

Noonan, Margaret E. 2013. *Mortality in Local Jails and State Prisons, 2000–2011: Statistical Tables.* NCJ 242186. Washington, DC: Bureau of Justice Statistics.

Ogletree, Charles J., Jr., and Austin Sarat. 2012. "Introduction: Lives on the Line: From Capital Punishment to Life without Parole." In *Life without Parole: America's New Death Penalty?* edited by Charles J. Ogletree, Jr., and Austin Sarat, 1–24. New York: New York University Press.

O'Hear, Michael M. 2010. "The Beginning of the End for Life without Parole?" *Federal Sentencing Reporter* 23:1–9.

"Outgoing Mississippi Governor Pardons Four Killers." 2012. *CNN*, January 10. Accessed December 19, 2013. http://www.cnn.com/2012/01/09/justice/mississippi-murder -pardons.

Paluch, James A., Jr. 2004. *A Life for a Life*, edited by Thomas J. Bernard and Robert Johnson. Los Angeles: Roxbury Publishing.

Paterson, A. 1951. *Paterson on Prisons*, edited by S. K. Ruck. London: Frederick Muller.

Penal Reform International. 2007. *Alternatives to the Death Penalty: The Problems with Life Imprisonment*. London: Penal Reform International.

Pennsylvania General Assembly. 2005. *Report of the Advisory Committee on Geriatric and Seriously Ill Inmates*. Harrisburg, PA: Pennsylvania General Assembly.

Petersilia, Joan. 2001. "Prisoner Reentry: Public Safety and Reintegration Challenges." *Prison Journal* 81:360–375.

Rasch, Wilfried. 1981. "The Effects of Indeterminate Detention: A Study of Men Sentenced to Life Imprisonment." *International Journal of Law and Psychiatry* 4:417–431.

Reed, Monkia B., and Francis D. Glamser. 1979. "Aging in a Total Institution: The Case of Older Prisoners." *The Gerontologist* 19:354–360.

Richards, Barry. 1978. "The Experience of Long-Term Imprisonment." *British Journal of Criminology* 18:162–169.

Rideau, Wilbert, and Billy Sinclair. 1984. "Dying in Prison." *The Angolite* 9:35–61.

Robinson, Paul H. 2012. "Life without Parole under Modern Theories of Punishment." In *Life without Parole: America's New Death Penalty?* edited by Charles J. Ogletree, Jr., and Austin Sarat, 138–166. New York: New York University Press.

Rubin, Herbert J., and Irene S. Rubin 1995. *Qualitative Interviewing: The Art of Hearing Data*. Thousand Oaks, CA: Sage.

Salive, Marcel E., Gordon S. Smith, and T. Fordham Brewer. 1989. "Suicide Mortality in the Maryland State Prison System, 1971 through 1987." *Journal of the American Medical Association* 262:365–369.

Sampson, Robert J., and John H. Laub. 1993. *Crime in the Making: Pathways and Turning Points through Life*. Cambridge, MA: Harvard University.

Sapsford, Roger J. 1978. "Life-Sentence Prisoners: Psychological Changes during Sentence." *British Journal of Criminology* 18:128–145.

Schimmel, Dennis, Jerry Sullivan, and Dave Mrad. 1989. "Suicide Prevention: Is It Working in the Federal System?" *Federal Prisons Journal* 1:20–24.

Seiter, Richard P., and Karen R. Kadela. 2003. "Prisoner Reentry: What Works, What Does Not, and What Is Promising." *Crime and Delinquency* 49:360–388.

Sheleff, Leon S. 1987. *Ultimate Penalties: Capital Punishment, Life Imprisonment, Physical Torture*. Columbus, OH: Ohio State University Press.

Silfen, Peter, Sarah B. David, Dina Kliger, Rachel Eshel, Hayah Heichel, and Dina Lehman. 1977. "The Adaptation of the Older Prisoner in Israel." *International Journal of Offender Therapy and Comparative Criminology* 21:57–65.

Simon, Jonathan. 2012a. "Dignity and Risk: The Long Road from *Graham v. Florida* to Abolition of Life without Parole." In *Life without Parole: America's Other Death Penalty?* edited by Charles J. Ogletree, Jr., and Austin Sarat, 282–310. New York: New York University Press.

———. 2012b. "You Should Know: Why Death Row Inmates Oppose LWOP." *Governing through Crime Blog*, September 25. http://governingthroughcrime.blogspot.com/2012/09/you-should-know-why-death-row-inmates.html.

Smyer, Tish, Marcia D. Gragert, and Sheena LaMere. 1997. "Stay Safe! Stay Healthy! Surviving Old Age in Prison." *Journal of Psychosocial Nursing* 35:10–17.

Snell, Tracy L. 2013. *Capital Punishment, 2011: Statistical Tables.* NCJ 242185. Washington, DC: Bureau of Justice Statistics.

Sorensen, Jon, and Robert D. Wrinkle. 1996. "No Hope for Parole: Disciplinary Infractions among Death-Sentenced and Life-Without-Parole Inmates." *Criminal Justice and Behavior* 23:542–552.

Stewart, Jim, and Paul Lieberman. 1982. "What Is This New Sentence That Takes Away Parole?" *Student Lawyer* 11:14–17, 39.

Stojkovic, Stan. 2007. "Elderly Prisoners: A Growing and Forgotten Group within Correctional Systems Vulnerable to Elder Abuse." *Journal of Elder Abuse and Neglect* 19:97–117.

Strupp, Heidi. 2010. *California's Older Prisoner Crisis: Facts and Figures.* San Francisco: Legal Services for Prisoners with Children.

Sundby, Scott E. 2005. *A Life and Death Decision: A Jury Weighs the Death Penalty.* New York: Palgrave Macmillan.

Sykes, Gresham M. 1958. *The Society of Captives: A Study of a Maximum Security Prison.* Princeton, NJ: Princeton University Press.

The Sentencing Project. 2011. *Juvenile Life without Parole.* Washington, DC: The Sentencing Project.

Tierney, John. 2012. "Life without Parole: Four Inmates' Stories." *New York Times*, December 12. Accessed December 19, 2013. http://www.nytimes.com/2012/12/12/science/life-without-parole-four-inmates-stories.html?_r=0.

Toch, Hans. 1992. *Mosaic of Despair: Human Breakdowns in Prison.* Rev. ed. Washington, DC: American Psychological Association.

Turley, Jonathan. 2007. *Testimony on Prisoner Reform and Older Prisoners before the House Judiciary Committee.* Accessed January 1, 2014. http://jonathanturley.org/2007/12/06/testimony-on-prisoner-reform-and-older-prisoners-before-the-house-judiciary-committee/.

Uniform Crime Reports. 2010. "State-by-State and National Crime Estimates by Year(s)." Washington, DC: Federal Bureau of Investigation. http://bjs.gov/ucrdata/Search/Crime/State/StatebyState.cfm?NoVariables=Y&CFID=1252692&CFTOKEN=48fb2be4cd3c4927-C6DC61D7-08EB-48FC-8ADCFB96E2F08616.

Unkovic, Charles M., and Joseph L. Albini. 1969. "The Lifer Speaks for Himself: An Analysis of the Assumed Homogeneity of Life-Termers." *Crime and Delinquency* 15:156–161.

van Wormer, Katherine. 1981. "To Be Old and in Prison." In *Contemporary Issues in Corrections*, edited by Sloan Letman, Laurence French, Herbert Scott, Jr., and Dennis Weichman, 79–101. Jonesboro, TN: Pilgrimage.

van Zyl Smit, Dirk. 2002. *Taking Life Imprisonment Seriously in National and International Law.* New York: Kluwer Law International.

Villaume, Alfred C. 2005. "'Life without Parole' and 'Virtual Life Sentences': Death Sentences by Any Other Name." *Contemporary Justice Review* 8:265–277.

Violent Crime Control and Law Enforcement Act of 1994, 42 U.S.C. § 20411 (1994).

Vito, Gennaro F., and Deborah G. Wilson. 1985. "Forgotten People: Elderly Inmates." *Federal Probation* 49:18–24.

W. Va. Code R. §61-2-2 (2013).

Waldo, Gordon P., and Raymond Paternoster. 2003. "Tinkering with the Machinery of Death: The Failure of a Social Experiment." In *Punishment and Social Control*, 2nd ed., edited by Thomas G. Blomberg and Stanley Cohen, 311–352. New York: Aldine de Gruyter.

Walker, Samuel, Cassia Spohn, and Miriam Delone. 2012. *The Color of Justice: Race, Ethnicity, and Crime in America*, 5th ed. Belmont, CA: Wadsworth.

Weisberg, Robert, Debbie A. Mukamal, and Jordan D. Segall. 2011. *Life in Limbo: An Examination of Parole Release for Prisoners Serving Life Sentences with the Possibility of Parole in California*. Stanford, CA: Stanford Criminal Justice Center.

Welch, Randy. 1987. "Can This Be Life? The Implications of Life without Parole." *Corrections Compendium* 11:1, 6–8.

Western, Bruce, Jeffrey R. Kling, and David F. Weiman. 2001. "The Labor Market Consequences of Incarceration." *Crime and Delinquency* 47:410–427.

Westervelt, Saundra D., and Kimberly J. Cook. 2012. *Life after Death Row: Exonerees' Search for Community and Identity*. New Brunswick, NJ: Rutgers University Press.

White, Herbert L. 2013. "Poll: NC Residents Reject Death Penalty." *Charlotte Post*, March 4. Accessed December 18, 2013. http://www.thecharlottepost.com/index.php?src=news&srctype=detail&category=News&refno=5418.

White, Thomas W., and Dennis J. Schimmel. 1995. "Suicide Prevention in Federal Prisons: A Successful Five-Step Program." In *Prison Suicide: An Overview and Guide to Prevention*, edited by L. M. Hayes, 48–59. Washington, DC: National Institute of Corrections.

Wikberg, Ronald, and Burk Foster. 1990. "The Long-Termers: Louisiana's Longest Serving Inmates and Why They Have Stayed So Long." *Prison Journal* 80:9–14.

Williams, Brie A., James McGuire, Rebecca G. Lindsay, Jacques Baillargeon, Irena Stijacic Cenzer, Sei J. Lee, and Margot Kushel. 2010. "Coming Home: Health Status and Homelessness Risk of Older Pre-release Prisoners." *Journal of General Internal Medicine* 25:1038–1044.

Wilson, Deborah G., and Gennaro F. Vito. 1986. "Imprisoned Elders: The Experience of One Institution." *Criminal Justice Policy Review* 1:399–421.

Wiser, Mike. 2012. "38 Iowa Life Sentences Commuted." *Quad-City Times*, July 16. Accessed December 19, 2013. http://qctimes.com/news/local/government-and-politics/iowa-life-sentences-commuted/article_89d7d576-cf63-11e1-8076-0019bb2963f4.html.

Wright, Julian H., Jr. 1990. "Life-Without-Parole: An Alternative to Death or Not Much of a Life at All?" *Vanderbilt Law Review* 43:529–568.

———. 1991. "Life without Parole: The View from Death Row." *Criminal Law Bulletin* 27:334–357.

Wyoming Board of Parole. 2012. "Frequently Asked Questions." Accessed December 18, 2013. http://boardofparole.wy.gov/faq/faq.htm.

Yates, Jeff, and William Gillespie. 2000. "The Elderly and Prison Policy." *Journal of Aging and Social Policy* 11:167–175.

Zamble, Edward. 1992. "Behavior and Adaptation in Long-Term Prison Inmates: Descriptive Longitudinal Results." *Criminal Justice and Behavior* 19:409–425.

Cases

Atkins v. Virginia, 536 U.S. 304 (2002).

Coker v. Georgia, 433 U.S. 584 (1977).

Ewing v. California, 538 U.S. 11 (2003).

Ford v. Wainwright, 477 U.S. 399 (1986).

Furman v. Georgia, 408 U.S. 238 (1972).

Graham v. Florida, 560 U.S. 48 (2010).

Gregg v. Georgia, 428 U.S. 153 (1976).

Harmelin v. Michigan, 501 U.S. 957 (1991).

Jackson v. Hobbs, 567 U.S. ____ (2012).

Kennedy v. Louisiana, 554 U.S. 407 (2008).

Lockyer v. Andrade, 538 U.S. 63 (2003).

Michigan v. Bullock, 440 Mich. 15 (1992).

Miller v. Alabama, 567 U.S. ____ (2012).

Roper v. Simmons, 543 U.S. 551 (2005).

Rummel v. Estelle, 445 U.S. 263 (1980).

Schick v. Reed, 419 U.S. 256 (1974).

Solem v. Helm, 463 U.S. 277 (1983).

Sumner v. Shuman, 483 U.S. 66 (1987).

Vinter and Others v. The United Kingdom. 66069/09 European Court of Human Rights (2013).

Woodson v. North Carolina, 428 U.S. 280 (1976).

Index

ABOUT THE AUTHOR

MARGARET E. LEIGEY IS an associate professor of criminology at the College of New Jersey in Ewing. She holds a BA in criminology/pre-law from Indiana University of Pennsylvania (Indiana) and an MA and a PhD in criminology from the University of Delaware (Newark). Her research focuses on the correctional experiences of special inmate populations including life-sentenced inmates, older inmates, female inmates, and juveniles incarcerated in adult prisons. She has authored or coauthored a dozen scholarly articles and book chapters that have appeared in the *International Journal of Offender Therapy and Comparative Criminology*, *The Prison Journal*, *Women and Criminal Justice*, the *Journal of Correctional Health Care*, the *Corrections Compendium*, the *Criminal Justice Policy Review*, and *Drug and Alcohol Dependence*. Her dissertation was awarded the George Herbert Ryden Prize for Best Dissertation in the Social Sciences from the University of Delaware in 2008.

Jodi Schorb, *Reading Prisoners: Literature, Literacy, and the Transformation of American Punishment, 1700–1845*

Susan F. Sharp, *Hidden Victims: The Effects of the Death Penalty on Families of the Accused*

Susan F. Sharp and Juanita Ortiz, *Mean Lives and Mean Laws: Oklahoma's Women Prisoners*

Robert H. Tillman and Michael L. Indergaard, *Pump and Dump: The Rancid Rules of the New Economy*

Mariana Valverde, *Law and Order: Images, Meanings, Myths*

Michael Welch, *Crimes of Power and States of Impunity: The U.S. Response to Terror*

Michael Welch, *Scapegoats of September 11th: Hate Crimes and State Crimes in the War on Terror*

Saundra D. Westervelt and Kimberly J. Cook, *Life after Death Row: Exonerees' Search for Community and Identity*

.

CPSIA information can be obtained at www.ICGtesting.com
Printed in the USA
LVOW06s2050221015

459347LV00004B/243/P

9 780813 569475